A BIBLIOGRAPHY OF THE WRITINGS OF ROBERT BROWNING.

A

COMPLETE BIBLIOGRAPHY

OF THE

WRITINGS IN PROSE AND VERSE

OF

ROBERT BROWNING

By

Thomas J. Wise

1971

DAWSONS OF PALL MALL

Folkestone & London

First published in 1897
Reprinted in 1971

Dawsons of Pall Mall
Cannon House
Folkestone, Kent, England
ISBN: 0 7129 0460 3

Printed in Great Britain
by Photolithography
Unwin Brothers Limited, Woking & London

A

COMPLETE BIBLIOGRAPHY

OF THE

WRITINGS IN PROSE AND VERSE

OF

ROBERT BROWNING.

By

Thomas J. Wise.

LONDON:

PRINTED ONLY FOR PRIVATE SUBSCRIBERS.

1897.

CONTENTS.

8 CONTENTS.

ILLUSTRATIONS.

PART I.
EDITIONES PRINCIPES, ETC.

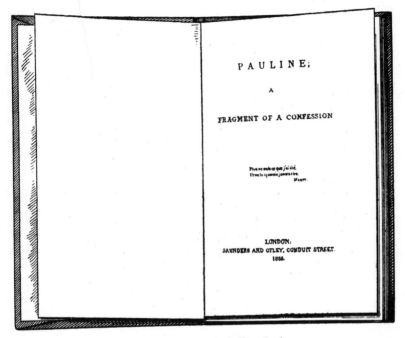

Pauline, Robert Browning's First Book.

From a copy in the original drab boards in the Library of Mr. Walter B. Slater.

A
COMPLETE BIBLIOGRAPHY OF THE WRITINGS IN PROSE AND VERSE OF ROBERT BROWNING.

PART I.

EDITIONES PRINCIPES, ETC.

(1.)

[PAULINE: 1833.]

Pauline ; / A / Fragment of a Confession. / Plus ne suis ce que j'ai été, / Et ne le scaurois jamais être. / Marot. / London : / Saunders and Otley, Conduit Street. / 1833.

Collation :—Large 12mo., pp. 71 : consisting of Title-page, as above (with imprint "*London : | Ibotson and Palmer, Printers, Savoy Street, Strand,*" at the foot of the reverse), pp. 1-2 ; Extract from "*H. Cor. Agrippa, De Occult. Phil.*" dated "*London, January,* 1833. *V.A. XX.*"[1] with blank reverse, pp. 3-4 ; and Text, pp. 5-71. The headline is *Pauline* throughout, upon both sides of the page. The imprint is repeated at the foot of p. 71. The poem is dated at the end, "*Richmond, October* 22, 1832."
Issued in drab boards, with white paper back-label bearing the single word 'Pauline.'

[1] In a letter dated November 5th, 1886, addressed to myself, Mr. Browning writes : "V.A. XX. is the Latin abbreviation of 'Vixi annos'—I was twenty years old—that is, the imaginary subject of the poem was of that age."

Reprinted in the 6 vol. edition of 1868, where it forms the first poem in Vol. I.

When inserting the poem in his collected Works, Mr. Browning recast entirely the whole of the punctuation, a change which rendered clear and simple several passages which had before seemed somewhat involved. The minute and careful manner in which this was done will be readily seen if a close comparison between the two versions be made, for the variations in the pointing number at least two or three in every line. Beyond the correction˙ of one or two printers' errors, however, the text was allowed to remain almost intact, only two fresh readings being introduced. The first of these is on page 30, where the asterisks are removed, and their place supplied by the following :—

> " And my choice fell
> Not so much on a system as a man——"

The second change will be found on page 33 of the original edition, where the last line

> " Well I remember * * * *"

is quietly dropped.

Pauline is one of the scarcest volumes in the list of modern poetical rarities. In the Crampon sale, at Sotheby's, June, 1896, a copy bound in morocco, with an interesting inscription in the poet's handwriting, realised £145. This attractive copy is now included in the collection of books and manuscripts formed by Mr. Stuart M. Samuel. An uncut copy in ordinary state has since been sold for £100.

Second Edition : 1886.

No other separate edition of *Pauline* was published until 1886, when a facsimile reprint was prepared with Mr. Browning's permission, and issued by the Browning Society to its members. The following is a transcript of the title-page :—

Pauline ; / A Fragment of a Confession. / By / Robert Browning. / A Reprint of the Original Edition of 1833. / Edited / by Thomas J. Wise. / London : / Printed by Richard Clay and Sons. / 1886.

The collation is identical with that given for the first edition, with the addition of twelve preliminary pages, as follows : Half-

Kathleen
    from her affec^{te}
        E. F.

I see with much interest this little work, the original publication of which can hardly have cost more than has been expended on a single copy by its munificent Proprietor and my friend – Mr Wise.

Feb. 12.'88,   Robert Browning.

Fac-simile of an inscription by Robert Browning upon the fly-leaf of a copy (uncut in boards) of the original edition of *Pauline* in the possession of Mr. Thomas J. Wise. The words "*Kathleen from her affec^{te}. E. F.*", at the head of the page, are in the handwriting of Edward Fitzgerald.

title, Title-page (as above), Certificate of issue, Fly-title to Prefatory Note (each with blank reverse), pp. i-viii; Prefatory Note pp. ix-xi ; and p. xii, blank.
Issued in drab boards, with white paper back-label, precisely similar to the binding of the first edition. Four hundred copies were printed. There were also twenty-five copies upon large hand-made paper, and four upon pure vellum. The size of these was demy octavo.

(2.)
[PARACELSUS: 1835.]

Paracelsus. / by Robert Browning. / London : / Published by / Effingham Wilson, Royal Exchange. / MDCCCXXXV.

Collation :—Small octavo, pp. xii + 216 : consisting of Half-title (with imprint : " *London : | Printed by G. Eccles,* 101 *Fenchurch Street,*" upon the centre of the reverse), pp. i-ii ; Title-page, as above (with blank reverse), pp. iii-iv ; Dedication " *To the Comte A. De Ripert-Monclar* " (with blank reverse) pp. v-vi ; Preface pp. vii-ix ; p. x is blank ; " Persons " (with blank reverse), pp. xi-xii ; Text, pp. 1-200 ; and *Note* pp. 201-216. There are headlines throughout. The imprint—" *G. Eccles, Printer,* 101 *Fenchurch street, London* "—is repeated at the foot of last page.
Issued in drab boards, with white paper back-label. The published price was Six Shillings.
First reprinted in the two volumes of collected Poems, issued by Chapman & Hall in 1849.

(3.)
[STRAFFORD: 1837.]

Strafford : / An Historical Tragedy. / By / Robert Browning / Author of ' Paracelsus.' / London : Printed for / Longman, Rees, Orme, Brown, Green, and Longman, / Paternoster-Row. / 1837.

Collation :—Octavo, pp. viii + 132 : consisting of Title-page, as
    above (with blank reverse, imprint at foot : " *London : |
    Printed by A. Spottiswoode, New-street-square* "), pp. i-ii ;
    Dedication, " *To William C. Macready, Esq.*" (with blank
    reverse), pp. iii-iv ; Preface, pp. v-vi ; Dramatis Personæ
    (with advertisement of *Sordello* upon the reverse) pp. vii-
    viii ; and Text, pp. 1-131.   There are headlines throughout.
    The imprint is repeated upon the reverse of the last page.
Issued in drab-coloured paper wrappers, with white paper label
on side, which reads—" *Strafford : | An Historical Tragedy, | By |
Robert Browning. | Price* 4s."
The Manuscript of *Strafford* is preserved in the Forster Library,
at South Kensington Museum.

In 1882 an " Acting Edition " was printed (in small 8vo.) for the
use of the pupils of the North London Collegiate School for Girls.
    Another edition, small 8vo., was published in 1884, with a preface
by Miss E. H. Hickey, and an introduction by S. R. Gardiner.

(4.)

[SORDELLO : 1840.]

Sordello. / By Robert Browning. / London : / Edward
Moxon, Dover Street. / MDCCCXL.

Collation :—Post octavo, pp. iv + 253 : consisting of Half-title
    (with blank reverse) pp. i-ii ; Title-page, as above (with
    imprint " *London : | Bradbury and Evans, Printers, |
    Whitefriars* " upon the centre of the reverse) pp. iii-iv ;
    and Text pp. 1-253.   The headline is *Sordello* throughout,
    upon both sides of the page.   The imprint is repeated
    upon the reverse of p. 253.
Issued in drab boards, with white paper back-label.   The
published price was Six Shillings and Sixpence.   The book
sold slowly, and whilst still on hand the change in fashion (from
'boards' to 'cloth') took place, and copies were afterwards made

up in dark-green cloth, lettered in gilt across the back, *Sordello* /
R. Browning. Some thirty years or so later the 'Remainder'
copies were put up in grass-green morocco-grained cloth, with the
original back-label. These were sold by Messrs. W. H. Smith
and Son, at 2*s.* apiece. The present value of the book, if in
original state, is about £5.

Sordello was also first reprinted in the two volumes of collected
Poems, issued by Chapman and Hall in 1849.

(5.)

[BELLS AND POMEGRANATES : 1841—6.]

No. 1.

Bells and Pomegranates. / No. 1.—Pippa Passes. / By
Robert Browning, / Author of " Paracelsus." / London : /
Edward Moxon, Dover Street. / MDCCCXLI.

Collation :—Royal octavo, pp. 16 : consisting of Title-page, as
    above (with *Advertisement* upon the reverse), pp. 1—2 ;
    and Text pp. 3—16. There are headlines throughout.

Issued in yellow paper wrappers,[1] with the title-page (enclosed
with an ornamental double ruled frame) reproduced upon the
front ; *Price Sixpence* being added at top, and the imprint—
" *Bradbury and Evans, Printers, Whitefriars* "—at foot.[2]

The *Advertisement* mentioned above, which has not been reprinted
in any later edition, reads as follows :—

" *Two or three years ago I wrote a Play, about which the chief matter
I much care to recollect at present, is, that a Pit-full of good-natured
people applauded it : ever since I have been desirous of doing something*

---

[1] The colour of these wrappers varies somewhat in different examples : some
being a pale cream colour, whilst others are a light brown.

[2] Page 4 of the wrappers of each part contains a list of " Cheap Editions of
Popular Works " published by Moxon. Advertisements of *Paracelsus, Sordello,*
and *Bells and Pomegranates* appear upon p. 3 of the wrappers of all except
No. 1.

in the same way that should better reward their attention. What follows I mean for the first of a series of Dramatical Pieces, to come out at intervals ; and I amuse myself by fancying that the cheap mode in which they appear will for once help me to a sort of Pit-audience again. Of course such a work must go on no longer than it is liked ; and to provide against a certain and but too possible contingency, let me hasten to say now—what, if I were sure of success, I would try to say circumstantially enough at the close—that I dedicate my best intentions most admiringly to the author of ' Ion '—most affectionately to Serjeant Talfourd.   *" Robert Browning."*

No. 2.

Bells and Pomegranates. / No. ii.—King Victor and King Charles. / By Robert Browning, / Author of " Paracelsus," / London : / Edward Moxon, Dover Street. / MDCCCXLII.

Collation :—Royal octavo, pp. 20 : consisting of Half-title [1] (with blank reverse) pp. 1—2 ; Title-page as above (with *Advertisement* upon the reverse), pp. 3—4 ; and Text pp. 5—20. There are headlines throughout.

Issued in yellow paper wrappers, with the title-page (enclosed within an ornamental double ruled frame) reproduced upon the front ; *Price One Shilling* being added at top, and· the imprint —as before—at foot.

No. 3.

Bells and Pomegranates. / No. iii.—Dramatic Lyrics. / By Robert Browning, / Author of " Paracelsus." / London : / Edward Moxon, Dover Street, / MDCCCXLII.

Collation :—Royal octavo, pp. 16 : consisting of Title-page as above (with *Advertisement* upon reverse) pp. 1—2 ; and Text, pp. 3—16. There are headlines throughout.

---

[1] When binding the eight numbers into one volume this Half-title should, of course, be inserted at the commencement of the book.

Issued in yellow paper wrappers, with the title-page (enclosed within an ornamental double ruled frame) reproduced upon tne front ; *Price One Shilling* being added at top, and the imprint—as before—at foot.

Contents.

No. 4.

Bells and Pomegranates. / No. iv.—The Return of the Druses. / A Tragedy. / In Five Acts. / By Robert Browning. / Author of " Paracelsus." / London : / Edward Moxon, Dover Street. / MDCCCXLIII.

Collation:—Royal octavo, pp. 19 : consisting of Title-page, as above (with list of *Persons* upon the reverse) pp. 1—2 ; and Text pp. 3—19. There are headlines throughout. Messrs. Bradbury and Evans' imprint is placed in the centre of the reverse of p. 19.

Issued in yellow paper wrappers, with the title-page (enclosed within an ornamental double ruled frame) reproduced upon the front ; *Price One Shilling* being added at top, and the imprint—as before—at foot.

The Return of the Druses was originally christened *Mansoor the Hierophant,* and under this title it was duly advertised at the end of

the 1840 edition of *Sordello*. Thanks are due to Mr. Edmund Gosse
for the loan of the following very interesting note :—

" 19, *Warwick Crescent*, *W.*,
June 4th, 1879.

" *Dear Mr. Gosse,*

"' *Mansoor* ' *was one of the names of the third Vatemite Caliph,
Biamvallah,—but the word* ' *Hierophant* ' *was used inadvertently.   I
changed the title to* ' *The Return of the Druses,*' *and the name to*
' *Djabal.*'   *It is very good of you to care about the circumstance.*

" *May I say how much I was delighted yesterday at the Grosvenor by
the two jewel-like pictures* * *which I had somehow failed to observe
before ?*

" *Ever truly yours,*
" *Robert Browning.*"

* Two landscapes by Mrs. Edmund Gosse.

No. 5.

Bells and Pomegranates. / No. v.—A Blot in the 'Scutcheon. /
A Tragedy, / In three Acts. / By Robert Browning, /
Author of " Paracelsus." / London : / Edward Moxon,
Dover Street. / MDCCCXLIII.

Collation :—Royal octavo, pp. 16 : consisting of Title-page, as above
(with list of *Persons* upon the reverse) pp. 1—2 ; and Text
pp. 3—16.   There are headlines throughout.   Messrs.
Bradbury and Evans' imprint occurs at the foot of p. 16.
Issued in yellow paper wrappers, with the title-page (enclosed
within an ornamental double ruled frame) reproduced upon the
front ; *Price One Shilling* being added at top, and the imprint—as
before—at foot.

Second Edition.

Part V. is the only one of the eight numbers of *Bells and Pomegranates* which passed into a Second Edition.   This latter agrees
with the First Edition in every particular, save that it has the words
Second Edition above the publisher's imprint upon both title-page
and wrapper.

No. 6.

Bells and Pomegranates. / No. vi.—Colombe's Birthday. / A Play, / in Five Acts. / By Robert Browning, / Author of " Paracelsus." / "*Ivy and violet, what do ye here,* / *With blossom and shoot in the warm spring-weather,* / *Hiding the arms of Monchenci and Vere ?* " / Hanmer. / London : / Edward Moxon, Dover Street. / MDCCCXLIV.

Collation :—Royal octavo, pp. 20 : consisting of Title-page, as above (with *Dedication—To Barry Cornwall*—and list of *Persons* upon the reverse) pp. 1—2 ; and Text pp. 3—20. There are headlines throughout. Messrs. Bradbury and Evans' imprint occurs at the foot of p. 20.

Issued in yellow paper wrappers, with the title-page (enclosed within an ornamental double ruled frame) reproduced upon the front ; *Price One Shilling* being added at top, and the imprint—as before—at foot.

The manuscript of *Colombe's Birthday* is in the possession of Mr. Buxton Forman. It is the only manuscript of one of the numbers of *Bells and Pomegranates* that has yet been traced. For a detailed account of it see *The Athenæum, September* 1*st* and 15*th*, 1894 ; also *Letters from Robert Browning to Various Correspondents*, Vol. i, 1895, pp. 55-56.

No. 7.

Bells and Pomegranates. / No. vii. / Dramatic Romances and Lyrics. / By Robert Browning, / Author of "Paracelsus."/ London : / Edward Moxon, Dover Street. / MDCCCXLV.

Collation :—Royal octavo, pp. 24 : consisting of Title-page, as above (with *Dedication—To John Kenyon*—and *Contents* upon the reverse) pp. 1—2 ; and Text pp. 3—24. There are headlines throughout. Messrs. Bradbury and Evans' imprint occurs at the foot of p. 20.

Issued in yellow paper wrappers, with the title-page (enclosed within an ornamental double ruled frame) reproduced upon the front; *Price Two Shillings* being added at top, and the imprint—as before—at foot.

Contents.

No. 8.

Bells and Pomegranates. / No. viii. and last. / Luria ; / and / A Soul's Tragedy. / By Robert Browning, / Author of "Paracelsus." / London : / Edward Moxon, Dover Street. / MDCCCXLVI.

Collation :—Royal octavo, pp. 32 : consisting of Title-page, as above (with imprint—*London : Bradbury and Evans, Printers, Whitefriars*—in the centre of the reverse) pp. 1—2 ; Dedication to *Walter Savage Landor* (with list of *Persons* upon the reverse) pp. 3—4 ; Text of *Luria* pp. 5—20 ; Fly-title to *A Soul's Tragedy* (with note of explanation upon the reverse) pp. 21—22 ; and Text of *A Soul's Tragedy* pp. 23—32. There are headlines throughout. Messrs. Bradbury and Evans' imprint occurs at the foot of p. 20.

Issued in yellow paper wrappers, with the Title-page (enclosed within an ornamental double ruled frame) reproduced upon the front : *Price Two Shillings and Sixpence* being added at top, and the imprint—as before—at foot.

The ' Note of explanation' mentioned above, which has not been reprinted, reads as follows :—

" *Here ends my first Series of* ' *Bells and Pomegranates*,' *and I take the opportunity of explaining, in reply to inquiries,* that I only meant by that title to indicate an endeavour towards something like an alternation, or mixture, of music with discoursing, sound with sense, poetry with thought ; which looks too ambitious, thus expressed so the symbol was preferred. It is little to the purpose, that such is actually one of the most familiar of the many Rabbinical (and Patristic) acceptations of the phrase ; because I confess that, letting authority alone, I supposed the bare words, in such juxtaposition, would sufficiently convey the desired meaning. ' Faith and good works' is another fancy, for instance, and perhaps no easier to arrive at : yet Giotto placed a pomegranate fruit in the hand of Dante, and *Raffaelle crowned his Theology (in the ' Camera della Segnatura')* with blossoms of the same ; as if the Bellari and Vasari would be sure to come after, and explain that it was merely ' simbolo delle buone opere—il qual Pomogranato fu però usato nelle vesti del Pontefice appresso gli Ebrei.'   " R. B."

NOTE.—The text of *Bells and Pomegranates* is printed in double columns, surrounded by plain rules.

Collected issue.

Upon the completion of the series ' remainder' copies of the eight numbers of *Bells and Pomegranates* were made up into one volume, and issued in dark stamped cloth of various colours. All such ' remainder' copies contain the *second* Edition of Part V., and, of course, do not include the original wrappers.

New Edition.

In *December*, 1896, the copyright of *Bells and Pomegranates* expired, and a new edition of the complete work was published by Messrs.

Ward, Lock & Co., Ltd., in two post octavo volumes. The text is an exact reprint of the first edition of 1841-6, and was edited—with *Preface* and *Notes*—by Thomas J. Wise. Vol. i. was issued in *December*, 1896, and Vol. ii. in *March*, 1897.

(6.)

[CHRISTMAS-EVE AND EASTER-DAY: 1850.]

Christmas-Eve / and / Easter-Day. / A Poem / By Robert Browning. / London: / Chapman & Hall, 186, Strand. / 1850.

Collation :—Post octavo, pp. iv + 142, consisting of: Half-title (containing advertisement of Poetical Works of Robert Browning and Elizabeth Barrett Browning upon the reverse) and Title-page, as above (with imprint in centre of the reverse—" *London: | Bradbury and Evans, Printers, Whitefriars* "), pp. i-iv ; and Text pp. 1-142. There are headlines throughout. The imprint—"*London: Bradbury and Evans, Printers, Whitefriars* "—is in centre of blank leaf at end of book.

Issued in 1850, in dark-green straight-grained cloth boards, lettered in gilt across the back: " *Christmas-Eve | and | Easter-Day | Robert Browning.*" ' Remainder' copies were put up in bright sand-grained cloth, with the lettering in gilt (enclosed within a gilt 'Oxford' frame) upon the side. The edges of these 're-mainder' copies were sadly trimmed. They were disposed of by Messrs. W. H. Smith & Co. at 2s. each.

Contents.

	Page			Page
Christmas-Eve	1		Easter-Day	80

The Manuscript of this book is preserved in the Forster Library, at South Kensington.

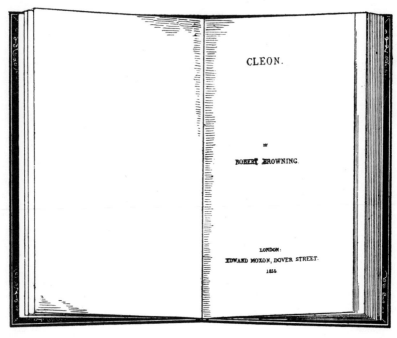

Cleon, as originally printed in pamphlet form.
From a copy in the Library of Mr. Buxton Forman.

(7.)

[CLEON : 1855.]

Cleon : / By / Robert Browning. / London : / Edward
Moxon, Dover Street. / 1855.

Collation :—Post octavo, pp. 1-23, consisting of : Half-title (with
blank reverse) pp. 1-2 ; Title-page, as above (with imprint :
"*London : / Bradbury and Evans, Printers, Whitefriars,*"
in centre of the reverse), pp. 3-4 ; and Text pp. 5-23.
There are headlines throughout. The imprint is repeated
at the foot of the last page.
Issued in coloured paper wrappers, unlettered. Printed the same
year in *Men and Women,* 1855, vol. ii. pp. 171-189.

(8.)

[THE STATUE AND THE BUST : 1855.]

The / Statue and the Bust. / By / Robert Browning. /
London : / Edward Moxon, Dover Street. / 1855.

Collation :—Post octavo, pp. 1-22, consisting of : Half-title (with
imprint on the centre of the reverse : "*London : / Bradbury
and Evans, Printers, Whitefriars*") pp. 3-4 ; and Text pp.
5-22. There are headlines throughout.
Issued in coloured paper wrappers, unlettered. Printed the same
year in *Men and Women,* 1855, vol. i. pp. 156-172.

(9.)

[MEN AND WOMEN : 1855.]

Men and Women. / By / Robert Browning. / In Two
Volumes. / Vol. i. [Vol. ii.] / London : / Chapman and
Hall, 193, Piccadilly. / 1855.

Collation : [Vol. i.] :—Foolscap octavo, pp. iv + 260, consisting of : Title-page, as above (with imprint—" *London : | Bradbury and Evans, Printers, Whitefriars* "—in centre of reverse), pp. i-ii ; Contents pp. iii-iv , and Text pp. 1-260. There are headlines throughout. The imprint—" *Bradbury and Evans, Printers, Whitefriars* "—is repeated at foot of last page.

Contents.

Collation : [Vol. ii.] :—Foolscap octavo, pp. iv + 242, consisting of : Title-page, as above (with imprint—" *London : | Bradbury and Evans, Printers, Whitefriars* "—in centre of reverse), pp. i-ii ; Contents pp. iii-iv ; and Text pp. 1-242. There are headlines throughout. The imprint—" *Bradbury and Evans, Printers, Whitefriars* "—is in centre of blank leaf of last page.

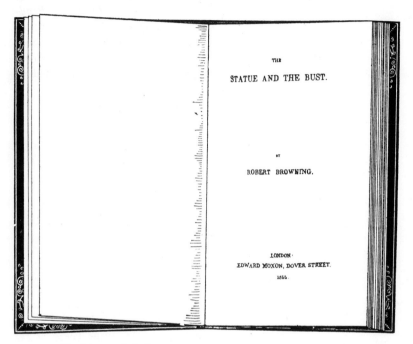

THE

STATUE AND THE BUST.

BY

ROBERT BROWNING.

LONDON:
EDWARD MOXON, DOVER STREET.
1855.

The Statue and the Bust, as originally printed in pamphlet form.
From a copy in the Library of Mr. Buxton Forman.

Contents.

Issued in green cloth boards, lettered in gilt across the back : *" Men | and Women, | Robt. Browning. | Vol.* i. [*Vol. ii.*] | *Chapman and Hall."* The published price was Twelve Shillings.

Men and Women was never reprinted separately. The Poems it contains were incorporated in the succeeding collected editions. With the exception of *In a Balcony* they were distributed under the respective headings of *Dramatic Lyrics, Dramatic Romances,* and *Men and Women.* It is to be noted that the three divisions into which *In a Balcony* was originally broken disappeared in this edition, where it was reprinted as a one-act drama.

Upon the publication of *Men and Women,* Mr. Browning forwarded a copy to Dante Gabriel Rossetti, and followed his gift by a letter (dated 102, *Rue de Grenelle, Paris, October* 29*th,* 1855) containing the following interesting list of *Errata :—*

" By the way, let me tell you something. I perceive some blunders in my poems, which I shall not, I think, draw attention to, but quietly

correct hereafter.[1] *But it happens unluckily that the worst of them occur just in a thing* [*Old Pictures in Florence*] *I would have you like if it might be—so, please alter the following in your copy, before you begin it, won't you?* "

Vol. II.

Page 34, line 3, all their work is—their work is.

           7, That a—*dele* That.

   35   4, there's its transit—then *sec tran.*

   36   3, Change the line to (" Earth here, rebuked by Olympus there ")

   36   4, You grew—And grew.

   39   6, His face—Man's face.

          13, the Hopes—new hopes.

   40   6, Which if on the earth—dele *the.*

          1, Change the line to : " Give these, I exhort you, their guerdon and glory."

   44   11, For " Rot or are left to the mercies still," read " Their pictures are left to the mercies still."

   46   11, For " But a kind of Witanagemot," read " But a kind of sober Witanagemot."

          13, For " To ponder Freedom restored to Florence," read, " Shall ponder, once Freedom restored to Florence."

   47   12, For " Turning the Bell-tower's altaltissimo," read " And turn the bell-tower's *alt* to *altissimo.*"

  188   18, one called—him called.

  189   3, one circumcised—and circumcised.

  231   4, with it—cried too.

[1] These corrections have all been made in the later editions of the poems.

(10.)

[Gold Hair : 1864.]

Gold Hair: / A Legend of Pornic. / By / Robert Browning. / 1864.

Collation :—Post octavo, pp. 1-15, consisting of : Half-title (with blank reverse) pp. 1-2 ; Title-page, as above (with imprint —" *London : Printed by W. Clowes and Sons, Stamford*

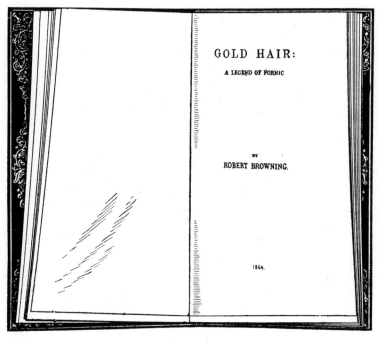

Gold Hair: the English " Copyright " Edition.

From a copy bound in morocco by Tout, in the Library of Mr. Buxton Forman.

Street and Charing Cross "—at foot of the reverse), pp.
3-4 ; and Text pp. 5-15. There are headlines throughout.
The imprint is repeated at the foot of the last page.
Stitched in paper wrappers, unlettered, and reserved for private
circulation only. Also printed in *The Atlantic Monthly*, vol. xiii.,
1864, pp. 596-599. Reprinted in *Dramatis Personæ*, 1864,
pp. 27, as one poem of twenty-seven stanzas.

The only variation that occurs in the text of *Gold Hair* as printed
privately in 1864, and as given in *The Atlantic Monthly*, is in the
spelling of the word " armour " in stanza 16—

> *"A baron with armour-adornments quaint "*—

and in the fact that the sections and stanzas are numbered in the
former, but not in the latter. The difference in spelling is, of course,
a mere matter of English and American printing offices.

The first edition of *Dramatis Personæ* also gives the poem textually
as in the private print ; but in the second edition three fresh stanzas
were added. For this addition George Eliot was responsible. The
great novelist remarked upon reading the poem that its motive was
not made sufficiently clear at the point where the money is discovered.
Browning took away her copy of the book after one of the renowned
Sunday gatherings at the Priory, and brought it back at another with
the following three stanzas added. These were intended for insertion
between two on page 32, but were written upon the blank space at
page 34, the final lines extending on to the half-title of the next poem,
The Worst of It :—

21.

> *Hid there ?   Why ?   Could the girl be wont*
> *(She, the stainless soul) to treasure up*
> *Money, earth's trash and Heaven's affront ?*
> *Had a spider found out the communion-cup,*
> *Was a toad in the christening font ?*

22.

> *Truth is truth : too true it was.*
> *Gold !   She hoarded and hugged it first,*
> *Longed for it, leaned o'er it, loved it—alas—*
> *Till the humour grew to a head and burst,*
> *And she cried, at the final pass,—*

23.

" Talk not of God, my heart is stone !
Nor lover nor friend—be gold for both !
Gold I lack ; and, my all, my own,
It shall hide in my hair.   I scarce die loth,
If they let my hair alone ! "

The copy of the book in which these stanzas were written passed into
the hands of Charles Lee Lewes, with the rest of the Priory treasures.

As a matter of minor bibliographical detail it may be mentioned
that copies of the separate print of *Gold Hair*—as also of the separate
issues of *Cleon* and *The Statue and the Bust*—occasionally occur bound
up at the end of cloth copies of the first collected edition of the *Poems*
(2 vols., 1849), and of the first edition of *Christmas Eve and Easter
Day ;* they may, however, have been so inserted in such copies only
of the books in question as were given away as presents by their
author.

(II.)

[DRAMATIS PERSONÆ: 1864.]

Dramatis Personæ. / By / Robert Browning. / London : /
Chapman and Hall, / 93 Piccadilly. / 1864.

Collation :—Crown octavo, pp. vi + 250, consisting of : Half-
title (with blank reverse) pp. i-ii ; Title-page, as above
(with imprint—" *London :   Printed by W. Clowes and
Sons, Stamford Street and Charing Cross* "—at foot of the
reverse), pp. iii-iv ; Contents pp. v-vi ; and Text pp.
1-250.   Each of the eighteen poems is preceded by a fly-
title (with blank reverse).   There are headlines throughout.
The imprint is repeated at the foot of the last page—
" *London : Printed by William Clowes and Sons, Stamford
Street | and Charing Cross.*"

Issued in 1864, in cloth boards of a dull red colour, lettered
in gilt across the back : " *Dramatis Personæ | Robert Browning.*"
The published price was Seven Shillings.

Contents.

Second Edition.

The Second Edition of *Dramatis Personæ* was also issued in 1864. The poems were afterwards incorporated in the collected edition of 1868, when several changes were made in the text. For instance, in the fifteenth section of *A Death in the Desert*, after the line " Is not His love at issue still with sin," there follows in the first edition the line " Closed with and cast and conquered, crucified." This line is omitted altogether in the 1868 edition. The changes in the text of *Gold Hair* and *James Lee* are highly interesting, and suffice to make the second edition of *Dramatis Personæ* a volume of considerable importance in the eyes of the Browning student.

(12.)

[THE RING AND THE BOOK: 1868–9.]

The / Ring and the Book. / By / Robert Browning, / M.A., / Honorary Fellow of Balliol College, Oxford. / In Four Volumes. / Vol. I. [Vol. II., &c.] / Smith, Elder and Co., London. / 1868. / [The Right of Translation is reserved.]

Collation [vol. i.] :—Post octavo, pp. iv + 246, consisting of : Title-page, as above (with blank reverse), pp. i-ii ; Contents (with blank reverse), pp. iii-iv ; and Text pp. 1-246. There are headlines throughout. The imprint—"*London : | Printed by Smith, Elder, and Co., | Old Bailey, E.C.*"—is in the centre of last page.

Contents.

	Page		Page
I. The Ring and the Book	1	III. The other Half-Rome	157
II. Half-Rome	75		

Collation [vol. ii.] :—Post octavo, pp. iv + 252, consisting of : Title-page, as above (with blank reverse), pp. i-ii ; Contents (with blank reverse), pp. iii-iv ; and Text pp. 1-252. There are headlines throughout. The imprint—"*London | Printed by Smith, Elder, and Co. | Old Bailey, E.C.*"—is in the centre of last page.

Contents.

	Page		Page
IV. Tertium Quid	1	chini	73
V. Count Guido Frances-		VI. Giuseppe Caponsacchi	161

Collation [vol. iii.] :—Post octavo, pp. iv + 250, consisting of : Title-page, as above (with blank reverse), pp. i-ii ; Contents (with blank reverse) pp. iii-iv ; and Text pp. 1-250. There are headlines throughout. The imprint—"*London | Printed by Smith, Elder, and Co., | Old Bailey, E.C.*"—is in centre of last page.

Contents.

	Page		Page
VII. Pompilia	1	IX. Juris Doctor Johannes-	
VIII. Dominus Hyacinthus		Baptista Bottinius, Fisci	
de Archangelis, Pauper-		et Rev. Cam. Apostol.	
um Procurator	90	Advocatus	175

Collation [vol. iv.] :—Post octavo, pp. iv + 236, consisting of : Title-page, as above (with blank reverse), pp. i-ii ; Contents (with blank reverse) pp. iii-iv ; and Text pp. 1-236. There are headlines throughout. The imprint—"*London | Printed by Smith, Elder, and Co., | Old Bailey, E.C.*"—is in centre of last page.

And so, although she has some other name,
we only call her Wild-pomegranate-flower
Balaustion; since, where'er the red bloom burst
'i' the dull dark verdure of the bounteous tree
dethroning, in the Rosy Isle, the rose,
You shall find food, drink, odours, all at once;
Cool leaves to bind about an aching brow,
And, never much away, the nightingale.

From "Balaustion's Adventure"

Robert Browning.

London,
Nov. 22. 71.

Contents.

Issued in dark-green cloth boards, bevelled, lettered in gilt across the back : " *The Ring and the Book | Robert Browning | Vol. I.* [*Vol. II. &c.*] | *Smith, Elder, & Co.*" The published price was Seven Shillings and Sixpence each volume.

The volumes were published separately :—Vol. i. in November, 1868 ; vol. ii. in December, 1868 ; vol. iii. in January, 1869 ; vol. iv. in February, 1869. A Second Edition was issued in *brown* cloth boards.

The manuscript of *The Ring and the Book* is in the possession of Mr. George Smith.

(13.)

[BALAUSTION'S ADVENTURE : 1871.]

Balaustion's Adventure : / Including / a Transcript from Euripides. / By / Robert Browning. / London : / Smith, Elder and Co., 15 Waterloo Place. / 1871. / The Right of Translation is reserved.

Collation :—Post octavo, pp. iv + 170, consisting of : Title-page, as above (with blank reverse), pp. i-ii ; Dedication *To the Countess Cowper* (with quotation from Mrs. Browning's *Wine of Cyprus* upon the reverse) pp. iii-iv ; and Text pp. 1-170. The head-line is *Balaustion's Adventure* throughout, upon both sides of the page. At the close of the book is an unnumbered leaf, with Messrs. Smith, Elder & Co.'s imprint upon its recto.

Issued in cloth boards, bevelled, of a reddish-brown colour, lettered in gilt across the back : "*Balaustion's | Adventure | By | Robert Browning | Smith | Elder & Co.*" The published price was Five Shillings.

This book is now in the Third Edition. No variations occur in the text.

(14.)

[Prince Hohenstiel-Schwangau : 1871.]

Prince Hohenstiel-Schwangau, / Saviour of Society. / By / Robert Browning. / Smith, Elder and Co., London. / 1871. / The Right of Translation is Reserved.

Collation :—Post octavo, pp. iv + 148, consisting of : Title-page, as above (with blank reverse), pp. i-ii ; Motto (with blank reverse), iii-iv ; and Text pp. 1-148. There are headlines throughout. The imprint— " *London : Printed by Smith, Elder & Co., Old Bailey, E.C.*"—is at foot of last page.

Issued in dark-blue bevelled cloth boards, lettered in gilt across the back: "*Prince | Hohenstiel-| Schwangau | By Robert | Browning | London | Smith, Elder & Co.*" The published price was Five Shillings.

(15.)

[Fifine at the Fair : 1872.]

Fifine at the Fair / By / Robert Browning / London / Smith, Elder and Co., 15 Waterloo Place / 1872 / The Right of Translation is reserved.

Collation :—Post octavo, pp. xii + 171, consisting of : Half-title (with blank reverse) pp. i-ii ; Title-page, as above (with blank reverse), pp. iii-iv ; extract from Molière's *Don Juan* (with translation upon reverse) pp. v-vi ; Prologue pp. vii-xii ; Text pp. 1-168 ; and Epilogue pp. 169-171. There are headlines throughout. The imprint—" *London : | Printed by Smith, Elder & Co., | Old Bailey, E.C.*"—is upon reverse of last page.

Issued in dark-brown bevelled cloth boards, lettered in gilt across the back : " *Fifine | at the | Fair | By | Robert | Browning | Smith | Elder & Co.*" The published price was Five Shillings.

(16.)

[RED COTTON NIGHT-CAP COUNTRY: 1873.]

Red Cotton Night-Cap Country / or / Turf and Towers / By / Robert Browning / London / Smith, Elder, & Co., 15 Waterloo Place / 1873 / The right of translation is reserved. The published price was Nine Shillings.

Collation :—Post octavo, pp. iv + 282, consisting of : Title-page, as above (with blank reverse), pp. i-ii ; Dedication " *To Miss Thackeray* " (with blank reverse) pp. iii-iv ; and Text pp. 1-282. There are headlines throughout. The imprint —" *London : Printed by | Spottiswoode and Co., New-street Square | and Parliament Street* "—is at the foot of the last page.

Issued in dark-green bevelled cloth boards, lettered in gilt across the back : " *Red Cotton | Night-Cap | Country | By | Robert Browning | Smith, Elder & Co.*"

The manuscript of *Red Cotton Night-Cap Country* is in the possession of Mrs. George Smith.

(17.)

[ARISTOPHANES' APOLOGY: 1875.]

Aristophanes' Apology / including / A Transcript from Euripides / Being the / Last Adventure of Balaustion / By / Robert Browning / London / Smith, Elder, & Co., 15 Waterloo Place / 1875 / All rights reserved.

Collation :—Post octavo, pp. vi + 366, consisting of : Half-title (with blank reverse) pp. i-ii ; Title-page, as above (with blank reverse), pp. iii-iv ; Motto (with blank reverse), pp. v-vi ; and Text pp. 1-336. There are headlines throughout. The imprint—" *London : Printed by | Spottiswoode & Co.,*

New-street Square | and Parliament Street"—is at the foot of the last page.

Issued in dark olive-green bevelled cloth boards, lettered in gilt across the back : *"Aristophanes' Apology | By | Robert Browning | Smith, Elder & Co."* The published price was Ten Shillings and Sixpence.

(18.)

[THE INN ALBUM: 1875.]

The / Inn Album / By / Robert Browning / London / Smith, Elder, & Co., 15 Waterloo Place / 1875 / All rights reserved.

Collation :—Post octavo, pp. iv + 211, consisting of : Half-title (with blank reverse) pp. i-ii ; Title-page, as above (with blank reverse), pp. iii-iv ; and Text pp. 1-211. Upon the reverse of the last page is a series of advertisements of poems of Robert Browning and Elizabeth Barrett Browning. There are headlines throughout. The imprint— *" London : Printed by | Spottiswoode and Co., | New-street Square | and Parliament Street"*—occurs at the foot of p. 211.

Issued in dark-green bevelled cloth boards, lettered in gilt across the back : *" The | Inn | Album | By | Robert | Browning | London | Smith, Elder, & Co."* The published price was Seven Shillings.

(19.)

[PACCHIAROTTO: 1876.]

Pacchiarotto / and / How he Worked in Distemper : / with other Poems. / By / Robert Browning. / London / Smith, Elder, & Co., 15 Waterloo Place. / 1876. / All rights reserved.

Collation :—Post octavo, pp. viii + 241, consisting of : Blank leaf
pp. i-ii ; Half-title (with blank reverse), pp. iii-iv ; Title-page,
as above (with blank reverse), pp. v-vi; Contents, pp. vii-viii ;
and Text, pp. 1-241. There are headlines throughout.
The imprint—"*London : Printed by | Spottiswoode and
Co., New-street Square | and Parliament Street*"—is in the
centre of the reverse of the last page.
Issued in slate-coloured bevelled cloth boards, lettered in gilt
across the back—"*Pacchiarotto | and | other Poems | By | Robert |
Browning | Smith, Elder & Co.*" The published price was
Seven Shillings and Sixpence.

Contents.

A letter addressed by Mr. Browning to Mr. Edmund Gosse on
July 25th, 1876, contains the following interesting reference to
Pacchiarotto : —

"*Let me tell you there are some odd pieces of oversight in the book—
attributable to my own carelessness, I believe. Especially, in a poem* [1]
*written while the earlier sheets were passing through the press,
read (page* 194*), for ' aloft '—' from bier '* [2] *: (*213*) for ' crowns '—*

[1] *Filippo Baldinucci on the Privilege of Burial. A Reminiscence of A.D.*
1676.

[2] Stanza 16, line 2 :
　　In just a lady borne aloft [*from bier*].

'*crowned*'[1]: *and* (214) *for* '*disbursed*'—'*unpursed.*'[2] *There is also* (*page* 164) *in the* 8*th line a* '*who*' *for* '*how.*'[3] *The punctuation* – *as is the way with printed verse—has been suffered to slip out of the endings, and confuse the sense in many instances. In Numpholeptos* (p. 97) *the* 8*th line should run:* '*So grant me—love—whole, sole,*' *etc.*"[4]

[1] Stanza 45, line 2 :
    Resolve me! Can it be, the crowns,—[crowned,—].
[2] Stanza 45, line 7 :
    Only for Mary's sake, disbursed [*unpursed*].
[3] *Cenciaja.* Page 164, line 8 :
    Relating who [*how*] *the penalty was paid.*
[4] As printed the line reads :
    Love, the love whole and sole without alloy!

(20.)

[THE AGAMEMNON OF ÆSCHYLUS: 1877.]

The Agamemnon of Æschylus / Transcribed by / Robert Browning / London / Smith, Elder, & Co., 15 Waterloo Place / 1877 / All rights reserved.

Collation :—Post octavo, pp. xii + 148, consisting of : Half-title (with blank reverse), pp. i-ii ; Title-page, as above (with blank reverse), pp. iii-iv ; Preface, pp. v-xi ; p. xii is blank ; Fly-title (with a list of *Persons of the Drama* upon the reverse), pp. 1-2 ; and Text, pp. 3-148. There are head-lines throughout. The imprint—"*London: Printed by Spottiswoode and Co., New-street Square / and Parliament Street*"—is at the foot of the last page.

Issued in dark-green bevelled cloth boards, lettered in gilt across the back : "*Agamemnon / of / Æschylus / Robert Browning / Smith / Elder & Co.*" The published price was Five Shillings.

(21.)

[LA SAISIAZ: 1878.]

La Saisiaz: / The Two Poets of / Croisic: / By / Robert Browning, / London: / Smith, Elder, & Co., 15 Waterloo Place. / 1878. / [All rights reserved.]

Collation :—Post octavo, pp. viii + 202, consisting of : Half-title (with blank reverse), pp. i-ii; Title-page, as above (with blank reverse), pp. iii-iv ; Dedication (with blank reverse) " *To Mrs. Sutherland Orr,*" pp. v-vi; Contents (with blank reverse), pp. vii-viii ; and Text, pp. 1-201. There are headlines throughout. The imprint—" *London : Printed by | Spottiswoode and Co., New-street Square | and Parliament Street*"—is upon the reverse of the last page. Each of the two poems is preceded by a fly-title, with blank reverse.

Issued in bluish-green bevelled boards, lettered in gilt across the back : " *La Saisiaz : | The | Two | Poets | of | Croisic | By | Robert | Browning | Smith, Elder & Co.*" The published price was Seven Shillings and Sixpence.

Contents.

	Page			Page
Prologue	1		Two Poets of Croisic	87
La Saisiaz	5		Epilogue	193
Prologue	85			

(22.)

[DRAMATIC IDYLS: FIRST SERIES: 1879.]

Dramatic Idyls / By / Robert Browning / London / Smith, Elder, & Co., 15 Waterloo Place / 1879 / *All rights reserved.*

Collation :—Post octavo, pp. vi—143, consisting of : Half-title, Title-page, and Contents (each with blank reverse), pp. i-vi ;

and Text, pp. 1-143. Each of the six poems composing the volume is preceded by a fly-title, with blank reverse. There are headlines throughout. The imprint—" *London : Printed by | Spottiswoode and Co., New-street Square | and Parliament Street*"—is at the foot of the last page.

Issued in 'old-gold' bevelled cloth boards, lettered in gilt across the back : " *Dramatic Idyls | Robert Browning | Smith, | Elder & Co.*" The published price was Five Shillings. Some copies were bound from quire stock, after the publication of the Second Series; these have " First Series " across the back, below the title.

Contents.

	Page		Page
Martin Relph.................	1	Ivàn Ivànovitch..............	57
Pheidippides	27	Tray.............................	101
Halbert and Hob	45	Ned Bratts	107

The first series of *Dramatic Idyls* passed into a Second Edition, but no variations were made in the text.

(23.)

[DRAMATIC IDYLS : SECOND SERIES : 1880.]

Dramatic Idyls / Second Series / By / Robert Browning / London / Smith, Elder, & Co., 15 Waterloo Place / 1880 / All rights reserved.

Collation :—Post octavo, pp. viii + 149, consisting of : Half-title (with blank reverse) pp. i-ii ; Title-page, as above (with blank reverse), pp. iii-iv ; Contents (with blank reverse), pp. v-vi ; Prologue (with blank reverse) pp. vii-viii ; and Text pp. 1-147 ; p. 148 is blank ; and Epilogue p. 149. There are headlines throughout. The imprint—" *London : Printed by | Spottiswoode and Co., New-street Square | and Parliament Street*"—is at the foot of last page, which is unnumbered.

Issued in dark-brown bevelled cloth boards, lettered in gilt across the back : " *Dramatic | Idyls | Second Series | Robert Browning | Smith | Elder & Co.*" The published price was Five Shillings.

Contents.

(24.)

[JOCOSERIA : 1883.]

Jocoseria / By / Robert Browning / London / Smith, Elder, & Co., 15 Waterloo Place / 1883 / [*All rights reserved.*]

Collation :—Post octavo, pp. vi + 144, consisting of : Half-title (with blank reverse) pp. i-ii ; Title-page, as above (with blank reverse), pp. iii-iv ; Contents (with blank reverse) pp. v-vi ; and Text pp. 1-144. There are headlines throughout. The imprint—" *London : Printed by | Spottiswoode and Co., New-street Square | and Parliament Street.*" —is at foot of last page. Each of the ten poems composing the volume is preceded by a fly-title, with blank reverse.

Issued in dark-red bevelled cloth boards, lettered in gilt across the back : " *Jocoseria | Robert | Browning | Smith | Elder & Co.*" The published price was Five Shillings.

Contents.

Three editions of *Jocoseria* have been published, but the text throughout has remained unchanged.

(25.)

[FERISHTAH'S FANCIES: 1884.]

Ferishtah's Fancies / By / Robert Browning / London / Smith, Elder, & Co., 15 Waterloo Place / 1884 / [*All rights reserved.*]

Collation :—Post octavo, pp. vi + 144, consisting of : Half-title (with quotations from Jeremy Collier and Shakspeare upon the reverse), pp. i-ii ; Title-page, as above (with blank reverse), pp. iii-iv ; Contents (with blank reverse), pp. v-vi ; and Text, pp. 1-144. There are headlines throughout. The imprint—" *Spottiswoode & Co., Printers, New-street Square, London* "—is at the foot of the last page.

Issued in November, 1884, in olive-green bevelled cloth boards, lettered in gilt across the back : " *Ferishtah's Fancies | Robert Browning | Smith | Elder & Co.*" The published price was Five Shillings.

Contents.

	Page		Page
Prologue	1	Two Camels	69
The Eagle	5	Cherries	78
The Melon-Seller	9	Plot Culture	87
Shah Abbas	13	A Pillar at Sebzevah	93
The Family	25	A Bean-Stripe : also Apple-	
The Sun	33	Eating	105
Mihrab Shah	46	Epilogue	140
A Camel-Driver	59		

Ferishtah's Fancies also has passed into a Third Edition, the text remaining unaltered.

(26.)

[PARLEYINGS: 1887.]

Parleyings with Certain People / of Importance in their Day : / To wit : Bernard de Mandeville, / Daniel Bartoli, / Christopher Smart, / George Bubb Dodington, / Francis

Furini, / Gerard de Lairesse, / and Charles Avison. / Introduced by / A Dialogue between Apollo and the Fates ; / concluded by / another between John Fust and his Friends. By Robert Browning. / London : / Smith, Elder, & Co., 15 Waterloo Place. / 1887. / [*All rights reserved.*]

Collation :—Post octavo, pp. viii + 268, consisting of : Half-title (with blank reverse), pp. i-ii ; Title-page, as above (with blank reverse), pp. iii-iv ; Dedication ("*In Memoriam /* J. Milsand / Obiit iv Sept. mdlxxxvi[1] / *Absens absentem auditque videtque*"), with blank reverse, pp. v-vi ; Contents (with blank reverse), pp. vii-viii ; and Text, pp. 1-268. There are headlines throughout. The imprint—"*Spottiswoode & Co., Printers, New-street Square, London* "—is at the foot of the last page.

Issued in light-brown bevelled cloth boards, lettered in gilt across the back : "*Parleyings / with / certain / people / By / Robert Browning / Smith, Elder & Co.*" The published price was Ten Shillings.

Contents.

	Page		Page
Apollo and the Fates—A Prologue	1	With George Bubb Dodington	97
With Bernard de Mandeville	29	With Francis Furini	121
With Daniel Bartoli	51	With Gerard de Lairesse	161
With Christopher Smart	77	With Charles Avison	191
		Fust and his Friends : an Epilogue	221

[1] This is of course a misprint for mdccclxxxvi.

(27.)

[ESSAY ON SHELLEY : 1888.]

An Essay / on / Percy Bysshe Shelley / By / Robert Browning / Being a Reprint of the Introductory Essay prefixed to the volume of / [25 spurious] Letters of Shelley published by / Edward Moxon in 1852. / Edited / By W. Tyas Harden / London / Published for the Shelley Society / By Reeves and Turner 196 Strand / 1888.

Collation :—Octavo, pp. 27, as follows : Half-title (with Certificate of Issue upon the reverse), pp. 1-2 ; Title-page, as above (with blank reverse), pp. 3-4 ; Fly-title to Introduction (with blank reverse), pp. 5-6 ; Introduction, pp. 7-8 ; Prelude (a reprint of Browning's *Memorabilia*—with blank reverse), pp. 9-10 ; and Text of the 'Essay,' pp. 11-27. The imprint—" *London : | Printed by Richard Clay & Sons, Bread Street Hill. | February,* 1888 "—is upon the reverse of the last page. There is a headline throughout.

Issued in green paper boards, lettered both upon the side and up the back. Five hundred copies were printed, all upon Dutch hand-made paper. Four additional examples were privately printed upon pure vellum. Some copies have an inserted slip containing two *Errata*. The volume was a gift to the Shelley Society from the editor, Mr. W. Tyas Harden. The published price was Six Shillings.

As duly set forth upon the title-page transcribed above, Mr. Browning's *Essay* was first printed in an octavo volume of *Letters*, presumably by Percy Bysshe Shelley, published by Moxon in 1852, with the following title :—*Letters | of | Percy Bysshe Shelley | With an Introductory Essay, | by | Robert Browning, | London : | Edward Moxon, Dover Street,*—1852. Pp. viii + 165. Mr. Browning's 'Essay' occupies pp. 1-44.

It is not necessary to enter here into any detailed account of the letters themselves, more especially as the matter belongs to the bibliography of Shelley rather than to that of Browning. Suffice it to say briefly that the letters, together with a number of spurious Byron manuscripts, were in all probability produced by an individual who styled himself the natural son of Lord Byron. They were in the first instance bought by William White, a bookseller of Pall Mall, who consigned them to Messrs. Sotheby's rooms for sale by public auction. They were there purchased by Mr. Edward Moxon, who at once proceeded

LETTERS

OF

PERCY BYSSHE SHELLEY.

WITH AN INTRODUCTORY ESSAY

BY

ROBERT BROWNING

LONDON.
EDWARD MOXON, DOVER STREET.
1852.

The suppressed volume of Shelley *Letters*, with Introduction by Robert Browning.
From a copy in the original purple cloth in the Library of Mr. Thos. J. Wise.

to publish them, and at whose suggestion Mr. Browning undertook to supply a suitable introduction. Mr. Browning (who was then—December, 1851—in Paris) assured me that he never saw the original holographs, having been provided either with manuscript copies of the letters, or printed proofs of the book, he was uncertain which. Upon ascertaining that the documents were forgeries, Moxon withdrew the volume from circulation. The whole of the facts were commented upon by the *Athenæum*, and White replied in a pamphlet (which ran to two editions, both of which have now become of considerable scarcity) entitled ' *The Calumnies of the " Athenæum" Exposed*,' &c.[1] The original letters were presented by Moxon to the Manuscript Department of the British Museum, where they may now be seen and consulted.

[1] *The | Calumnies | of | The " Athenæum" Journal exposed. | Mr. White's | Letter | to | Mr. Murray, | on the subject of the | Byron, Shelley, and Keats MSS. | " Calumny will sear Virtue itself."—Shakespeare. London: | William White, Pall Mall | mdccclii.*—Octavo, pp. 15. The Second Edition extended to pp. 16, and was considerably revised. The tract has never been reprinted.

(28.)

[ASOLANDO: 1890.]

Asolando : / Fancies and Facts. / By / Robert Browning. / London : / Smith, Elder, & Co., 15 Waterloo Place. / 1890. / [All rights reserved.]

Collation :—Post octavo, pp. viii + 158, consisting of : Half-title (with blank reverse), pp. i-ii ; Title-page, as above (with blank reverse), pp. iii-iv ; Dedication " *To Mrs. Arthur Bronson*," pp. v-vi ; Contents, pp. vii-viii ; and Text, pp. 1-158. There are headlines throughout. The imprint— " *Printed by | Spottiswoode and Co., New-street Square | London*"—is at the foot of the last page.

Though dated "1890," this volume was issued in December, 1889, in bright-red bevelled cloth boards, lettered in gilt across back : "*Asolando | Robert Browning | Smith | Elder & Co.*" It was published at Five Shillings.

Contents.

The demand for *Asolando* (which was published on the day of Browning's death) was very considerable, and it passed rapidly into a Seventh Edition. The text of all is uniform.

(29.)

[PROSE LIFE OF STRAFFORD: 1892.]

(*Attributed to Robert Browning.*)

Robert Browning's / Prose / Life of Strafford, / with an Introduction / by C. H. Firth, M.A., Oxon., / and / Forewords / by F. J. Furnivall, M.A., Hon. Dr. Phil. / Publisht for / The Browning Society / By Kegan Paul, Trench, Trübner & Co. / London. 1892.

Collation :—Crown octavo, pp. lxxvi + 319 : consisting of Half-title (with blank reverse), pp. i-ii ; Title-page, as above (with imprint : " *Richard Clay & Sons, Limited* / *London and Bungay*" upon the centre of the reverse), pp. iii-iv ;

Forewords by F. J. Furnivall, pp. v-xii; Introduction by C. H. Firth, pp. xiii-lxxvi; Text, pp. 1-278; Appendices, pp. 279-303; and Index, pp. 304-319. There are headlines throughout. The imprint is repeated upon the reverse of the last page.

Issued in cloth boards, lettered across the back, uniform with the 17 Vol. edition of Robert Browning's *Works*. The published price was 7s. 6d. Five hundred copies were printed.

Two Hundred and Fifty large hand-made paper copies were also printed in demy octavo, and bound in straw-coloured buckram, with white paper back-label, uniform with the large paper copies of the 17 Vol. edition of the Works. The price of these was 12s. 6d. *net*. The book was issued simultaneously in America by Messrs. Estes and Lauriat, of Boston.

The above *Life of Strafford*, only in 1892 first attributed to Robert Browning, was originally published in 1836 as the work of John Forster in a volume of *Lives of Eminent British Statesmen* in Lardner's *Cabinet Cyclopædia*. Dr. Furnivall's reasons for fathering the work upon Browning are set forth at length in his clever *Fore-words*. His arguments, however, are far from being convincing, though the following passage is, as evidence, sufficiently direct :—

Three times during his life did Browning speak to me about his prose Life of Strafford. The first time he said only—in the course of chat—that very few people had any idea of how much he had helpt John Forster in it. The second time he told me at length that one day he went to see Forster and found him very ill, and anxious about the '*Life of Strafford*,' *which he had promist to write at once, to complete a volume of* '*Lives of Eminent British Statesmen*' *for Lardner's Cabinet Cyclopædia. Forster had finisht the Life of Eliot—the first in the volume—and had just begun that of Strafford, for which he had made full collections and extracts; but illness had come on, he couldn't work, the book ought to be completed forthwith, as it was due in the serial issue of volumes; what* was *he to do?* '*Oh*,' *said Browning,* '*don't trouble about it. I'll take your papers and do it for you.*' *Forster thankt his young friend heartily, Browning put the Strafford papers under his arm, walkt off, workt hard, finisht the Life, and it came out*

to time in 1836, *to Forster's great relief, and past under his name.   A
third time—in the spring of* 1889, *I think, almost the last time I saw
Browning—he began to tell me how he had written almost all Forster's
' Life of Strafford' ; but I stopt him by saying that he'd told me before,
and we went on to chat of something else.*

*At the first and second times, I had the ' Eminent British Statesmen'
on my shelves, and once thought of reading the Life of Strafford and
asking the poet to point out his large share of it to me.   But life in
London is such a hurry that anything which gets into a busy man's
head is driven out by another thing within the next half-hour.   Later,
my ' Statesmen' volumes went to one of the Free Libraries that
appeald to me for books, and I never lookt at the ' Life of Strafford'
till after Browning's death.   Then Prof. S. R. Gardiner one day in
the British Museum renewd our talk of some years before about this
Life.   I took it off the shelves, read the last paragraph and felt—as
every other Browning student will feel—that I could swear it was
Browning's.*

On tne other hand it is only fair to state that the surviving relatives
of both Browning and Forster are firm in their assertions that the
Life was the work of the Biographer, and not that of the Poet.   But
perhaps it is best to print without further comment the two following
letters which sufficiently introduce and explain themselves :—

Palace-Gate House, Kensington, W.

July 30*th,* 1894.

Dear Sir,

*An announcement that you are preparing a Bibliography of
Mr. Browning's Works must be my plea for troubling you with this
note.   It has reference to the extraordinary claim which has been set
up by Dr. Furnivall for Mr. Browning's authorship of nearly the
whole of my husband's " Life of Strafford."   Against this claim, so
distressing to me, I make the most emphatic protest.   I enclose you a
copy of a letter from Mr. Browning's son on the subject, and also add
an extract from a subsequent letter to my niece, in which he says :
" Mrs. Forster is most welcome to make what use she likes of the whole
of mine dated Feb.* 27*th,* 1893."

*Mr. Browning's own acknowledgment to his friend Mr. Forster is
to be found in the first edition of his tragedy of " Strafford."   I also*

*take leave to forward you a copy of the letter Mr. Charles Kent sent
to " The Times" after Dr. Furnivall brought out the book in* 1892,
which may have escaped your notice.

I am, dear Sir,

Yours faithfully,

Eliza Ann Forster.

T. J. Wise, Esq.

Palazzo Rezzonico, Venice.

February 27th, 1893.

My Dear Mrs. Forster,

     *Your kind letter reached me after some little delay, or I would
have written to thank you sooner.*

     *Let me say at once that I have long ceased having anything to do
with Dr. Furnivall, nor have I seen his book; but I presume, and
gather from what you write, that he has been claiming the authorship
of Mr. Forster's " Life of Strafford" for my father—in which case he
has done this in spite of all I could do to prevent him, and in oppo-
sition to my earnest desire, expressed soon after my father's death. It
is a fact that my father assisted Mr. Forster, who was more or less
incapacitated from working by indisposition and domestic anxiety—I
believe his father was ill—but I need not say that* that *would not
justify any claim of authorship! No letters of Mr. Forster could be
found throwing any light on the matter, and the only ones in my
possession are of a later date. These, of course, I will lend you with
great pleasure when I return to Venice.*

     *I am indeed sorry that you have been pained in this way. My
father would, I am sure, have been indignant at such a proceeding,
and I, as I have said, opposed it to my utmost when the subject was
brought up by Dr. Furnivall. I am much obliged for the copy of my
father's letter which you kindly send me, although I needed no
reminding of the friendship between him and Mr. Forster. My aunt,
who is with me, asks to be affectionately remembered.*

Believe me, my dear Mrs. Forster, always

and with warmest regard,

Yours very sincerely,

R. Barrett Browning.

I am writing from Asolo.

But the weightiest argument against Mr. Browning's assumed authorship of the prose *Life of Strafford* is probably the second paragraph of the Preface to the first edition (published in 1837) of his own Historical Tragedy :—

" *The portraits are, I think, faithful; and I am fortunate in being able, in proof of this, to refer to the subtle and eloquent exposition of the characters of Eliot and Strafford, in the Lives of Eminent British Statesmen now in course of publication in Lardner's Cyclopædia, by a writer whom I am proud to call my friend; and whose biographies of Hampden, Pym, and Vane will, I am sure, fitly illustrate the present year—the Second Centenary of the Trial concerning Ship-Money. My Carlisle, however, is purely imaginary : I at first sketched her singular likeness roughly in, as suggested by Matthew and the memoir writers —but it was too artificial, and the substituted outline is exclusively from Voiture and Waller.*"

It is difficult to believe that Mr. Browning would have referred to the *Life* as " subtle and eloquent " had the major portion of the work in question been the product of his own pen.

(30.)

[LETTERS : 1895-6.]

Letters / from / Robert Browning / to / Various Corre-spondents. / Edited by Thomas J. Wise. / Volume One. [Volume Two, &c.] / London : Privately Printed. / 1895.

Vol. I.

Collation :—Post octavo, pp. xii + 98, consisting of : Half-title (with blank reverse) pp. i-ii ; Title-page, as above (with blank reverse), pp. iii-iv ; Certificate of issue (with blank reverse) pp. v-vi ; Contents, pp. vii-xii ; and Text, pp. 1-98. There are headlines throughout,—" *Letters of* " upon each verso, and " *Robert Browning* " upon each recto. Following the last page is a leaf with the colophon of *The Ashley Library* upon its recto.

Issued (in *June*, 1895) in plum-coloured cloth boards, bevelled, lettered in gilt across the back : "*Letters | Vol. I. | Robert | Browning | 1895.*" Thirty copies were printed upon Whatman's hand-made paper, and Four upon fine Vellum. An additional Forty copies were printed on ordinary paper for distribution to the members of the Browning Society. These were stitched in pale green paper wrappers, lettered "*The Browning Society. | Robert Browning's Letters. | Vol. I. | London : | Printed for Members of the Browning Society only. | 1895*" upon the front cover. All copies contain as frontispiece a *facsimile*, upon 'Japanese-vellum' paper, of a holograph letter from Robert Browning to the Editor.

The xxxiii. letters which the volume contains are addressed to : Miss Eliza Flower (1 letter), John Macready (1 letter), Mr. Christopher Dowson, Junr. (1 letter), Richard Henry Horne (2 letters), Edward Moxon (1 letter), Dante G. Rossetti (1 letter), Mr. E. S. Dallas (1 letter), Mr. W. G. Kingsland (1 letter), Rev. Alexander B. Grosart (1 letter), Mr. John H. Ingram (4 letters), a 'Lady Correspondent' (1 letter), Mr. Edmund Gosse (4 letters), Mr. H. Buxton Forman (3 letters), Mr. George Barnett Smith (1 letter), and Dr. F. J. Furnivall (10 letters).

Vol. II.

Collation :—Post octavo, pp. xii + 98, consisting of Half-title (with blank reverse) pp. i-ii; Title-page, as above (with blank reverse), pp. iii-iv; Certificate of issue (with blank reverse) pp. v-vi; Contents pp. vii-xii; and Text pp. 1-98. There are headlines throughout, as in Vol. I. Following the last page is a leaf with the colophon of *The Ashley Library* upon its recto.

Issued (in *June*, 1896) in plum-coloured cloth boards, uniform with Vol. I. The same number of copies also were printed ; namely Four upon fine Vellum, Thirty upon Whatman's hand-made paper, and an additional Forty upon ordinary paper for distribution to the Members of the Browning Society.

PART II.

CONTRIBUTIONS TO PERIODICAL
LITERATURE.

PART II.

CONTRIBUTIONS TO PERIODICAL LITERATURE, ETC.

(1.)

The Monthly Repository, Vol. viii, New Series, 1834, p. 712.

SONNET. ("*Eyes, calm beside thee, Lady, couldst thou know !*")

> Reprinted in *Browning Society's Papers*, Part XII, p. 36*.
> Not included in any edition of Robert Browning's collected works.

(2.)

The Monthly Repository, Vol. ix, New Series, 1835, pp. 707—708.

THE KING. ("*A King lived long ago.*")

> Reprinted (with considerable variations) in *Bells and Pomegranates*, No. I, 1841, p. 12, where it forms one of Pippa's songs in *Pippa Passes*.

(3.)

The Monthly Repository, Vol. x, New Series, 1836, pp. 43—44.

PORPHYRIA. (" *The rain set early in to-night.*")

> Reprinted (under the title of *Madhouse Cells—*II) in *Bells and Pomegranates*, No. III, 1842, p. 13.

(4.)

The Monthly Repository, Vol. x, New Series, 1836, pp. 45—46.

JOHANNES AGRICOLA. (" *There's Heaven above ; and night by night.*")

> Reprinted (under the title of *Madhouse Cells—*I) in *Bells and Pomegranates*, No. III, 1842, p. 13.

(5.)

The Monthly Repository, Vol. x, New Series, 1836, pp. 270—271.

LINES.   ("*Still ailing, wind ?   Wilt be appeased or no ?*")

> Reprinted in *The Atlantic Monthly*, Vol. xiii, *July*, 1864, pp. 737—738. Afterwards included in *Dramatis Personæ*, 1864, where it forms the first six stanzas of Section VI of *James Lee*.

(6.)

Hood's Magazine, Vol. i, No. VI, *June*, 1844, pp. 513—514.

THE LABORATORY (ANCIEN RÉGIME).

> Reprinted (under the title of *France and Spain*) in *Bells and Pomegranates*, No. VII, 1845, p. 11.

(7.)

Hood's Magazine, Vol. i, No. VI, *June*, 1844, p. 525.

CLARET AND TOKAY.

> Reprinted in *Bells and Pomegranates*, No. VII, 1845, pp. 20—21.

(8.)

Hood's Magazine, Vol. ii, No. VII, *July*, 1844, pp. 45—48.

GARDEN FANCIES.   I. *The Flower's Name ;* II. *Sibrandus Schafnaburgensis.*

> Reprinted in *Bells and Pomegranates*, No. VII, 1845, pp. 10—11.

(9.)

Hood's Magazine, Vol. ii, No. VIII, *August*, 1844, pp. 140—142.

THE BOY AND THE ANGEL.

> Reprinted (with considerable variations, and the addition of five new couplets) in *Bells and Pomegranates*, No. VII, 1845, pp. 19—20.

(10.)

Hoods Magazine, Vol. iii, No. III, *March*, 1845, pp. 237—239.

THE TOMB AT ST. PRAXED'S (*Rome* 15—).

Reprinted in *Bells and Pomegranates*, No. VII, 1845, p. 9.

(11.)

Hood's Magazine, Vol. iii, No. IV, *April*, 1845, pp. 313—318.

THE FLIGHT OF THE DUCHESS. Part the First.

Reprinted in *Bells and Pomegranates*, No. VII, pp. 12—19.

(12.)

Letters of Percy Bysshe Shelley, London, 1852, pp. 1—44.

INTRODUCTORY ESSAY BY ROBERT BROWNING.

Reprinted separately, as follows :—*An Essay | on | Percy Bysshe Shelley | By | Robert Browning | . . . . | Edited | by W Tyas Harden | London | . . . . | 1888.* Octavo, pp. 27.
Also included in the *Browning Society's Papers*, Part I, pp. 5—19.

(13.)

The Keepsake, 1856, p. 16.

BEN KARSHOOK'S WISDOM. ("' *Would a man 'scape the rod' ?*")

Reprinted in the *Browning Society's Papers*, Part I, p. 56. This poem has not been included in any collection of Mr. Browning's poems.

(14.)

The Keepsake, 1857, p. 164.

MAY AND DEATH. ("*I wish that when you died last May.*")

Reprinted (with some variations) in *Dramatis Personæ*, 1864, p. 145.

(15.)

Last Poems.   By Elizabeth Barrett Browning.   London, 1862.

DEDICATION ("To Grateful 'Florence'") BY ROBERT BROWNING, p. v.

PREFATORY NOTE (styled *Advertisement*) BY ROBERT BROWNING, p. vii.

> Mrs. Browning died at Florence on *June 29th*, 1861, and the volume was posthumous. It was arranged and edited by Robert Browning.

(16.)

The Greek Christian Poets and the English Poets.   By Elizabeth Barrett Browning.   London, 1863, pp. iii—iv.

PREFACE (styled *Advertisement*) BY ROBERT BROWNING.

> This volume was also posthumous. Its contents were reprinted from the pages of *The Athenæum.*

(17.)

Royal Academy Exhibition Catalogue, 1864, p. 13.

ORPHEUS AND EURYDICE.   ("*But give them me—the mouth, the eyes, the brow !* ")

> Reprinted in the *Selections from the Works of Robert Browning* ("Moxon's Miniature Poets"), 1865, p. 215, under the title "*Eurydice to Orpheus.   A Picture by Frederick Leighton, A.R.A.*"; and in the *Poetical Works* of 1868, where it is inserted in *Dramatis Personæ.*

(18.)

The Atlantic Monthly, Vol. xiii, *May,* 1864, pp. 596—599.

GOLD HAIR : A LEGEND OF PORNIC.

> Printed privately in pamphlet form, for copyright purposes, as follows :—*Gold Hair : | A Legend of Pornic. | By | Robert Browning. |* 1864.   Post octavo, pp. 15.

Also reprinted in *Dramatis Personæ*, 1864, pp. 27—34. In the Second Edition of *Dramatis Personæ*, 1864, three fresh stanzas were added. They were inserted between stanzas 20 and 21.

(19.)

The Atlantic Monthly, Vol. xiii, *June*, 1864, p. 694.

PROSPICE. (" *Fear death ?—to feel the fog in my throat.*")

Reprinted, with slight changes in one or two lines, in *Dramatis Personæ*, 1864, pp. 149—150.

(20.)

A Selection from the Poetry of Elizabeth Barrett Browning. First Series. London, 1866, p. v.

PREFATORY NOTE BY ROBERT BROWNING.

Reprinted in all later editions of the *Selections*.

(21.)

The Cornhill Magazine, Vol. xxiii, *March*, 1871, pp. 257—260.

HERVÉ RIEL.

Reprinted in *Pacchiarotto and other Poems*, 1876, p. 117.

(22.)

The Hour will Come. By Wilhelmine von Hillern. Translated from the German by Clara Bell. London [1879], Vol. ii, p. 174.

SONG. (" *The Blind Man to the Maiden said.*")

Reprinted in the *Whitehall Review*, March 1, 1883; also in *Browning Society's Papers*, Part IV, p. 410. This *Song* has not been included in any edition of Robert Browning's collected works.

(23.)

Euripides. By J. P. Mahaffy. (*Macmillan's Classical Writers.*)
London, 1879, p. 116.

LYRIC OF EURIPIDES. (" *Oh Love, Love, thou that from the eyes diffusest.*")

> Reprinted in the *Browning Society's Papers*, Part I, p. 69.
> This Translation has not been included in any edition of Robert Browning's collected works.

(24.)

The Century. Vol. xxv, 1882, pp. 159—160.

TEN NEW LINES TO " *Touch him ne'er so lightly* " (*Dramatic Idyls*, Second Series, 1880, p. 149). (" *Thus I wrote in London, musing on my betters.*")

> These lines were printed in *The Century* without Mr. Browning's consent; they have not been added to any reprint of the original verses, as they were not intended to form a permanent addition thereto. They were reprinted in the first edition of the *Browning Society's Papers*, Part IV, p. 48. At Mr. Browning's request the lines were cancelled, and did not appear in later issues of the Part.

(25.)

The Pall Mall Gazette, Dec. 8, 1883.

SONNET ON GOLDONI. (" *Goldoni,—good, gay, sunniest of souls,—*")

> Reprinted in the *Browning Society's Papers*, Part V, p. 98*.
> This *Sonnet* has not been included in any edition of Robert Browning's collected works.

(26.)

The Pall Mall Gazette, Dec. 13, 1883.

PARAPHRASE FROM HORACE. (*"All singers, trust me, have this common vice."*)

Reprinted in the *Browning Society's Papers*, Part V, p. 99*.
This *Paraphrase* has not been included in any edition of Robert Browning's collected works.

(27.)

The Pall Mall Gazette, Dec. 28, 1883.

HELEN'S TOWER. (*" Who hears of Helen's Tower, may dream perchance."*)

Reprinted in the *Browning Society's Papers*, Part V, p. 97*.
This *Sonnet* has not been included in any edition of Robert Browning's collected works.

(28.)

The Century Magazine, Vol. xxvii, *February,* 1884, p. 640.

SONNET ON RAWDON BROWN. (*"Sighed Rawdon Brown : 'Yes, I'm departing, Toni !'"*)

Reprinted in the *Browning Society's Papers*, Part V, p. 132*.
This *Sonnet* has not been included in any edition of Robert Browning's collected works.

(29.)

The World, April 16, 1884.

THE FOUNDER OF THE FEAST. (*"'Enter my palace,' if a prince should say—"*)

Reprinted in the *Browning Society's Papers*, Part VII, p. 18*.
This *Sonnet* has not been included in any edition of Robert Browning's collected works.

(30.)

The Divine Order and other Sermons and Addresses. By the late Thomas Jones. London, 1884.

INTRODUCTION BY ROBERT BROWNING.

(31.)

The Shaksperean Show Book, 1884, p. 1.

THE NAMES. (" *Shakespeare ?—to such name's sounding, what succeeds.*")

> Reprinted in the *Browning Society's Papers*, Part V, p. 105*. This *Sonnet* has not been included in any edition of Robert Browning's collected works.

(32.)

Why am I a Liberal? Edited by Andrew Reid. London, 1885, p. 11.

WHY AM I A LIBERAL? (" ' *Why ?* ' *Because all I haply can and do.*")

> Reprinted in the *Browning Society's Papers*, Part VIII, p. 92*. This *Sonnet* has not been included in any edition of Robert Browning's collected works.

(33.)

The New Amphion. The Book of the Edinburgh University Union Fancy Fair, 1886, p. 1.

SPRING SONG. (" *Dance, yellows and whites and reds !*"), with a full page illustration by Elizabeth Gulland.

> Reprinted in *Parleyings*, VI, " Gerard de Lairesse," p. 189.

(34.)

Poems by Elizabeth Barrett Browning, London :
Smith, Elder & Co., 1887.

PREFATORY NOTE BY ROBERT BROWNING, occupying
three unnumbered pages inserted between Title-page
and Dedication.

Only a portion of the copies issued contain this *Preface*, which
was designed to controvert certain statements made by the
author of a (then) recent *Memoir* of Elizabeth Barrett
Browning.

(35.)

*Lines accompanying Memorial of the Queen's Jubilee, in St.
Margaret's Church, Westminster* [1887].

MEMORIAL LINES. (*"Fifty years' flight ! wherein should
he rejoice."*)

Reprinted in the *Browning Society's Papers*, Part X, p. 234*.
These *Lines* have not been included in any edition of Robert
Browning's collected works.

(36.)

The Athenæum, No. 3,220, *July* 13, 1889, p. 64.

TO EDWARD FITZGERALD. (*" I chanced upon a new book
yesterday."*) Dated *"July* 8, 1889."

Reprinted in the *Browning Society's Papers*, Part XI, p. 347*

These unhappy lines were occasioned by the following passage
in one of FitzGerald's letters printed by Mr. Aldis Wright
in *The Life and Letters of Edward FitzGerald :—*

*" Mrs. Browning's death is rather a relief to me, I must say.
No more Aurora Leighs, thank God ! A woman of real genius,
I know ; but what is the upshot of it all ! She and her sex had*

better mind the kitchen and the children; and perhaps the poor. Except in such things as little novels, they only devote themselves to what men do much better, leaving that which men do worse or not at all."

Despite the fact that the words do not bear the meaning Mr. Browning attached to them, their retention in a letter published during the life-time of the husband of the dead poetess betrayed a sad lack of editorial discretion. Although Mr. Browning afterwards acknowledged that the conclusion at which he had arrived upon a first hasty perusal of the letter was erroneous, he never formally withdrew his bitter verses; at the same time he refrained from reviving them when issuing the final (17 vol.) edition of his collected works.

In the succeeding number (*July 20th*) of *The Athenæum* appeared the following letter :—

Trinity College,
Cambridge, July 16, 1889.

I find that by a grave oversight I have allowed a sentence to stand in one of Edward FitzGerald's letters which has stirred the just resentment of Mr. Browning. FitzGerald's expression was evidently thrown off with the freedom that men permit themselves in correspondence with their intimate friends; and I feel how great an injustice I have done to FitzGerald in making public what was but the careless outburst of a passing mood, and thus investing it with a significance which was never designed. That I should have allowed a passage to remain which has so wronged the dead and pained the living causes me, I need not say, extreme vexation, and I can only beg publicly to express my sincere regret.

William Aldis Wright.

(37.)

Poet Lore, Vol. i, *August* 1889, p. 398.

LINES ADDRESSED TO LEVI LINCOLN THAXTER.

These lines, written in 1885, are inscribed upon the boulder on the Maine sea-coast that marks the grave of Thaxter. From

Poet Lore they were widely reprinted by the various journals of the day.   They have not yet been included in any edition of Robert Browning's collected works.

> *Thou, whom these eyes saw never, say friends true*
> *Who say my soul, helped onward by my song,*
> *Though all unwittingly, has helped thee too!*
> *I gave but of the little that I knew :*
> *How were the gift requited, while along*
> *Life's path I pace, couldst thou make weakness strong.*
> *Help me with knowledge—for Life's Old—*
> > *Death's New!*
>
> > > *R. B. to L. L. T., April,* 1885.

PART III.

PUBLISHED LETTERS OF ROBERT BROWNING.

PART III.

PUBLISHED LETTERS OF ROBERT BROWNING.

This list includes only such letters as have appeared at various times in scattered volumes, in magazines, or in the columns of the public press. They are arranged according to the date of *publication.* For Mr. Browning's ' collected ' letters see *ante,* Part I. pp. 398–399.

(1.)

Life of William Etty, R.A. By Alexander Gilchrist. London, 8vo., 1855. Letter to William Etty.

(2.)

The Correspondence of Leigh Hunt. Edited by his Eldest Son. London : 8vo, 1862, Vol. ii, pp. 264—266. Letter to Leigh Hunt on *Aurora Leigh,* Keats's *Lamia, Isabella, &c.,* and a manuscript (originally preserved by Captain Roberts) of Shelley's *Indian Serenade.* Some interesting variations of the text between this MS. and the version of the *Serenade* printed in the *Posthumous Poems* are given by Mr. Browning. The close of the letter mentions the lock of Milton's hair given by Hunt to Mr. Browning.[1] Signed " R. B.," and dated *Bagni di Lucca, 6th October,* 1857.

---

[1] This lock of Milton's hair was one of Mr. Browning's most cherished treasures. He never tired of exhibiting it to his friends.

(3.)

The Daily News, February 10*th,* 1871. Letter to the Editor stating that his contribution to the French Relief Fund was the payment by his publishers for a lyrical poem [*Hervé Riel*]. Signed " Robert Browning," and dated " 19 *Warwick Crescent, W. Feb.* 9" [1871].

(4.)

The Daily News, November 21*st,* 1874. Letter to the Editor of *The Daily News,* referring to the " Doctrine of the enclitic *De*" in the poem of the *Grammarian's Funeral.* Signed "R. B.," and dated "*Nov.* 20" [1874].

(5.)

The Poetical Works of Laman Blanchard, London, 8vo, 1876, pp. 6–8. Letter to Laman Blanchard.

(6.)

The Prose Works of William Wordsworth. Edited by Rev. Alexander B. Grosart. London, 1876. Vol. i. p. xxxvii. Letter to the Rev. Alexander B. Grosart, on the poem of *The Lost Leader* and Wordsworth. Signed " Robert Browning," and dated " 19 Warwick Crescent, *Feb.* 24, 1875." Reprinted in *Letters from Robert Browning to Various Correspondents, Edited by Thos. J. Wise,* 1895, Vol. i., pp. 28–29.

(7.)

Works of Percy Bysshe Shelley, Edited by H. Buxton Forman. London, 1876–1880, Vol. ii, pp. 418–420,

Letter to Mr. Buxton Forman on the value to be attached to the termination " aia " in the poem *Cenciaja.* Signed " Robert Browning," and dated " 19 *Warwick Crescent, W., July, 27 '76.*"

(8.)

Letters of Elizabeth Barrett Browning addressed to R. H. Horne. Edited by S. R. Townshend Mayer. 2 Vols. London, 8vo, 1877.

(1) Page 182. Letter to R. H. Horne, chiefly regarding Mrs. Browning's improvement in health. Signed " R. Browning," and dated " *Pisa, Dec.* 4."

(2) Page 194. Letter to R. H. Horne [in the hand-writing of Mrs. Browning], announcing their departure from England, and the despatch of the new editions of their works. Signed " Robert and Elizabeth Barrett Browning," and dated " *London, September 24th,* [1851]."

(9.)

The Times, November 20th, 1877. Letter to the Editor of *The Times* concerning his nomination as a candidate for the Lord Rectorship of St. Andrews. He explains that directly he heard of his nomination he wrote declining the honour, " as I had found myself compelled to do on some former occasions." Signed " Robert Browning," and dated " 19 *Warwick Crescent, Nov.* 19." [1877.]

(10.)

The Academy, December 20th, 1878. Letter to Dr. Furnivall.

(11.)

The Pall Mall Gazette, June, 1888. Letter to a correspondent on the beauty of the vale of Llangollen : " I received àn impression of the beauty around me which continued ineffaceable during all subsequent experience of varied foreign scenery, mountain, valley, and river." Signed " Robert Browning," and dated " 29 *De Vere Gardens, June* 5, 1888."

(12.)

The Athenæum, December 21*st,* 1889, p. 860. Letter to Mr. Charles Kent, accompanying a copy of Volume 3 of the new collected edition of the *Poetical Works.* Signed " Robert Browning," and dated " 29 *De Vere Gardens, W.,* 28 *August,* 1889."

(13.)

The Browning Society's Papers, 1889–90, Part XI, p. 338*. Extract (undated and unsigned) from a Letter to Dr. Furnivall on the meaning of the poem *Numpholeptos.*

(14.)

The Browning Society's Papers, 1889–1890, *Part XII.*
(1) Page 41*. Letter to Alfred, Lord Tennyson, congratulating him upon his birthday. Signed " Robert Browning," and dated " 29 *De Vere Gardens, W. August* 5*th,* 1889."

Also printed in *The Academy,* No. 922, for *January* 4*th,* 1892, p. 8.— thence copied extensively by the Daily Press.

(2) Page 65*. Letter to Theodore Tilton: " I have lost the explanation of American affairs, but I assure you of my belief in the justice and my confidence in the triumph of the great cause. For the righteousness of the principle I want no information. God prosper it and its defenders." Signed " Robert Browning," and dated " *St. Enogat, près Dinard, France, Sept.* 11, 1861."

(3) Page 122*. Letter to Mrs. Bloomfield Moore, thanking her for her " goodness in caring so effectually for my interest with Messrs. Houghton and Mifflin." Signed " Robert Browning," and dated " 19 *Warwick Crescent W., Nov. 7,* '84."

(15.)

Life of Robert Browning   By William Sharp. London, 8vo, 1890.

(1) Page 53. Letter to Mr. Sharp on " Rossetti's *Pauline* letter "—" It was to the effect that the writer, personally and altogether unknown to me, had come upon a poem in the British Museum ... that he judged to be mine, but could not be sure, and wished me to pronounce in the matter—which I did." Neither signature nor date is given.

(2) Page 189. Letter to Mr. Edmund Yates, *à propos* of the Browning Society: " I cannot wish harm to a Society of—with a few exceptions—names unknown to me, who are busied about my books so disinterestedly." The signature and date are not given.

(3) Page 191. Letter to " Alma " [a child-friend of

Mr. Browning's], detailing a conversation with the Shah, in which the latter requested the gift of a volume of his poems. Signed " Robert Browning," and dated " 29 *De Vere Gardens, W., 6th July,* 1889."

(16.)

The Times, Monday, December 30*th* 1889, p. 10. Letter to Lord Tennyson, congratulating him upon his birthday. Signed " Robert Browning," and dated " 29 *De Vere Gardens, W. Aug.* 5, 1889."

(17.)

Alma Murray,[1] *Portrait as Beatrice Cenci, with Critical Notice, containing four Letters from Robert Browning.* London, 8vo, 1891.

(1) Page 6. Letter to Mrs. Forman, upon her " admirable impersonation of that most difficult of all conceivable characters to personate " (*i.e. Beatrice Cenci*). Signed " Robert Browning," and dated "*May 8th,* 1886." This letter is also printed in the *Note-book of the Shelley Society,* Part I., 1888, p. 105.

(2) Page 6 (*at foot*). Letter to Mrs. Forman, acknowledging receipt of her " charming photograph " in character as *Beatrice Cenci.* Signed " Robert Browning," and dated " 29 *De Vere Gardens, W. May 9th,* 1888."

(3) Page 7. Letter to Mrs. Forman, upon her performance of *Colombe* in *Colombe's Birthday.* Signed " Robert Browning," and dated " *Venice, December* 29*th,* 1885."

---

[1] " *Alma Murray,*" the stage-name of Mrs. Alfred Forman.

(4) Page 8. Letter to Mrs. Forman, mentioning " how beautifully and how powerfully she acted the part of *Mildred* in *A Blot in the 'Scutcheon.*" Signed " Robert Browning," and dated "*March*, 1888."

(18.)

Poet Lore, Vol. ii, No. 2, *February*, 1890, p. 101. Letter to the printers of *Asolando* [Messrs. Spottiswoode & Co.] expressing his " gratitude for the admirable supervision of the gentleman whose care to correct my mistakes or oversights has so greatly obliged me." Signed " Robert Browning," and dated " 29 *De Vere Gardens, June* 5, 1889."

(19.)

The Jewish Chronicle, 1890. Letter to Mr. O. J. Simon on the religious persecutions in Russia in the winter of 1881–82. Signed " Robert Browning," and dated "*Feb.* 2, '82."

(20.)

The Nonconformist, 1890. Letter to a lady on the love and power of God : " It is a great thing, the greatest that a human being should have passed the probation of life, and sum up its experience in a witness to the power and love of God." Signed "Robert Browning," and dated " 19, *Warwick Crescent, W., May* 11, '76." This letter is also printed in *Kingsland's Robert Browning : Chief Poet of the Age*, p. 83. Also in *Letters from Robert Browning to Various Correspondents, Edited by Thos. J. Wise*, 1895, Vol. i, pp. 35–38.

(**21.**)

Robert Browning : Chief Poet of the Age. New Edition. By William G. Kingsland. London, 8vo, 1890.

(1) Page ii. Letter to Mr. W. G. Kingsland : " How can I be other than most grateful to you for your generous belief in me ?—unwarranted as it may be by anything I have succeeded in doing, although somewhat justified, perhaps, by what I would fain have done if I could." Signed " Robert Browning," and dated " 19, *Warwick Crescent, W., March* 17*th,* 1887."

(2) Page 6. Letter to Mr. Thos. J. Wise on " the early editions of Shelley. . . obtained for me some time before 1830 (or even earlier), in the regular way, from Hunt and Clarke, in consequence of a direction I obtained from the *Literary Gazette.* . . I got at the same time, nearly, *Endymion,* and *Lamia,* &c., just as if they had been published a week before—and not years after the death of Keats." Dated " *March* 3*rd,* 1886." Signature not given.

(3) Page 8. Letter to Mr. Thos. J. Wise concerning his facsimile reprint of the original edition of *Pauline :* " I really have said my little say about the little book already elsewhere, and should only increase words without knowledge. . . There was a note of explanation in the copy I gave John Forster,—which contained also a criticism by John Mill." Signed " Robert Browning," and dated " *November* 5, 1866."

(4) Page 13. Extract from a letter referring to his having re-written *Sordello :* " I did certainly at one time

intend to re-write much of it, but changed my mind."
Signature and date not given.

(5) Page 25. Letter to Mr. Thos. J. Wise, answering certain queries concerning *The Statue and the Bust.* Signed " Robert Browning," and dated "*Jan. 8th, '87.*"

(6) Page 32. Letter to Mr. W. G. Kingsland explanatory of the poem *Fears and Scruples.* Signed " Robert Browning," and dated " 19, *Warwick Crescent, W., Feb. 9th, '85.*"

(7) Page 35. Letter to Mr. W. G. Kingsland on the subject of a proposed cheap volume of selections from his poems. Signed " Robert Browning," and dated " 19 *Warwick Crescent, Jan. 6th, '86.*"

(8) Facing Page 36. Facsimile of a letter addressed to Mr. W. G. Kingsland telling of the death of "my belovedest of friends, Milsand." Signed " Robert Browning," and dated "*Hand Hotel, Llangollen, N. Wales, Sept. 6, '86.*"

(9) Page 46. Letter to Mr. W. G. Kingsland acknowledging receipt of magazines [*Poet Lore*] from America. Signed " Robert Browning," and dated " 29 *De Vere Gardens, W., Aug. 26, '89.*"

(10) Page 56. Letter to Mr. W. G. Kingsland on the alleged obscurity of his poems : " I can have little doubt but that my writing has been, in the main, too hard for many I should have been pleased to communicate with ; but I never designedly tried to puzzle people, as some of my critics have supposed. On the other hand, I never pretended to offer such literature as should be a substitute for a cigar, or a

game at dominoes to an idle man." Signed " Robert
Browning," and dated " 19 *Warwick Crescent, W.,
Nov. 27, '68.*" Reprinted in *Letters from Robert
Browning to Various Correspondents, Edited by
Thomas J. Wise,* 1895, Vol. i, pp. 25–26.

(22.)

Poet Lore, 1890, p. 108. Letter to Mr. Halliwell-Phillipps
concerning the New Shakspere Society and Mr.
Browning's position as president. Signed " Robert
Browning," and dated "*Jan.* 27, '81."

(23.)

Merry England, 1890. Letter to Mr. Meynell concerning
the merits of some " prose and verse " brought to his
notice. Signed "Robert Browning," and dated "*Asolo,
Veneto, Italia, Oct. 7,* '89."

(24.)

Browning's Message to his Time. By Edward Berdoe.
London, 8vo, 1890.
(1) Page 6. Letter to Dr. Berdoe acknowledging a communication concerning the help received from Mr.
Browning's writings. Signed " Robert Browning,"
and dated " 19 *Warwick Crescent, W. Jan.* 12,
1885."
This letter is also given in facsimile upon an unnumbered leaf facing p. 6.
(2) Letter (given in facsimile upon an unnumbered leaf
facing p. 127) to Dr. Berdoe, expressing " my sense

of the obligation your goodness lays me under by the paper in which you so generously estimate my attempts to make use of the few materials of a scientific nature I have had any opportunity of collecting." Signed " Robert Browning," and dated " 19, *Warwick Crescent, W. June* 11, '85."

(3) Page 218. Letter to Dr. Berdoe stating his willingness to become a patron of a proposed Anti-vivisectionist Hospital. Signed " Robert Browning," dated " 29 *De Vere Gardens, W. August 27th*, 1889."

This letter is also given in facsimile upon an unnumbered leaf, facing p. 218.

(25.)

Poet Lore, Vol. ii, No. 5, *May*, 1890, p. 283.

An article containing many extracts from various letters of Robert Browning.

(26.)

The Critic (New York), *Oct. 25th*, 1890.

Letter to Mr. Irving concerning a reminiscence of Kean, and asking his acceptance of the empty purse found upon Kean after his death. Signed " Robert Browning ; " undated.

(27.)

Poet Lore, vol. iii, No. 10, *October* 1891, p. 524.

Article upon Mrs. Sutherland Orr's *Life of Robert Browning*, containing extracts from various letters *not* quoted by Mrs. Orr.

(28.)

Life and Letters of Robert Browning. By Mrs. Sutherland Orr.   London, 8vo, 1891.

(1) Page 55. Letter to Rev. W. J. Fox concerning the approaching issue of *Pauline.* Signed " R. B." (Undated.)

(2) Page 55. Letter to Rev. W. J. Fox accompanying copies of *Pauline.* Signed " R. Browning." (Undated.)

(3) Page 56. Letter to Rev. W. J. Fox referring to a probably favourable notice of *Pauline.* Signed " R. B." (Undated, but post-marked " *March* 29, 1833.")

(4) Page 57. Letter to Rev. W. J. Fox conveying thanks for the notice of *Pauline.* Signed " Robert Browning," and dated " *March* 31, 1833."

(5) Page 68. Letter to Rev. W. J. Fox on *Paracelsus :* " I hope my poem will turn out not utterly unworthy your kind interest, and more deserving your favour than anything of mine you have as yet seen." Signed " Robt. Browning," and dated " *April* 2, 1835."

(6) Page 69. Letter to Rev. W. J. Fox on the securing a publisher for *Paracelsus,* and other matters. Unsigned, but dated " *April* 16."

(7) Page 90. Two letters to Rev. W. J. Fox on *Strafford.* Both signed " Robert Browning," and both undated.

(8) Page 95. Letter to John Robertson, Esq., informing him that he had that morning sailed for Venice, " intending to finish my poem [*Sordello*] among the scenes it describes." Signed " Robert Browning," and dated " *Good Friday,* 1838."

(9) Page 96. Letter to Miss Haworth relating his adventures in Italy, and other matters. Signed " R. B.," and dated " 1838."

(10) Page 102. Letter to Miss Haworth on Rev. W. J. Fox —" who used to write in reviews when I was a boy, and to whom my verses, written at the ripe age of twelve and thirteen, were shown : which verses he praised not a little ; which praise comforted me not a little." (Signature and date not given.)

(11) Page 110. Letter to Miss Flower : " Praise what you can praise, do me all the good you can, you and Mr. Fox (as if you will not !) for I have a head full of projects." Signed " Robert Browning." Date not given. This letter is printed in full in *Letters from Robert Browning to Various Correspondents. Edited by Thomas J. Wise*, 1895, vol. i, pp. 3–4, where it is dated " *London, March 9th* [1842]."

(12) Page 118. Letter to Mr. Hill on Macready and the performance of *A Blot in the 'Scutcheon* at Drury Lane, in February 1843. Signed " Robert Browning," and dated " 19 *Warwick Crescent : Dec.* 15, 1884."

(13) Page 123. Letter to Mr. Hill containing a last word regarding the reputed failure of *A Blot in the 'Scutcheon* at Drury Lane in Feb. 1843 : " I would submit to anybody drawing a conclusion from one or two facts past contradiction, whether that play could have thoroughly failed which was not only not withdrawn at once, but acted three nights in the same week." Signed " Robert Browning," and dated *December* 21, 1884."

(14) Page 132.   Letter to Miss Lee on the *Lost Leader* and Wordsworth contr*o*versy : " I thought of the great Poet's abandonment of liberalism, at an unlucky juncture, and no repaying consequence that I could ever see.   But—once call my fancy portrait *Words-worth*—and how much more ought one to say—how much more would not I have attempted to say." Signed " Robert Browning," and dated " *Villers-sur-mer, Calvados, France : Sept. 7, '75.*"

(15) Page 133.   Extract from an undated letter to Miss Haworth, detailing the writing an impromptu verse for a picture by Maclise.   Signed " Robert Browning."   Undated.

(16) Page 135.   Letter to Miss Flower relating apparently to the publication of *Hymns*, &c.   Signed " Robert Browning," and headed " *New Cross, Hatcham, Surrey : Tuesday morning.*"   Precise date not given.

(17) Page 135.   Letter to Miss Flower expressing his admiration for her music.   Signature and date not given.

(18) Page 193.   Letter to Lady (then Mrs. Theodore) Martin [Helen Faucit] on the projected performance of *Colombe's Birthday.*   Signature not given, but dated " *Florence : Jan.* 31, '53."

(19) Page 222.   Letter to W. J. Fox (written in continuation of a letter of Mrs. Browning's), asseverating his old feelings of friendship and goodwill.   Signed ' Robert Browning," but undated.

(20) Page 226.   Letter to Mr. (now Sir Frederic) Leighton, on various matters.   Signed " R. Browning," and dated " *Kingdom of Piedmont, Siena : Oct.* 9, '59."

(21) Page 242. Letter to Mr. (now Sir Frederick) Leighton anticipatory of his movements. Signed "Robert Browning," and dated "Florence: *July* 19, '61."

(22) Page 249. Letter to Miss Haworth, narrating the circumstances of his wife's death: "At four o'clock there were symptoms that alarmed me. . . . Then came what my heart will keep till I see her again, and longer—the most perfect expression of her love to me within my whole knowledge of her. Always smilingly, happily, and with a face like a girl's—and in a few minutes she died in my arms ; her head on my cheek." Signed "Robert Browning," and dated "*Florence : July* 20, 1861."

(23) Page 251. Extract from a letter to Miss Blagden, on the subject of the provisional disinterment of his wife's remains. Unsigned, but dated "*Sept.* '61."

(24) Page 256. Letter to Madame du Quaire concerning the best course to pursue as to the education of his son. Signed "Robert Browning," and dated "*M. Chauvin St.-Enogat près Dinard, Ile et Vilaine : Aug.* 17, '61."

(25) Page 258. Letter to Miss Blagden : "My heart is sore for a great calamity just befallen poor Rossetti. . . . There has hardly been a day when I have not thought, 'if I can, to-morrow, I will go and see him, and thank him for his book; and return his sister's poems.' Poor, dear fellow !" Signature not given : dated "*Feb.* 15, '62."

(26) Page 259. Letter to Miss Blagden, on his stay at St.

Jean de Luz.   Signature not given : dated "*Biarritz, Maison Gastonbide : Sept.* 19, '62."

(27) Page 261.   Letter to Miss Blagden on his being " pestered with applications for leave to write the *Life* of my wife—I have refused—and there's an end."   Signature not given : dated "*Jan.* 19, '63."

(28) Page 268.   Letter to Miss Blagden on the " gossiping going about" concerning himself and his books. Signature not given : dated "*August* '65."

(29) Pages 271—273.   Short extracts from letters to Miss Blagden.   Unsigned : dated respectively "*Sept.* '65," "*Feb.* 19, '66," and "*May* 19, '66."

(30) Page 273.   Letter to Miss Blagden on the death of his father—" this good, unworldly, kind-hearted religious man, whose powers, natural and acquired, would so easily have made him a notable man, had he known what vanity or ambition or the love of money or social influence meant."   Signature not given : dated "*June* 20, '66."

(31) Page 276.   Letter to Dr. Scott, Master of Balliol, acknowledging the distinction of Honorary Fellow of Balliol College which had been conferred upon him. Signed " Robert Browning," and dated "19, *Warwick Crescent : Oct.* 21, '67."

(32) Pages 277—284.   Short extracts from letters to Miss Blagden, and others, on various topics.

(33) Page 286.   Letter to Miss Blagden : " Florence would be irritating, and, on the whole, insufferable—Yet I never hear of anyone going thither but my heart is twitched."   Signature not given : dated "*Feb.* 24."

(34) Page 287.   Letter to Miss Blagden, touching on various reminiscences.   Signature not given : dated " *St. Aubin : August* 19, 1870."

(35) Letter to Mr. George Smith, asking him to buy the right of printing a poem [*Hervé Riel*] in the *Pall Mall,* or the *Cornhill Magazine,* the proceeds to go to the relief of the distressed people of Paris : " Would, for the love of France, that this were a *Song of a Wren*—then should the guineas equal the lines ; as it is, do what you safely may for the song of a Robin— Browning," dated "*Feb.* 4, '71."

(36) Page 291.   Letter to Miss Blagden on the poem *Prince Hohenstiel-Schwangau :* " I am told my little thing is succeeding—sold 1,400 in the first five days, and before any notice appeared."   Signature not given : dated "*Jan.* 1872."

(37) Page 309.   Letter to Mrs. Fitz-Gerald on his visit to Oxford.   Signed " R. Browning," and dated "*Jan.* 20, 1877."

(38) Page 312.   Letter to Mrs. Fitz-Gerald on " the harm- less drolleries of the young men" [at Oxford]. Signed " R. Browning" ; date not given.

(39) Page 314.   Letter to Mrs. Fitz-Gerald on his sojourn at La Saisiaz.   Signature not given : dated "*August* 17, 1877."

(40) Page 324.   Letter to Mrs. Fitz-Gerald describing his visit to Asolo after an absence of forty years.   Signed " Robert Browning," and dated "*Sept.* 28, 1878."

(41) Page 332.   Letter to Mrs. Fitz-Gerald giving an account of his residence in Venice.   Signature not

given : dated "*Albergo dell' Universo, Venezia, Italia :
Sept.* 24, '81."

(42) Pages 336—339.   Extracts from letters, signatures and
dates not given.

(43) Page 346.   Letter to Mrs. Fitz-Gerald on the Browning Society and the close of its first session : "They
always treat me gently in *Punch*—why don't you do
the same by the Browning Society ?   They give
their time for nothing, offer their little entertainment
for nothing, and certainly get next to nothing in the
way of thanks—unless from myself, who feel grateful to the faces I shall never see, the voices I shall
never hear."   Signed "R. Browning:" date not given.

(44) Page 353.   Letter to Miss Hickey on her annotated
edition of *Strafford* for the use of students.   Signed
" Robert Browning " : and dated " 19, *Warwick Crescent, W., February* 15, 1884."

(45) Page 354.   Letter to Professor Knight on the variations in the text of Wordsworth's poem, *The Daisy :*
" Your method of giving the original text, and sub-
joining in a note the variations, each with its proper
date, is incontestably preferable to any other."
Signed " Robert Browning," and dated "19, *Warwick
Crescent, W. : July* 9, '80."

(46) Page 355.   Letter to Professor Knight on the classify-
ing of Wordsworth's poems : " In my heart I fear I
should do it almost chronologically—so immeasurably superior seem to me the 'first sprightly run-
nings.' "   Signed " Robert Browning," and dated
" 19, Warwick Crescent, W. : *March* 23, '87."

(47) Page 359. Letter to Mrs. Charles Skirrow on his anticipated purchase of the Manzoni Palace, on the Canal Grande, Venice. Signed " Robert Browning " : and dated " *Palazzo Giustiniani Recanati, S. Moïse : Nov.* 15, '85."

(48) Page 378. Letter to Mrs. Hill on an " impromptu sonnet "—correctly printed in the *Century*, but incorrectly extracted by the *Pall Mall :* " So does the charge of unintelligibility attach itself to your poor friend—who can kick nobody." Signed " Robert Browning " : dated "*Jan.* 31, 1884."

(49) Page 391. Letter to Professor Knight on his unwillingness to speak at public festivals. Signed " Robert Browning," and dated " 19, *Warwick Crescent, W. : May* 9, '84."

(50) Page 402. Letter to Mr. George Bainton on any special "influence" that may have moulded his " style." Signed " Robert Browning," and dated " 29, *De Vere Gardens : Oct.* 6, '87."

(51) Page 403. Letter to Mr. Smith concerning certain corrections in *Pauline*. Signed " Robert Browning," and dated " 29, *De Vere Gardens, W. : Feb.* 27, '88."

(52) Page 405. Letter to Lady Martin, mentioning the acquisition, by his son, of the Rezzonico Palace, in Venice. Signed " Robert Browning," and dated " 29, *De Vere Gardens, W. : Aug.* 12, '88."

(53) Page 407. Letter to Miss Keep, on his sojourn at Primiero : " It is, I am more and more confirmed in believing, the most beautiful place I was ever

resident in." Signature not given : dated " *Primiero : Sept.* 7, '88."

(54) Page 409. Letter to Professor Knight on his view of
the position and function of Poetry : " Philosophy
first, and Poetry, which is its highest outcome, after-
ward—and much harm has been done by reversing
the natural process." Signed "Robert Browning,"
and dated " 29, *De Vere Gardens, W.: June* 16,
1889."

(55) Page 413. Letter to Mrs. Fitz-Gerald on Asolo. The
signature is not given : dated " *Oct.* 8, 1889."

(56) Page 414. Letter to Mrs. Skirrow, on his stay at
Asolo. Signed " Robert Browning " : dated
" *Oct.* 15."

(57) Page 415. Letter to Mr. George Smith descriptive of
Asolo : " The one thing I am disappointed in is to
find that the silk-cultivation with all the pretty
girls who were engaged in it are transported to
Cornuda and other places." Signed " Robert
Browning," and dated " *Asolo, Veneto, Italia : Oct.*
22, '89."

(58) Page 420. Letter to Mr. George Moulton-Barrett
descriptive of Asolo—" which strikes me,—as it did
fifty years ago, which is something to say, considering that, properly speaking, it was the first spot
of Italian soil I ever set foot upon—having proceeded to Venice by sea, and thence here." The
signature is not given : dated " *Asolo, Veneto : Oct.*
22, '89."

(59) Page 423. Letter to Miss Keep on his arrival at

Venice—" magnificently lodged in this vast palazzo
which my son has really shown himself fit to possess,
so surprising are his restorations and improvements."
The signature is not given, but dated " *9th of
November.*"

(29.)

Poet Lore, Vol. IV, No. 5, *May*, 1892, p. 233. Article
entitled *Excerpts from a Sheaf of Browning Letters*,
containing extracts from many letters by Robert
Browning.

(30.)

Poet Lore, Vol. IV, Nos. 8 and 9, *Aug.–Sept.* 1892, p. 473.
Letter to a correspondent distinguishing " between
the good of having the poetical temperament, and
the not-good of attempting to make poetry one's
self, except in the extraordinary cases where there
is original creative power added to the merely sensitive and appreciative,—valuable and distinguishing
as these are." Signed " Robert Browning," and
dated " 19, *Warwick Crescent, Upper Westbourne
Terrace, W. Apr. 27,'66.*"

(31.)

Poet Lore, Vol. V, No. 5, *May*, 1893, p. 231.
(1) Page 231. Letter to Mr. W. G. Kingsland explanatory of his apparent neglect in replying to a
communication. Signed " Robert Browning," and
dated " *June*, 1889."

(**32.**)

(2) Page 232. Letter to a lady [Miss C. G. Barnard] stating how much he valued "all such sympathy as you are pleased to express;" and assuring her that "I am the better for having heard of your care to see me while it was yet possible." Signed "Robert Browning," and dated "*Warwick Crescent, May,* 1884."

(**33.**)

The Life and Work of John Ruskin. By W. G. Collingwood, M.A. London : Methuen & Co., 1893, pp. 199–202.

Letter to John Ruskin. Signed "Robert Browning," and dated "*Paris, Dec.* 10*th,* '55." "Do you think poetry was ever generally understood—or can be? Is it the business of it to tell people what they know already, as they know it? . . . . . It is all teaching, and the people hate to be taught. . . . . . . A poet's affair is with God, to whom he is accountable, and of whom is his reward : look elsewhere, and you find misery enough."

(**34.**)

The Daily Chronicle, July 19*th,* 1895. Letter to Messrs. Fields, Osgood & Co. regarding the Trans-Atlantic publishing arrangements for *The Ring and the Book.* Signed "Robert Browning," and dated "*September 2nd,* 1868."

*** The *Chronicle* avowedly reproduced this letter from the Catalogue of an American firm of Autograph-dealers.

(35.)

The Critic (New York). Letter to Mr. Edmund Gosse selecting the four of his poems he would prefer to have inserted in a volume of poetical selections : " Let me say — at a venture—lyrical : *Saul* or *Abt Vogler ;* narrative : *A Forgiveness ;* dramatic : *Caliban upon Setebos ;* idyllic (in the Greek sense): *Clive.*" Signed " Robert Browning," and dated " 19 *Warwick Crescent, W., March* 15, 1885."

(36.)

The Table-Talk of Shirley [*i.e.* John Skelton]. William Blackwood & Sons, Edinburgh and London, 1895.

(1) Page 288. Letter to Dr. Skelton. Signed " Robert Browning," and dated " *March* 31*st,* 1863."

(2) Page 289. Letter to Dr. Skelton. Signed " Robert Browning," and dated " *November* 15, 1878."

(37.)

The Athenæum, January 11*th,* 1896. Letter to F. T. Palgrave, " in reply to some remonstrance I [F. T. P.] had ventured to make on the quantity which Browning somewhere assigned to the word ' metamorphosis,' the penultimate syllable of which is long in Greek." Signed " Yours unirrĩtatedly, R.B.," and dated " *April* 1*st,* 1869."

PART IV.

COMPLETE VOLUMES OF BIOGRAPHY AND CRITICISM.

PART IV.

COMPLETE VOLUMES OF BIOGRAPHY AND CRITICISM.

(I.)

Essays / on / Robert Browning's / Poetry / by / John T. Nettleship / London / Macmillan and Co. / 1868.

Collation :—Post octavo, pp. viii + 305 : consisting of Half-title (with publishers' Monogram on reverse) pp. i–ii ; Title-page (with imprint in centre of reverse) pp. iii–iv ; Preface v–vi ; Contents (with blank reverse) pp. vii–viii ; and Text pp. 1–305. The imprint is repeated on the reverse of last page.

Issued in light brown cloth boards, lettered in gilt across the back : "*Essays / on / Robert / Browning's / Poetry / Nettleship / Macmillan & Co.*"

[*New Edition.*]

Robert Browning / Essays and Thoughts / by / John T. Nettleship / London / Elkin Mathews, Vigo Street, W. / 1890.

Collation :—Post octavo, pp. xii + 454 : consisting of Half-title (with blank reverse) pp. i–ii ; Title-page (with imprint in centre of blank reverse) pp. iii–iv ; Dedication to Robert Browning (with blank reverse) pp. v–vi ; Prefatory note (with blank reverse) pp. vii–viii ; Contents pp. ix–x ; Preface xi–xii ; and Text pp. 1–454.

Issued in brown buckram bevelled boards, lettered in gilt across back "*Robert Browning / Essays / and / Thoughts / J. T. Nettleship / Elkin Mathews.*" There were also seventy-five copies on large Whatman paper.

(2.)

Balaustion's Adventure. / Reprinted from the London Quarterly Review, / January, 1872. / For Private Circulation. / [By H. Buxton Forman.] London : / Printed by Beveridge and Fraser, / Fullwood's Rents, Holborn.

Collation :—Demy octavo, pp. 24 : consisting of Title-page p. 1, and Text pp. 2–24.

Issued without wrapper, stitched, the text commencing on the reverse of the title-page.

(3.)

Browning's Women / by / Mary E. Burt / With an Introduction by / Rev. Edward Everett Hale, D.D., LL.D. / Chicago / Charles H. Kerr & Company / 175 Dearborn Street / 1877.

Collation :—16mo, pp. xii + 1–225 : consisting of Title-page (with imprint and " copyright " on blank reverse) pp. i–ii ; Dedication to " Jenkin Lloyd Jones and his first Browning Club " (with blank reverse) pp. iii–iv ; Contents (with blank reverse) pp. v–vi ; Preface (with blank reverse) pp. vii–viii ; Introduction (with blank reverse) pp. ix–xii ; and Text pp. 1–225.

Issued in dark blue cloth boards, with gilt top, and lettered in gilt on front cover : " *Browning's Women* / *Mary E. Burt.*" Also gilt lettered across the back " *Browning's Women* / *Burt.*"

(4.)

Sordello / A Story from Robert Browning / By / Frederick May Holland / Author of the " Reign of the Stoics " / New York / G. P. Putnam's Sons / 27 and 29 West 23d Street / 1881.

Collation :—Small square octavo, pp. 29 : consisting of Title-
page, as above (with imprint upon the reverse) pp. 1–2 ;
and Text pp. 3–29.

Issued in stiff drab paper wrappers, with *"Sordello | Frederick May
Holland"* printed upon the front. The pamphlet was issued as
an experiment, very few copies being printed. It was afterwards
included (with considerable alterations) in *Stories from Robert
Browning, by F. May Holland, London,* 1882—(See *post,* No. 7).

(5.)

The / Browning Society's Papers. / 1881–4 / [*Contents.*]
Publisht for / The Browning Society / by N. Trübner &
Co., 57 & 59, Ludgate Hill, / London, E.C., 1881–4 /
Price Five Shillings.

Issued in grey paper wrappers, the second and third pages of
which contain Advertisements of other Societies ; the fourth page
being devoted to an announcement of the officers, list of meetings,
&c., of the Browning Society. The Papers were issued in
" Parts," the intention being to complete them in Three
Volumes. Thirteen Parts in all have been issued, as
follows : Vol. i, Parts i–v ; Vol. ii, Parts vii–xi ; Vol. iii, Parts
xii–xiii. Several of the earlier numbers have been reprinted,
many corrections being made in the text—particularly in the
Bibliography contained in Part I. The *First* edition of Part I
was issued at 5/-. Later editions of this Part, and *all* editions of
the succeeding Parts, were 10/- each.

Part I.

	Page		Page
Title......................	I	The Browning Society	19–20
Foretalk, by F. J. Fur-		A Bibliography of	
nivall	3–4	Robert Browning,	
Browning's Essay on		1833–1881, by F J.	
Shelley	5–19	Furnivall	21–72

Part II.

Part III.

Part XI.

Part XII.

Part XIII.

(*Illustrations.*)

(6.)

Illustrations / to / Browning's Poems / Part I. / [*Contents :* Part II. *with Contents*] With a / Notice of the Artists and the Pictures / by / Ernest Radford. / Published for / the Browning Society / by N. Trübner & Co., 57 and 59, Ludgate Hill, / London, E.C. 1882 / Price Ten Shillings.

Collation :—Quarto, pp. i–viii : consisting of Title-page (with notice of *Illustrations* on reverse), pp. i–ii ; and Text, pp. iii-viii.

Issued in mottled-grey paper boards, Part I. in 1882, and Part II. in 1883.

Contents.
Part I.

1. The Coronation of the Virgin, from the Painting by Fra Lippo Lippi in the *Accademia delle Belle Arti* at Florence, described in Browning's *Fra Lippo Lippi*, lines 347–387.

2. Andrea del Sarto and his Wife, from the Painting by Andrea del Sarto in the Pitti Palace, Florence, which gave rise to Browning's *Andrea del Sarto.*

3. The Angel and the Child, from the Picture by Guercino in a chapel at Fano, on the Adriatic, which is the subject of Browning's *Guardian Angel.*

Part II.

4. A Photogravure, by Dawson's process, of Mr. C. Fairfax Murray's

Copy of Andrea del Sarto's painting of himself and his wife, which gave rise to Browning's *Andrea del Sarto.*

5. A Woodbury Type engraving of Robert Browning, from a Photograph by Fradelle. (Presented by Mrs. Sutherland Orr.)

Note.—With this Part was issued Woodbury-type engravings of Robert Browning (from Fradelle's photograph), in demy octavo for the Society's *Papers ;* and in foolscap octavo for any volume of Browning's poems (both presented by Mrs. Sutherland Orr). Also reductions in foolscap octavo, for Browning's poems, of the Andrea (No. 4, Part II.) ; and of Fra Lippo's Coronation, and Guercino's Angel and Child (Nos. 1 and 2 of the *Illustrations*, Part I.).

(7.)

Stories from Robert Browning. / By / Frederick May Holland, / Author of / ' The Reign of the Stoics.' / With an Introduction by / Mrs. Sutherland Orr. / London : George Bell and Sons, / York Street, Covent Garden. / 1882.

Collation :—Crown octavo, pp. xlviii + 228 : consisting of Half-title (with blank reverse), pp. i–ii ; Title-page (with imprint at foot of the reverse), pp. iii–iv ; Contents (with blank reverse), pp. v–vi ; Preface pp. vii–ix ; p. x is blank ; Introduction pp. xi–xlvii; p. xlviii is blank; and Text pp. 1–228. The imprint is repeated at the foot of the last page.

Issued in orange coloured bevelled cloth boards, lettered in gilt across the back : " *Stories | from | Browning | Holland | G. Bell & Sons.*" Also lettered in gilt upon the front cover.

The "Stories" included are those of *Strafford—Sordello—Luria— The Adventures of Balaustion—A Blot on the 'Scutcheon—The Ring and the Book—Pippa Passes—The Return of the Druses—* and *Colombe's Birthday.*

(8.)

The Browning Society / 1884-5 / Hercules Wrestling with

Death / for the body of Alcestis / A Picture painted in 1871 by / Sir Frederick Leighton / P.R.A.

This print was taken by kind permission of Sir B. Samuelson, Bart., M.P., and presented to the members of the Browning Society by the painter (one of its Vice-Presidents) in Sept. 1884. It was issued in a wrapper, on the inside of which is printed the lines from *Balaustion's Adventure* illustrated by the picture.

(9.)

Robert Browning / The Thoughts of a Poet on Art and Faith. / A Lecture / Delivered to the Birmingham Central Literary Association, / March 27th, 1885. / By / Howard S. Pearson. / Price Sixpence. / Published for the Committee of the Birmingham Central Literary Association, by / Cornish Brothers, 37, New Street.

Collation :—Demy quarto, pp. 27 : consisting of Title-page, as above (with imprint in centre of reverse), pp. 1–2 ; and Text, pp. 3–27.

Issued in drab-coloured paper wrappers, with the title-page reproduced upon the front.

(10.)

A Handbook / to the Works of / Robert Browning / by / Mrs. Sutherland Orr. / " No pause i' the leading and the light ! " / *The Ring and the Book*, vol. iii., p. 70. / London : George Bell & Sons, / York Street, Covent Garden. / 1885. / [*The right of translation is reserved.*]

Collation :—Foolscap octavo, pp. xiii + 332 : consisting of Half-title (with blank reverse), pp. i–ii; Title-page, as above (with imprint at bottom of reverse), pp. iii–iv; Preface, pp. v–vi; Errata and Note to " Artemis Prologizes," p. vii; p. viii is blank ; Contents pp. ix–xiii; Text, pp. 1–328 ; and Index, pp. 329–332.

Issued in olive-green cloth boards, lettered in gilt across the back :
" *Handbook | to | Robert | Browning's | Works | Mrs. S. Orr |
George Bell and Sons.*"

The above is a description of the first edition of this work ; but there
have been several subsequent editions, in which various corrections, &c.,
have been made.

(11.)

Miss Alma Murray's | Constance | in | Robert Brown-
ing's " In a Balcony." | A paper by | B. L. Mosely, LL.B. |
Barrister-at-Law. | Read to the Browning Society | on the
27th of February, 1885. | *Reprinted from* THE THEATRE
for May, 1885. | For private distribution only. | London,
1885.

Collation :—Octavo, pp. 8 : consisting of Title-page, as above
(with blank reverse) pp. 1–2 ; and Text, pp. 3–8.
Issued in cream-tinted wrapper, lettered " *Miss Alma Murray's |
Constance | in | Robert Browning's ' In a Balcony.' | A paper by |
B. L. Mosely, LL.B. | Barrister-at-Law,*" upon the front.

(12.)

Sordello's Story | Retold in Prose | by | Annie Wall |
[*Publishers' device.*] Boston and New York | Houghton,
Mifflin and Company | The Riverside Press, Cambridge |
1886.

Collation :—Crown octavo, pp. 145 : consisting of Title-page,
as above (with " copyright " in centre and imprint at foot of
reverse), pp. 1–2 ; Dedication (with blank reverse), pp. 3–4 ;
Quotation from Dante (with blank reverse), pp. 5–6 ; and
Text, pp. 7–145.
Issued in dark yellow cloth boards, gilt lettered across the back,
" *Sordello's Story | Annie Wall | Houghton, Mifflin & Co.*"

(**13.**)

An / Introduction / to the Study of / Robert Browning's Poetry. / By / Hiram Corson, LL.D., / Professor of Rhetoric and English Literature in the / Cornell University. / "*Subtlest Assertor of the Soul in song.*" / Boston : / D. C. Heath & Co., Publishers. / 1886.

Collation :—Crown octavo, pp. x + 338 : consisting of Title-page, as above (with "copyright" in centre, and imprint at foot, of the reverse), pp. i–ii ; motto (with blank reverse), pp. iii–iv ; Preface, pp. v–vii ; p. viii is blank ; Contents, pp. ix–x ; and Text, pp. 1–338.

Issued in dark-blue cloth boards, lettered in gilt across the back : "*Introduction | to | Browning | Corson | D. C. Heath & Co | Boston.*"

(**14.**)

Robert Browning's Poetry / "*The development of a soul ; little else is worth study*" / Outline Studies / Published for the Chicago Browning Society / Chicago / Charles H. Kerr & Company / 175 Dearborn Street / 1886.

Collation :—Crown octavo, pp. 50 : consisting of Title-page (with "copyright" in centre of reverse), pp. 1—2 ; Contents (with prefatory note on reverse), pp. 3—4 ; and Text, pp. 5-50.

Issued in light yellow paper wrapper, with "*Robert Browning's Poetry*" printed across centre. A limited number of copies were placed on sale in London.

(**15.**)

Sordello : / A History and a Poem. / By Caroline H. Dall. / Boston : / Roberts Brothers. / 1886.

Collation :—Octavo, pp. 36 : consisting of Title-page, as above

(with reverse containing notice of copyright, and imprint, in centre and at foot respectively), pp. 1—2 : prefatory "note," pp. 3—4 ; and Text, pp. 5—36.
Issued in light grey wrapper, with the Title-page reproduced upon the front cover.

(16.)

An / Introduction / to / the study of / Browning / by / Arthur Symons / Cassell & Company, Limited / London, Paris, New York, & Melbourne / 1886 / [All rights reserved.]

Collation :—Crown octavo, pp. viii + 216 : consisting of Title-page (with quotation from Landor on reverse), pp. i–ii ; Dedication to George Meredith (with blank reverse), pp. iii–iv ; Preface, pp. v–vi ; Contents (with blank reverse), pp. vii–viii ; and Text, pp. 1–216.
Issued in dark green bevelled boards, lettered in gilt across the back " *Introduction / to / Browning / Symons.*"

(17.)

Swedenborg and the / Brownings / By / James Spilling / Author of " The Evening and the Morning," etc. etc. / James Speirs / 36 Bloomsbury Street, London / 1886.

Collation :—Foolscap octavo, pp. 16 : consisting of Title-page, as above (with blank reverse), pp. 1–2 ; and Text, pp. 3–16.
Issued stitched, and without wrappers. The imprint, " *Morrison and Gibb, Edinburgh, / Printers to Her Majesty's Stationery Office,*" occurs at the foot of the last page.

(18.)

Studies in the Poetry / of / Robert Browning / by / James Fotheringham / London / Kegan Paul, Trench & Co., 1 Paternoster Square / 1887.

Collation :—Crown octavo, pp. xii + 382 : consisting of Title-page (with quotations on reverse), pp. i–ii ; Preface, pp. iii–viii ; Contents, pp. ix–x ; Reference List of Poems, pp. xi–xii ; and Text, pp. 1–382.

Issued in dark blue cloth boards, gilt lettered across the back " *Studies | in the | Poetry | of | Robert | Browning | Fothering-ham | Kegan Paul, Trench & Co.*" The front cover is also lettered " *Studies in the Poetry | of Robert Browning.*"

(19.)

Robert Browning : / Chief Poet of the Age. / An Essay / Addressed primarily to beginners in the Study of / Browning's Poems / By / William G. Kingsland / London / J. W. Jarvis & Son / 28 King William Street, Strand / 1887.

Collation :—Square 16mo., pp. 47 : consisting of Title-page (with blank reverse), pp. 1–2 ; Dedicatory Sonnet "to Robert Browning" (with blank reverse), pp. 3–4 ; and Text, pp. 5–47. The imprint is placed upon the centre of the reverse of the last page.

Issued in drab-coloured paper boards ; with the title-page reprinted upon the front. A portrait of Mr. Browning forms the frontispiece. Thirty copies on large hand-made paper were also issued.

[*Second Edition.*]

Robert Browning : / Chief Poet of the Age. / By / William G. Kingsland / New Edition, / With Biographical and other Additions / London : / J. W. Jarvis & Son, / 28 King William Street, Strand / 1890.

Collation :—Small octavo, pp. vi + 136 : consisting of Half-
        title (with blank reverse), pp. i–ii ; Title-page (with imprint
        on reverse), pp. iii–iv ; Preface, pp. v–vii ; Dedicatory
        Sonnet, p. viii ; and Text, pp. 1–136. The imprint is re-
        peated at the foot of the last page.

Issued in fawn-coloured cloth boards, gilt lettered across the back
" *Browning* | *Kingsland* | 1890." A portrait of Mr. Browning
forms the frontispiece. Fifty copies were also printed on large
hand-made paper.

(20.)

Sordello / An Outline Analysis of / Mr. Browning's Poem /
by / Jeanie Morison / author of / ' The Purpose of the
Ages ; ' ' Gordon : an Our Day Idyll ; " / ' Ane Booke of
Ballades,' etc. / William Blackwood and Sons / Edinburgh
and London / MDCCCLXXXIX. | *All Rights reserved.*

Collation :—Crown octavo, pp. vi + 115 : consisting of Half-title
        (with blank reverse), pp. i–ii ; Title-page (with blank
        reverse), pp. iii–iv ; Dedication to the Members of the
        Edinburgh Women-Students' Browning Club, with blank
        reverse, pp. v–vi ; and Text, pp. 1–115. The imprint is
        at the foot of the last page.

Issued in dark red cloth boards, with trimmed edges, and lettered
in gilt across the back : " *Analysis* | *of* | *Sordello* | *Jeanie* |
Morison | *Wm. Blackwood* | *&* Sons."

(21.)

Robert Browning. / Nineteenth Century Authors. / Louise
Manning Hodgkins. / D. C. Heath & Co., Boston. [1889.]

Collation :—Small octavo, pp. ii + 8 : consisting of Title-page,
        as above (with blank reverse), pp. i–ii ; Text, pp. 1–4 ;
        blank pages headed *Notes*, pp. 5–7 ; and notices of the
        series of *Guides*, p. 8.

Issued stitched, without wrappers.　Circulated gratis.　A number of copies were distributed among the Members of the Browning Society.

(22.)

Robert　Browning / Personalia / by / Edmund　Gosse / Boston and New York / Houghton, Mifflin and Company / The Riverside Press, Cambridge / 1890.

Collation :—Crown octavo, pp. 96 : consisting of Title (with imprint in centre of reverse), 1–2 ; Preface, 3–9 (blank reverse, 10) ; Contents (with blank reverse), 11–12 ; Half-title (with blank reverse), 13–14 ; Text, 15–96.

Issued in Indian red cloth boards, with gilt top, and lettered in gilt on front cover : " *Robert Browning | Personalia | By Edmund | Gosse*" / ; also lettered across back " *Robert | Browning | Per-sonalia | Gosse | Houghton | Mifflin & Co.*"　There is a portrait of Robert Browning as frontispiece.

A portion of the impression of this book was purchased by T. Fisher Unwin, who issued these copies in London with his own imprint upon the title-page, and upon the cover, in place of that of Messrs. Houghton, Mifflin & Co. as detailed above. They were put up in vellum bevelled boards, gilt lettered.

There were also ten copies printed upon large paper.

(23.)

A Sequence of Sonnets / on the Death of Robert Browning / By / A. C. Swinburne / London / Printed for Private Circulation / MDCCCXC.

Collation :—Small quarto, pp. 13 ; consisting of Half-title (with blank reverse), pp. 1–2 ; Title-page, as above (with blank reverse), pp. 3–4 ; Prefatory Note (with blank reverse), pp.

5–6 ; * and Text, pp. 7–13.   The head-line is *A Sequence of Sonnets* throughout, on both sides of the page.   There is no imprint.

Issued in dark slate coloured paper wrappers, with the title-page reproduced upon the front.

These *Sonnets* also appeared in *The Fortnightly Review* for *January*, 1890.   They were afterwards reprinted in *Astrophel, and other Poems*, 1894, pp. 136-142.   There is a copy of the pamphlet in the British Museum.

* This *Prefatory Note* states that " A few copies only have been printed in this separate form more befitting the occasion."   It may safely be prophesied that these " few copies," forming as they do a connecting link between two of the foremost poets of the age, will at no distant date prove to occupy a conspicuous position in the list of modern poetical rarities.

(24.)

Robert Browning. / Read before the / Literary and Philosophical Society of Liverpool. / April 28th, 1890 / By / Gerald H. Rendall.

Collation :—Demy octavo, pp. ii + 20 : consisting of Title-page, as above (with blank reverse), pp. i—ii ; and Text, pp. 1—20.

Issued in light mottled-grey wrapper, with the Title-page reprinted upon the front.

(25.)

Life / of / Robert Browning / by / William Sharp / London : / Walter Scott, 24 Warwick Lane. / 1890. / (*All rights reserved.*)

Collation :—Post octavo, pp. ii + 219 + xxii: consisting of Half-title, pp. i–ii ; Title-page, as above (with blank reverse), pp. 1–2 ; Contents, pp. 3–8 ; prefatory "note" pp. 9–10 ; Text, pp. 11–212 ; Index, pp. 213–219 ; and Bibliography, pp. i–xxii.

Issued in dark blue cloth boards, lettered in gilt across the back, " *Life of | Robert Browning | William Sharp | Walter Scott.*"

This work formed one of the volumes of the " Great Writers' " series. Large Paper copies were also printed, the size being demy octavo.

(26.)

Browning's / Message to his Time : / His Religion, Philosophy, and Science / By Edward Berdoe / Member of the Royal College of Surgeons of England ; / Licentiate of the Royal College of Physicians (Edinburgh) ; / Member of the British Medical Association ; / etc., etc. / [*Quotation from Emerson*] London : / Swan Sonnenschein & Co., / Paternoster Square. / 1890.

Collation :—Octavo, pp. iv + 222 : consisting of Title-page, as above (with imprint in centre of reverse), pp. i–ii ; Dedication (with contents in centre of reverse), pp. iii–iv ; and Text, pp. 1–222.

Issued in dark red bevelled cloth boards, gilt lettered across the back : " *Browning's | Message | to | his Time | Berdoe | Sonnenschein.*"

(27.)

Life and Letters / of / Robert Browning / by / Mrs. Sutherland Orr / London / Smith, Elder, & Co., 15 Waterloo Place / 1891 / [*All rights reserved.*]

Collation :—Crown octavo, pp. xiii + 451 : consisting of Half-title (with blank reverse), pp. i–ii ; Title-page, as above (with blank reverse), pp. iii–iv ; Preface, pp. v–vi ; Contents, pp. vii–xiii ; Text, pp. 1–438 ; and Index, pp. 439–451.

Issued in dark yellow cloth boards, gilt lettered across the back, " *Life | and | Letters | of | Robert | Browning | Mrs. Sutherland Orr | Smith, Elder & Co.*"

(28.)

Robert Browning / and the Drama / With special reference to the point of view afforded by / Miss Alma Murray's / Performances of his Heroines. / A Note / by / Walter Fairfax / London / Reeves and Turner 196 Strand / 1891.

Collation :—Octavo, pp. 20 : consisting of Title-page, as above (with blank reverse), pp. 1–2 ; and Text, pp. 3–20. The imprint occurs at the foot of the last page.

Issued in light grey wrappers, with the Title-page reproduced upon the front, and on the reverse an advertisement of a forthcoming work by the same author.

(29.)

A Primer on Browning / By F. Mary Wilson / London / Macmillan and Co. / and New York / 1891 / *All rights reserved.*

Collation :—Small octavo, pp. viii + 248 : consisting of Half-title (with publishers' monogram upon the reverse), pp. i–ii ; Title-page, as above (with blank reverse), pp. iii–iv; Contents, pp. v–vii ; p. viii is blank ; and Text, pp. 1–248. The imprint occurs at the foot of the last page.

Issued in bright red coloured cloth boards, with trimmed edges, lettered in gilt across the back : " *A | Primer | on | Browning | F. Mary | Wilson | Macmillan & Co.*" Also lettered in black upon the front cover.

(30.)

Browning / as a / Philosophical and Religious / Teacher. / By / Henry Jones, M.A., / Professor of Philosophy in the

University College / of North Wales. / Glasgow : / James
Maclehose & Sons, / Publishers to the University. / 1891. /
All rights reserved.

Collation :—Crown octavo, pp. xii + 367 : consisting of Half-title
　　　　　(with publishers' imprint upon the reverse), pp. i–ii ; Title-
　　　　　page, as above (with blank reverse), pp. iii–iv ; Dedication
　　　　　(with blank reverse), pp. v–vi ; Preface, pp. vii–ix ; p. x is
　　　　　blank ; Contents, pp. xi–xii ; and Text, pp. 1–367. The
　　　　　imprint occurs at the foot of the last page.

Issued in dark red coloured cloth boards, lettered in gilt across
the back : " *Browning / as a / Philosophical / and / Religious /
Teacher / Henry Jones / Maclehose.*" The book passed into a
Second Edition.

(31.)

Browning's / Criticism of Life / By / William F. Revell /
Author of " Ethical Forecasts," etc. / With a Frontispiece /
[*Publishers' device*] London / Swan Sonnenschein & Co. /
New York : Macmillan & Co. / 1892.

Collation :—Post octavo, pp. x + 116 : consisting of Half-title
　　　　　(with advertisements of *The Dilettante Library* upon the
　　　　　reverse), pp. i–ii ; Title-page, as above (with imprint in the
　　　　　centre of the reverse), pp. iii–iv ; Dedication ("To my
　　　　　Wife"—with blank reverse), pp. v–vi ; Preface, pp. vii–viii ;
　　　　　Contents (with blank reverse), pp. ix–x ; and Text, pp. 1–116.
　　　　　The imprint is repeated at the foot of the last page.

Issued in dark brown bevelled cloth boards, with trimmed edges,
and lettered in gilt across the back : " *Browning's / Criticism / of
Life / Revell / Sonnenschein.*" The Frontispiece is a portrait of
Robert Browning, taken after death.

(32.)

Of / " Fifine at the Fair " / " Christmas Eve and Easter

Day " / and / other of Mr. Browning's Poems / by / Jeanie Morison / William Blackwood and Sons / Edinburgh and London / MDCCCXCII.

Collation :—Crown octavo, pp. viii + 99 : consisting of Half-title (with blank reverse), pp. i–ii ; Title-page (with blank reverse), pp. iii–iv ; Dedication to Miss Browning (with blank reverse), pp. v–vi ; Contents (with quotation from *Easter Day* on reverse), pp. vii–viii ; and Text, pp. 1–99. The imprint is at foot of last page.

Issued in dark red cloth boards, with trimmed edges, and lettered in gilt across the back : " *Of | Fifine | at the | Fair | Jeanie | Morison | Wm. Blackwood | & Sons.*"

(33.)

The / Browning Cyclopædia / A Guide to the Study of the Works / of / Robert Browning. / With / Copious Explanatory Notes and References / on all Difficult Passages. / By / Edward Berdoe, / Licentiate of the Royal College of Physicians, Edinburgh ; member of / the Royal College of Surgeons, England, etc., etc. / Author of " Browning's Message to his Time," " Browning as a Scientific / Poet," etc., etc. / London : Swan Sonnenschein & Co. / New York : Macmillan & Co. / 1892.

Collation :—Post octavo, pp. xx + 572 : consisting of Half-title (with advertisement on reverse), pp. i–ii ; Title-page, as above (with imprint at foot of reverse), pp. iii–iv ; Dedication (with blank reverse), pp. v–vi ; Preface vii–x ; " Unsolved Difficulties," study-books, etc., pp. xi–xx ; and Text, pp. 1–572.

Issued in dark red cloth boards, lettered in gilt across the back : " *The | Browning | Cyclopædia | Berdoe | Sonnenschein.*"

(34.)

Browning Studies / being / Select Papers by Members / of the / Browning Society / Edited, with an Introduction / by / Edward Berdoe, M.R.C.S., &c., / Author of " The Browning Cyclopædia," " Browning's Message to his Time," &c., &c. / London / George Allen, 156, Charing Cross Road / 1895 / [*All rights reserved.*]

Collation :—Octavo, pp. xiv + 331 : consisting of Half-title (with the publisher's imprint upon the reverse), pp. i–ii ; Title-page, as above (with the printers' imprint upon the reverse), pp. iii–iv ; Introduction, pp. v–xii ; Contents, pp. xiii–xiv ; and Text, pp. 1–331. The printers' imprint is repeated at the foot of the last page.

Issued in dark red cloth boards, lettered in gilt across the back : "*Browning | Studies | Edited by | E. Berdoe. | George Allen*" ; with " *Browning Studies* " added in gilt upon the front cover.

The entire Contents of this volume were reprinted from the Browning Society's Papers.

(35.)

An Introduction / to / Robert Browning. / A Criticism of the Purpose and / Method of his Earlier / Works. / By / Bancroft Cooke. / London : Simpkin, Marshall & Co. / Liverpool : Adam Holden, 48, Church Street. / Price one shilling.

Collation :—Demy octavo, pp. ii + 40 : consisting of Half-title (with blank reverse), pp. i–ii ; Title-page, as above (with blank reverse), pp. 1–2 ; and Text, pp. 3–40.

Issued in light grey paper wrappers, lettered "*An Introduction | to | Robert Browning*," upon the front. The pamphlet is undated.

(36.)

Browning / and the Christian Faith / The Evidences of
Christianity from / Browning's Point of View / By / Edward
Berdoe / Member of the Royal College of Surgeons of
England ; Licentiate of the / Royal College of Physicians
(Edinburgh) ; / Author of / ' The Browning Cyclopædia,'
' Browning's Message to his Time,' / Etc. / [Quotation from
' A Death in the Desert.'] / London / George Allen, 156,
Charing Cross Road / 1896 / [*All rights reserved.*]

Collation :—Crown octavo, pp. xx and 233 : consisting of Half-
title (with blank reverse), pp. i–ii ; Title-page, as above
(with blank reverse), pp. iii–iv ; Dedication (with blank
reverse), pp. v–vi ; Preface, pp. vii–ix ; p. x is blank ; Contents (with blank reverse), pp. xi–xii ; Introduction, pp.
xiii–xx ; and Text, pp. 1–233. The imprint, " *Richard Clay
& Sons, Limited,* | *London and Bungay,*" is placed upon the
centre of the reverse of the last page.

Issued in dark green cloth boards, lettered in gilt across the back
" *Browning* | *and the* | *Christian* | *Faith* | *Dr. Berdoe* | *George
Allen.*"

PART V

AN ALPHABETICAL LIST OF ROBERT BROWNING'S
POEMS, WITH REFERENCES TO THE POSITIONS
OF EACH IN THE PRINCIPAL EDITIONS
OF HIS WORKS.

PART IV.

An alphabetical list of Robert Browning's Poems, with references to the positions of each in the principal editions of his works.

A BLOT IN THE 'SCUTCHEON.

First appeared in *Bells and Pomegranates*, 1843, No. v. pp. 3–20.

Reprinted, *Poems*, 1849, Vol. ii. p. 1–60.

Ditto   ditto   1863, Vol. ii. p. 216–274.

Ditto   ditto   1868, Vol. iv. p. 1–60.

Ditto   *Poetical Works*, 1889, Vol. iv. p. 1–70.

This play was first performed at Drury Lane on February 11th, 1843, when Miss Helen Faucit (now Lady Martin) took the part of *Mildred Tresham*, Mrs. Stirling that of *Guendolen Tresham*, Mr. Phelps *Lord Tresham*, Mr. Hudson *Austin Tresham*, Mr. Anderson Henry *Earl Mertoun*, and Mr. Bennett *Gerard.* The circumstances attending the production of the play, as also its rehearsal, were by no means favourable to its success, and must in any case have militated against it. *The Examiner* (Feb. 18, 1843) remarks that " of the performance we have little to say, but that we think it was on the whole under-acted." Some measure of success, however, was vouchsafed the play—for we are told that at the close of the performance " the applause greatly predominated."

On the 27th of November, 1848—some five years later—the play was revived by Mr. Phelps, at Sadler's Wells Theatre, and on this occasion was a decided success. Mr. Phelps himself took the part of *Lord Tresham*, Miss Cooper that of *Mildred Tresham*, and Miss Huldart *Guendolen Tresham*, Mr. Dickinson representing *Earl Mertoun.* It was excellently mounted, and well acted—evidently giving satisfaction to a numerous audience.

Not for some seven-and-thirty years after Mr. Phelps's revival was *A Blot in the 'Scutcheon* again put on the boards : when on May 2nd, 1885, it was performed at St. George's Hall, under the direction of Mr. Charles Fry, and was a most interesting performance, Mr. Browning himself being present in a private box. Three years later (March 18th, 1888) a still more interesting revival of the play has to be recorded, on this occasion under the auspices of the Browning Society. It was performed in the Olympic Theatre, and there was an excellent caste—Miss Alma Murray (now Mrs. Alfred Forman) taking the part of *Mildred Tresham*, a part which was rendered with refined delicacy and grace of conception, and was indeed an intellectual performance of a very high order. Mr. Browning and his sister were present on this occasion also.

In March, 1885, Mr. Lawrence Barrett gave a very successful performance of the play at Boston, U.S.A.

À propos of the first performance of *A Blot in the 'Scutcheon.* Lady Martin (formerly Miss Helen Faucit) writes as follows in *Blackwood's Magazine* for March, 1881 : " It seems but yesterday that I sat in the green-room at the reading of Robert Browning's beautiful drama *A Blot in the 'Scutcheon.* As a rule, Mr. Macready always read the new plays. But owing, I suppose, to some stress of business, the task was entrusted on this occasion to the head prompter, a man . . . wholly unfitted to bring out, or even to understand, Mr. Browning's meaning, Consequently, the delicate, subtle lines were twisted, perverted, and sometimes even made ridiculous in his hands. My ' cruel father ' (Mr. Elton) was a warm admirer of the poet. He sat writhing and indignant, and tried by gentle asides to make me see the real meaning of the verse. But somehow the mischief proved irreparable, for a few of the actors during the rehearsals chose to continue to misunderstand the text, and never took the interest in the play which they would have done had Mr. Macready read it—for he had great power as a reader. I always thought it was chiefly because of this *contretemps* that a play so thoroughly dramatic failed, despite its painful story, to make the great success which was justly its due."

Writing in 1842 to Forster, Charles Dickens says :—" Browning's play [*A Blot in the 'Scutcheon*] has thrown me into a perfect passion of sorrow. To say that there is anything in its subject save what is lovely, true, deeply affecting, full of the best emotion, the most earnest feeling, and the most true and tender source of interest, is to say that there is no light in the sun, and no heat in the blood. It is full of genius, natural and great thoughts, profound and yet simple, and yet beautiful in its vigour. I know nothing that is so affecting, nothing in any book I have ever read, as Mildred's recurrence to that : ' I was so young—I had no mother.' I know no love like it, no passion like it, no moulding of a splendid thing after its conception, like it. And I swear it is a tragedy that MUST be played : and must be played, moreover, by Macready. There are some things that I would have changed if I could (they are very slight, mostly broken lines) ; and I assuredly would have the old servant *begin his tale upon the scene;* and be taken by the throat, or drawn upon, by his master, in its commencement. But the tragedy I shall never forget, or less vividly remember than I do now. And if you tell Browning that I have seen it, tell him that I believe from my soul there is no man living (and not many dead) who could produce such a work."

In reference to this letter, it may be desirable to note that Mr. Browning had lent the manuscript of his tragedy to John Forster, who took upon himself to pass it on to Charles Dickens —in the belief, as he says, " that it would profoundly touch him." That Forster was not mistaken in this belief is evident from the above letter. Unfortunately, however, he kept its contents to himself—and some thirty years were to elapse ere the poet knew how deeply his work had touched the great novelist. The letter was made public for the first time in *Forster's Life of Dickens* [vol. ii. pp. 24–25] ; and Mr. Browning made no secret of his regret that the nature of its contents had been so long withheld : naturally feeling that such an expression of opinion from one so prominently before the public would have been invaluable to himself and his work at that period of his career.

A CAMEL-DRIVER.

First appeared in *Ferishtah's Fancies,* 1884, pp. 59–67.
Reprinted, *Poetical Works,* 1889, Vol. xvi. pp. 40–46.

A Death in the Desert.

First appeared in *Dramatis Personæ*, 1864, pp. 89–119.
Reprinted, *Poems*, 1868, Vol. vi. pp. 110–135.
Ditto *Poetical Works*, 1889, Vol. vii. pp. 120–148.

In revising this poem for subsequent editions, no alteration seems to have been made save in one instance—when a whole line was omitted. It would be interesting to know whether this was deleted by the poet, or was a mistake on the part of the printer : this latter, however, being hardly a tenable hypothesis, as such a blunder would scarcely have escaped the notice of the printer's " reader." In the original edition, from line 212, the reading was as follows :

> " Is not his love at issue still with sin,
> Closed with and cast and conquered, crucified
> Visibly when a wrong is done on earth ? "

The poem now reading—

> " Is not his love at issue still with sin,
> Visibly when a wrong is done on earth ? "

A Grammarian's Funeral.

First appeared in *Men and Women*, 1855, Vol. ii. pp. 210–217.
Reprinted, *Poems*, 1863, Vol. i. pp. 278–284.
Ditto   ditto 1868, Vol. iv. pp. 270–275.
Ditto *Poetical Works*, 1889, Vol. v. pp. 154–160.

In the *Daily News* of Nov. 21, 1874, appeared the following letter from Mr. Browning : " Sir—In a clever article this morning you speak of ' the doctrine of the enclitic *De*'—' which, with all deference to Mr. Browning, in point of fact does not exist. No, not to Mr. Browning : but pray defer to Herr Buttmann, whose fifth list of ' enclitics ' ends with ' the inseparable *De*'— or to Curtius, whose fifth list ends also with ' *De* (meaning *"towards,"* and as a demonstrative appendage).' That this is not to be confounded with the accentuated ' *De*, meaning *but,*' was the ' doctrine' which the Grammarian bequeathed to those capable of receiving it."

A FACE.

First appeared in *Dramatis Personæ*, 1864, pp. 161–162.
Reprinted, *Poems*, 1868, Vol. vi. p. 158.
Ditto *Poetical Works*, 1889, Vol. vii. pp. 176–177.

A FORGIVENESS.

First appeared in *Pacchiarotto*, 1876, pp. 131–161.
Reprinted, *Poetical Works*, 1889, Vol. xiv. pp. 86–103.

A LIGHT WOMAN.

First appeared in *Men and Women*, 1855, Vol. i. pp. 151–155.
Reprinted, *Poems*, 1863, Vol. i. pp. 226–228.
Ditto   ditto   1868, Vol. iv. pp. 217–220.
Ditto *Poetical Works*, 1889, Vol. v. 92–95.

A LIKENESS.

First appeared in *Dramatis Personæ*, 1864, pp. 163 168.
Reprinted, *Poems*, 1868, Vol. vi. pp. 159–161.
Ditto *Poetical Works*, 1889, Vol. vii. pp. 178–181.

A LOVER'S QUARREL.

First appeared in *Men and Women*, 1855, Vol. i. pp. 7–18.
Reprinted, *Poems*, 1863, Vol. i. pp. 42–48.
Ditto   ditto   1868, Vol. iii. pp. 115–122.
Ditto *Poetical Works*, 1889, Vol. vi. pp. 58–65.

A PEARL, A GIRL.

First appeared in *Asolando*, 1889, pp. 14–15.
Reprinted, *Poetical Works*, 1894, Vol. xvii. p. 12.

A PILLAR AT SEBZEVAH.

First appeared in *Ferishtah's Fancies*, 1884, pp. 93–103.
Reprinted, *Poetical Works*, 1889, Vol. xvi. pp. 62-68.

A Pretty Woman.

First appeared in *Men and Women*, 1855, Vol. i. pp. 128–134.
Reprinted, *Poems*, 1863, Vol. i. pp. 125–128.
Ditto   ditto   1868, Vol. iii. pp. 197–200.
Ditto *Poetical Works*, 1889, Vol. vi. pp. 163–167.

A Serenade at the Villa.

First appeared in *Men and Women*, 1855, Vol. i. p. 117–121.
Reprinted, *Poems*, 1863, Vol. ii. pp. 119–122.
Ditto   ditto   1868, Vol. iii. pp. 191–194.
Ditto *Poetical Works*, 1889, Vol. vi. pp. 155–158.

A Soul's Tragedy.

First appeared in *Bells and Pomegranates*, 1845, No. viii. pp. 21–32.
Reprinted, *Poems*, 1849, Vol. ii. pp. 211–251.
Ditto   ditto   1863, Vol. ii. pp. 428–467.
Ditto   ditto   1868, Vol. v. pp. 1–41.
Ditto *Poetical Works*, 1889, Vol. iii. pp. 257–302.

So well known and so widely circulated is the anecdote about Douglas Jerrold and *Sordello*, that the following extract from that writer's magazine (*Douglas Jerrold's Shilling Magazine*, June 1846) will be of more than ordinary interest: "*A Soul's Tragedy* is one of the most intensely dramatic works ever penned. The deepest emotions and the nicest traits of character are developed by the mere external conduct and expression. The villain of the piece is a thorough human villain, and the unfolding his villainy is a masterly exposition of the degradations and weakness of human nature. The truly good and the noble are equally powerfully pourtrayed, and Mr. Browning has fulfilled the mission of the poet and the dramatist by giving new and valuable illustrations of our human nature. The theatre and Mr. Browning's dramas are never likely to come in contact ; not at all events until, as in the early days of our true drama, the most refined minds, and therefore the comparatively few, again visit the playhouse as a place to study nature and philosophy. The high drama was always played in its entirety, and always must be, to the reflecting few. When we have another ' Globe ' or ' Blackfriars,' containing a few hundred cultivated spectators, Mr. Browning's dramas may be performed."

A Toccata of Galuppi's.

First appeared in *Men and Women*, 1855, Vol. i. pp. 56–62.
Reprinted, *Poems*, 1863, Vol. i. pp. 54–58.
Ditto   ditto   1868, Vol. iii. pp. 127–130.
Ditto *Poetical Works*, 1889, Vol. vi. pp. 72–76.

In her *Studies of the Eighteenth Century in Italy*, " Vernon Lee " says of the Venetian Baldassarre Galuppi, surnamed Buranello, that he was " an immensely prolific composer, and abounded in melody, tender, pathetic, and brilliant, which in its extreme simplicity and slightness occasionally rose to the highest beauty. . . He defined the requisites of his art to Burney in very moderate terms—' Chiarezza, vaghezza, e buona modulazione '—clearness, beauty, and good modulation, without troubling himself much about any others. . . Galuppi was a model of the respectable modest artist, living quietly on a moderate fortune, busy with his art and the education of his numerous children ; beloved and revered by his fellow artists ; and, when some fifteen years later [than 1770] he died, honoured by them with a splendid funeral, at which all the Venetian musicians performed, the great Pachierotti writing to Burney that he had ' sung with much devotion to obtain a rest for Buranello's (Galuppi's) soul.' "

Ritter, in his *History of Music* (p. 245), has a concise but expressive notice of Galuppi : " *Balthasar Galuppi*, called Buranello (1706–1785), a pupil of Lotti, also composed many comic operas. The main features of his operas are melodic elegance, and lively and spirited comic forms ; but they are rather thin and weak in their execution. He was a great favourite during his lifetime."

Concerning the technical musical allusions in this poem, which are all found in the seventh, eighth, and ninth verses, Miss Helen A. Clarke writes as follows [*Poet Lore*, Vol. ii. pp. 546–547]: The " lesser thirds " are of course minor thirds, and are

of common occurrence, but the diminished sixth is an interval
rarely used, ordinarily a diminished sixth (seven semitones),
exactly the same interval as a perfect fifth, instead of giving a
plaintive, mournful or minor impression, would suggest a feeling
of rest and satisfaction. As I have said, however, there is one
way in which it can be used,—as a suspension, in which the root
of the chord on the *lowered* super-tonic of the scale is suspended
from above into the chord with added seventh on the super-
tonic, making a diminished sixth between the root of the first
and the third of the second chord. The effect of this pro-
gression is most dismal, and possibly Browning had it in mind,
though it is doubtful almost to certainty if Galuppi knew anything of it. Whether it be an anachronism or not, or whether
it is used in a scientifically accurate way or not, the figure is
true enough poetically, for a diminished interval—namely, something less than normal—would naturally suggest an effect of
sadness.

Suspensions are notes which are held over from one chord into
another, and must be made according to certain musical rules
as strict as the laws of the Medes and Persians. This holding
over of a note always produces a dissonance, and must be
followed by a concord,—in other words a *solution*. Sevenths
are very important dissonances in music, and a commiserating
seventh is most likely the variety called a minor seventh. Being
a somewhat less mournful interval than the lesser thirds and
the diminished sixths, whether real or imaginary, yet not so final
as "those solutions" which seem to put an end to all uncertainty,
and therefore to life, they arouse in the listeners to Galuppi's
playing a hope that life may last, although in a sort of disson-
antal, Wagnerian fashion. The "commiserating sevenths"
are closely connected with the "dominant's persistence" in the
next verse.

"Hark ! the dominant's persistence till it must be answered to :
So an octave struck the answer."

The dominant chord in music is the chord written on the fifth
degree of the scale, and it almost always has a seventh added
to it, and in a large percentage of cases is followed by the tonic,

the chord on the first degree of the scale. Now, in fugue form a theme is first presented in the tonic key, then the same theme is repeated in the dominant key, the latter being called the answer ; after further contrapuntal wanderings of the theme the fugue comes to what is called an episode, after which the theme is presented first, in the dominant. " Hark ! the dominant's persistence " alludes to this musical fact ; but according to rule this dominant must be answered in the tonic an octave above the first presentation of the theme, and " So an octave struck the answer." Thus the inexorable solution comes in after the dominant's persistence. Although life seemed possible with commiserating sevenths, the tonic, a resistless fate, strikes the answer that all must end—an answer which the frivolous people of Venice failed to perceive, and went on with their kissing. The notion of the tonic key as a relentless fate seems to suit well with the formal music of the days of Galuppi, while the more hopeful tonic key of *Abt Vogler*, "the C major of this life," indicates that fate and the tonic key have both fallen more under man's control.

A WOMAN'S LAST WORD.

First appeared in *Men and Women*, 1855, Vol. i. pp. 31-34.
Reprinted, *Poems*, 1863, Vol. i. pp. 34-35.
Ditto   ditto   1868, Vol. iii. pp. 108-109.
Ditto *Poetical Works*, 1889, Vol. vi. pp. 48-50.

ABT VOGLER.

First appeared in *Dramatis Personæ*, 1864, pp. 67-75.
Reprinted, *Poems*, 1868, Vol. vi. pp. 92-98.
Ditto *Poetical Works*, 1889, Vol. vii. pp. 101-108.

Abt Vogler (Georg Joseph Vogler)[1] was born at Pleicchart, a suburb of Würtzburg, on June 15, 1749. He was educated by

---

[1] See *Abt Georg Joseph Vogler: sein Leben, Charakter, und musikalischer System*, &c., by Dr. Karl Emil von Schafhäutl ; also Sir G. Grove's *Dictionary of Music and Musicians*. An excellent epitome of the life and work of Abt Vogler, from the pen of Miss Helen Ormerod, will be found in the *Browning Society's Papers*, Part x. p. 221.

Jesuits, and soon gave evidence of those brilliant qualities by which he was distinguished. At an early age—and indeed throughout his life—he was possessed by an untiring industry, courage and piety ; while he was specially endowed with an aptitude for music, and an extraordinary linguistic facility. As an instance of this latter, it is related that during five months spent in Spain, Africa and Greece he confessed fifteen hundred persons in twelve different languages ! It was an important moment in his life when, on the point of entering the Franciscan monastery at Würtzburg, he received the appointment of almoner to the Elector. His fame as a musician soon spread, and Weber, at the age of seven, was placed under his tuition. In 1773 he visited Italy, studying under the best teachers Padua could afford. In 1775 he returned to Mannheim, where he was appointed Court chaplain and *Vice-Kapellmeister*. It was at Mannheim he founded his first school of music. In 1780 he followed the Elector to Munich, and visited Paris in the December of that year, giving a series of organ recitals. He then passed over to England, and expounded to the Royal Society, under the presidency of Sir Joseph Banks, his views upon organ-construction. In 1784 he was *Kapellmeister* at Munich, where he brought out his opera of *Castor and Pollux* ; thence he proceeded to Berlin and Düsseldorf—where he was led to endeavour to render in music the impression made upon him by the pictures in the galleries of these two places. In 1786 he visited Sweden—two years later departing thence for Russia, where he made a tour of the celebrated organs and organ-builders of that country. Now it was that he came to a decision to construct on his own plan a portable organ, which he called " orchestrion "—engaging the Swedish organ-builder Racknitz to carry out his plans. It had been his life-long endeavour to invent a portable organ on which to perform at his recitals, and his efforts were at last to meet with success. He had now the " instrument of his own invention " of which Browning speaks, and the plan of it led him to form schemes for the remodelling and simplification of existing organs. In his own " orchestrion " he combined his inventions and improvements ; conveying it with him from place to place. " It was about three feet square, and higher in the middle than the sides ; it contained about 900 pipes, had shutters for crescendos and diminuendos, and naturally the reed stops were free reeds." In 1790, Vogler again visited England ; afterwards proceeding to Darmstadt, where he received a series of ovations. In 1796 he was in Paris, amid the throes of events happening there, and where he studied the national songs of the Revolution. In 1798 he again left Stockholm, where he had founded his second school of music. In 1803 he was invited to Vienna, and there produced his *Castor and Pollux*—returning to Munich two years later to superintend the performance of his opera before Napoleon. He subsequently accepted an invitation to Darmstadt, where for some years he resided in peace and honour, and whither Weber and Meyerbeer went to be his pupils. He died of apoplexy on May 6, 1814, loaded with honours, and with every proof of love and esteem.

ADAM, LILITH, AND EVE.

First appeared in *Jocoseria*, 1883, pp. 51-54.
Reprinted, *Poetical Works*, 1889, Vol. xv. pp. 197-198.

AFTER.

First appeared in *Men and Women*, 1855, Vol. ii. pp. 19-20.
Reprinted, *Poems*, 1863, Vol. i. pp. 141-142.
Ditto   ditto 1868, Vol. iii. pp. 213-214.
Ditto *Poetical Works*, 1889, Vol. vi. p. 186.

"ALL SINGERS, TRUST ME, HAVE THIS COMMON VICE."

First appeared in *The Pall Mall Gazette*, Dec. 13, 1883.
Reprinted in the *Browning Society's Papers*, Part v. p. 99*.

These lines were not included by Mr. Browning in the final, 17 vol., edition of his works.
This stanza is a translation of the well-known lines of Horace—

> Omnibus hoc vitium est cantoribus inter amicos
> Ut nunquam inducant animum cantare rogati ;
> Injussi, nunquam desistant.

They were Englished (impromptu) for Mr. Felix Moscheles, the painter ; who, having asked Mr. Browning if he knew of a good

translation of them, was answered by the Poet himself supply-
ing the following free version :—

> " All singers, trust me, have this common vice :
> To sing 'mid friends, you'll have to ask them twice.
> If you don't ask them, 'tis another thing,
> Until the judgment-day be sure they'll sing."

AMPHIBIAN (" The fancy I had to-day ").

First appeared in *Fifine at the Fair*, 1872, pp. vii-xii.
Reprinted, *Poetical Works*, 1889, Vol. xi. pp. 215-219.
This poem forms the prologue to *Fifine at the Fair*.

AN EPISTLE CONCERNING THE STRANGE MEDICAL EXPERIENCE OF KARSHISH, THE ARAB PHYSICIAN.

First appeared in *Men and Women*, 1855, Vol. i. pp. 90-106.
Reprinted, *Poems*, 1863, Vol. i. pp. 332-343.
Ditto   ditto 1868, Vol. v. pp. 218-229.
Ditto *Poetical Works*, 1889, Vol. iv. pp. 186-198.

ANDREA DEL SARTO.

First appeared in *Men and Women*, 1855, Vol. ii. pp. 1-14.
Reprinted, *Poems*, 1863, Vol. i. pp. 360-369.
Ditto   ditto 1868, Vol. v. pp. 248-257.
Ditto, *Poetical Works*, 1889, Vol. iv. p. 221-231.

As is probably known to most readers, this poem was suggested
to Mr. Browning by Andrea del Sarto's portrait of himself and
his wife Lucrezia, in the Pitti Palace, Florence. Writing from
Florence [to Dr. Furnivall] *à propos* of this picture, Mr. Ernest
Radford says : " Any one who has sat, as I have, looking at the
picture of which I write, will feel that the poem is *true*—not
merely typically, but historically. The catalogue says : The
painter, seen in three-corner face, appears by the gesture of his
left hand to appeal to his wife, Lucrezia Fede. His right hand
rests on her shoulder [his arm is around her, I may remark—an
act of tenderness which has much to do with the pathos of the
composition]. Lucrezia is presented in full face, with a golden

chain on her neck, and a letter in her hand.' The artist and his wife are represented at half length. Andrea turns towards her with a pleading expression on his face—a face not so beautiful as that in the splendid portrait in the National Gallery ; but when once felt it strikes a deeper chord. It wears an expression that cannot be forgotten—that nothing can suggest but the poem of Browning. Andrea's right arm, as I said, is round her ; he leans forward as if searching her face for the strength that has gone from himself. She is beautiful. I have seen the face (varied as a musician varies his theme) in a hundred pictures. She holds the letter in her hand, and looks neither at that nor at him, but straight out of the canvas. And the beautiful face, with the red-brown hair, is passive and unruffled, and awfully expressionless. Byron speaks of the ' one simile for a *proud angry woman*, and that's thunder !' There is ' silent thunder' in this face, if ever there was, though there is no anger. It suggests only a very mild, and at the same time immutable determination to have ' her own way.' It seems rather a personification of obstinacy in the female type than a portrait. She is a magnificent *Rosamund Viney*, and will lure her husband to his own damnation as kindly and surely as George Eliot's heroine does the unfortunate Lydgate. . . . Really, whilst looking at it the words of the poem come little by little into my mind, and it seems as if I had read them in Andrea's face. And so now, when I read it in my room, the picture is almost as vividly before me as when I am in the gallery, so completely do the two seem complementary."—[*Browning Society's Papers*, Part ii., pp. 160–161. Dr. Furnivall remarks that the letter of Mr. Radford (who at the time was not aware that the poem had been *directly* inspired by the picture) "is at once a witness to his own penetration, and to the power and truth of Browning's creative art—which makes us claim him as the greatest ' Maker' and master of characterisation since Shakespere."]

Of Lucrezia as seen in Andrea's pictures, Mr. William Mercer also writes : " Lucrezia may be traced beyond dispute in the *Madonna del Sacco* and in the *Birth of the Virgin*, to be seen in the cloister and *cortile* of the church of the Annunziata, also in the Madonna called ' of the Harpies' in the Tribuna of the

Uffizi Gallery.   Most exquisite among all, she appears in the girlish profile of the Madonna in the Pitti Palace in the painting of the *Holy Family*, so called for want of a better title, although San Giuseppe is absent.   But there is no need to travel outside the cloister of the Scalzo ; for in one of the scenes depicting the life of St. John the Baptist, the soft, sweet face that haunted and pursued the painter even to the Court of the French King Francis, is ever present, and as Herodias glances across a table in seeming confidence of sure recognition."

As to the accuracy of Browning's reading of the painter's life-history, Mr. Frederick Wedmore (a very high authority) says : " All the real Andrea del Sarto—at all events as men knew him when Mr. Browning wrote—is in this poem.   That is his portrait, his history ; its form, almost autobiography : incidents in the development—yes, also in the decay—of a soul."

ANOTHER WAY OF LOVE.

> First appeared in *Men and Women*, 1855, Vol. ii. pp. 220-222.
> Reprinted, *Poems*, 1863, Vol. i. pp. 123-124.
> Ditto   ditto   1868, Vol. iii. pp. 195-196.
> Ditto *Poetical Works*, 1889, Vol. vi. pp. 161-162.

ANY WIFE TO ANY HUSBAND.

> First appeared in *Men and Women*, 1855, Vol. i. pp. 81-89.
> Reprinted, Poems, 1863, Vol. i. pp. 110-115.
> Ditto   ditto   1868, Vol. iii. pp. 182-187.
> Ditto *Poetical Works*, 1889, Vol. vi. pp. 142-149.

APOLLO AND THE FATES.

> First appeared in *Parleyings*, 1887, pp. 1-28.
> Reprinted, *Poetical Works*, 1889, Vol. xvi. pp. 97-116.

> This poem forms the Prologue to the volume called *Parleyings with certain People of Importance in their Day.*

APPARENT FAILURE.

> First appeared in *Dramatis Personæ*, 1864, pp. 237-242.
> Reprinted, *Poems*, 1868, Vol. vi. pp. 219-221.
> Ditto *Poetical Works*, 1889, Vol. vii. pp. 246-249.

Written to keep alive the memory of a once famous building in Paris, Mr. Browning in this poem sits in judgment on the bodies of three drowned men, which he saw exposed in the Morgue in that city in the summer of 1856.

APPEARANCES.

First appeared in *Pacchiarotto*, 1876, pp. 106–107.
Reprinted, *Poetical Works*, Vol. xiv. p. 70.

ARCADES AMBO.

First appeared in *Asolando*, 1889, pp. 56–57.
Reprinted, *Poetical Works*, 1894, Vol. xvii. p. 47.

ARISTOPHANES' APOLOGY ; including a Transcript from Euripides.   Being the last Adventure of Balaustion.

First appeared (1875) in one vol.   See *ante*, p. 383, No. 17.
Reprinted, *Poetical Works*, 1889, Vol. xiii. pp. 1–258.

" It appears," says Mr. Bury, "that Browning has been peculiarly drawn to a period in the history of the Hellenic spirit which, unlike his own century in other respects, resembles it in a moral and religious restlessness which produces a need of escape.   In *Aristophanes' Apology* he shows how Euripides met this need, and exhibits the saving power, which he ascribes to his poetry, in the hopefulness of *Balaustion*.   It may be objected that in many respects the character of *Balaustion* is an anachronism, that she is not a Greek but a modern woman. As a point of fact the objection is true as well as obvious ; but there is a reason for this modern character.   Euripides was the first Greek who pointed beyond the Greek to a new world ; the beginnings of the modern spirit appear in him.   And *Balaustion* is the interpretess of Euripides, who brings forth to light what is latent in his poetry, and therefore her soul must have a certain consonance with the modern world."—[*Browning Society's Papers*, Part viii. p. 79.]

ARTEMIS PROLOGIZES.

First appeared in *Bells and Pomegranates*, No. iii. p. 9.
Reprinted, *Poems*, 1849, Vol. ii. pp. 280–284.
   Ditto   ditto   1863, Vol. i. pp. 327–331.

Reprinted, *Poems*, 1868, Vol. v. pp. 213-217.
Ditto *Poetical Works*, 1889, Vol. iv. pp. 181-185.

This poem had been destined to form part of a longer composition, and was suggested by the *Hippolytos* of Euripides.
Mr. Browning writes concerning it : " I had better say perhaps
that the above is nearly all retained of a tragedy I composed,
much against my endeavour, while in bed with a fever two years
ago—it went farther into the story of Hippolytus and Aricia ;
but when I got well, putting only thus much down at once, I
soon forgot the remainder."
Some deviations from the first version of this poem may be
duly noted here. For instance, lines 24-26, originally reading—

> " But when Hippolutos exclaimed with rage
> Against the miserable Queen, she judged
> Intolerable life,"

now reads—

> " Hippolutos exclaiming in his rage
> Against the fury of the Queen, she judged
> Life insupportable."

And in the last line, for the more sonorous—

> " In fitting silence the event await,"

we now have—

> " Await, in fitting silence, the event."

" Ask not one least word of praise."

First appeared in *Ferishtah's Fancies*, 1884, p. 104.
Reprinted, *Poems*, 1889, Vol. xvi. p. 68.

At the " Mermaid."

First appeared in *Pacchiarotto*, 1876, pp. 47-59.
Reprinted, *Poetical Works*, 1889, Vol. xiv. pp. 31-38.

" At the midnight in the silence of the sleep time."

First appeared in *Asolando*, 1889, pp. 156-157.
Reprinted, *Poetical Works*, 1894, Vol. xvii. pp. 130-131.

This poem is the Epilogue to *Asolando*; and is of especial interest in that it is understood to have been the last poem written by Mr. Browning.

AVISON, CHARLES, PARLEYING WITH.

First appeared in *Parleyings*, 1887, pp. 191–220.
Reprinted, *Poetical Works*, 1889, Vol. xvi. pp. 221–240.

Charles Avison, a musician, was born in Newcastle about 1710. After studying in Italy, he returned to England and became a pupil under Geminiani. He was appointed organist of St. Nicholas Church, Newcastle, in 1736. His celebrated *Essay on Musical Expression* appeared in 1752, and startled the musical world by putting the French and Italian schools of music above the German, headed by Handel himself. This book led to a controversy with Dr. Hayes, in which, according to the *Dictionary of National Biography* (from which we glean these facts), " Hayes had the best of the argument, though Avison was superior from a literary point of view." Avison was said to be a man of much culture and polish, and issued several sets of sonatas and concertos. He died in 1770.

It is interesting to note that, on May 28, 1890, a new tombstone, erected over the grave of Charles Avison, in St. Andrew's Churchyard, Newcastle, was unveiled, with all due ceremony. In connection with this event, Mr. Barrett Browning wrote : " The ceremony would have a deep interest for me, as you can understand ; for my father was really pleased to think he had been able to call attention to Charles Avison with such good result." The following lines from Mr. Browning's poem were inscribed on the tombstone :—

> " On the list
> Of worthies who by help of pipe or wire
> Expressed in sound rough rage or soft desire
> Thou whilom of Newcastle organist."

BAD DREAMS. I.

First appeared in *Asolando*, 1889, p. 19.
Reprinted, *Poetical Works*, 1894, vol. xvii. p. 16.

BAD DREAMS. II.

> First appeared in *Asolando*, 1889, pp. 20-26.
> Reprinted, *Poetical Works*, 1894, Vol. xvii pp. 17-22.

BAD DREAMS. III.

> First appeared in *Asolando*, 1889, pp. 27-29.
> Reprinted, *Poetical Works*, 1894, Vol. xvii. pp. 23-25.

BAD DREAMS. IV.

> First appeared in *Asolando*, 1889, pp. 30-33.
> Reprinted, *Poetical Works*, 1894, Vol. xvii. pp. 26-28.

BALAUSTION, THE LAST ADVENTURE OF. See *Aristophanes' Apology*.

BALAUSTION'S ADVENTURE; INCLUDING A TRANSCRIPT FROM EURIPIDES.

> First appeared (1871) in one Vol. See *ante*, p. 381, No. 13.
> Reprinted, *Poetical Works*, 1889, Vol. xi. pp. 1-122.

> The structure upon which *Balaustion's Adventure* was raised may be found in the following description by Plutarch of the fate of the Athenians defeated under Nikias by the Syracusans : Some there were who owed their preservation to Euripides. Of all the Grecians, his was the muse whom the Sicilians were most in love with. From every stranger that landed in their island they gleaned every small specimen or portion of his works, and communicated it with pleasure to each other. It is said that on this occasion a number of Athenians, upon their return home, went to Euripides, and thanked him in the most respectful manner for their obligations to his pen ; some having been enfranchised for teaching their masters what they remembered of his poems, and others having got refreshments when they were wandering about after the battle for singing a few of his verses. Nor is this to be wondered at, since they tell us that when a ship from Caunus, which happened to be pursued by pirates, was going to take shelter in one of

their ports, the Sicilians at first refused to admit her, but upon asking the crew whether they knew any of the verses of Euripides, and having answered in the affirmative, they received both them and their vessel.

BARTOLI, DANIEL, PARLEYING WITH.

First appeared in *Parleyings*, 1887, pp. 51-75.
Reprinted, *Poetical Works*, 1889, Vol. xvi. pp. 132-147.

Daniel Bartoli—who was born at Ferrara in 1608 and died at Rome in 1685—was a learned Jesuit : his chief work being a history of his Order, in six volumes, published at various times. It is crowded with stories of miracles, and is enriched with facts drawn from the Vatican records, and from memoires sent him by friends in England. His style is much esteemed by Italians for its purity and precision ; while his manner of life is said to have been correct and virtuous.

BEATRICE SIGNORINI.

First appeared in *Asolando*, 1889, pp. 76-98.
Reprinted, *Poetical Works*, 1894, Vol. xvii. pp. 62-81.

BEFORE.

First appeared in *Men and Women*, 1855, Vol. ii. pp. 15-18.
Reprinted, *Poems*, 1863, Vol. i. pp 139-141.
Ditto   ditto, 1868, Vol. iii. pp. 211-213.
Ditto, *Poetical Works*, 1889, Vol. vi. pp. 183-185.

BELLS AND POMEGRANATES.

i.	*Pippa Passes,*	first appeared in	1841, pp. 1-16.
ii.	*King Victor and King Charles,*	,,	,,	1842, pp. 1-20.
iii.	*Dramatic Lyrics,*	,,	,,	1842, pp. 1-16.
iv.	*The Return of the Druses,*	,,	,,	1843, pp. 1-19.
v.	*A Blot in the 'Scutcheon,*	,,	,,	1843, pp. 1-16.
vi.	*Colombe's Birthday,*	,,	,,	1844, pp. 1-24.
vii.	*Dramatic Romances and Lyrics,*	,,	,,	1845, pp. 1-24.
viii.	*Luria* and *A Soul's Tragedy,*	,,	,,	1845, pp. 1-32.

"I had hardly ended my first conversation [in their student days] with Rossetti," says Mr. W. Holman Hunt, "when he asked me if I knew Browning. I confessed I did not. Quickly he lent me the paper-covered volume of *Bells and Pomegranates.* . . . We discussed together the English and Tuscan poets; but there was no poet more honoured by us than Browning. At that time Browning was not found in every house; few knew his name—but that made him the more welcome to them. At that time, he remembered a certain barrister, Serjeant Thomas, saying that 'a great fuss had been made about one Browning, but it had all ended in smoke,' and that was then the general opinion. Since then, however, his reputation had grown and was still growing, and was now built on a sound and solid basis."—[*Browning Society's Papers*, Part iv, 64*.]

BEN KARSHOOK'S WISDOM.

First appeared in *The Keepsake*, 1856, p. 16.
Reprinted in *Browning Society's Papers*, Part i. p. 56.
Ditto, W. G. Kingsland's *Robert Browning: Chief Poet of the Age*, p. 26; also in *Sharpe's Life of Robert Browning*, p. 167.

"*Karshook* (Heb.: a Thistle)," writes Mr. Browning, in 1881, "belongs to the snarling verses I remember to have written, but forget for whom."

This poem appeared in *The Keepsake* for 1856, under the editorship of Miss Power, and was dated "Rome, April 27th 1854." As the "snarling verses" have not been reprinted in any edition of Mr. Browning's works, they are inserted here—in the exact form in which they appeared in *The Keepsake* :—

I.

"Would a man 'scape the rod?"
Rabbi Ben Karshook saith,
"See that he turn to God,
The day before his death."

"Ay, could a man inquire,
When it shall come!" I say.
The Rabbi's eye shoots fire—
"Then let him turn to-day!"

II.

Quoth a young Sadducee :
 " Reader of many rolls,
Is it so certain we
 . Have, as they tell us, souls?"

" Son, there is no reply ! "
 The Rabbi bit his beard :
" Certain, a soul have *I*—
 We may have none," he sneered.

—————

Thus Karshook, the Hiram's-Hammer,
 The Right-hand Temple-column,
Taught babes in grace their grammar,
 And struck the simple, solemn.

BIFURCATION.

First appeared in *Pacchiarotto*, 1876, pp. 91–94.
Reprinted, *Poetical Works*, 1889, Vol. xiv. pp. 61-62.

BISHOP BLOUGRAM'S APOLOGY.

First appeared in *Men and Women*, 1855, Vol. i. pp. 205-258.
Reprinted, *Poems*, 1863, Vol. i. 374–410.
Ditto   ditto, 1868, Vol. v. pp. 262-298.
Ditto, *Poetical Works*, 1889, Vol. iv. pp. 238–278.

Writing to Dr. Furnivall in August 1881, Mr. Browning says :
"The most curious notice I ever had was from Cardinal
Wiseman on *Blougram—i.e.*, himself. It was in the *Rambler*,
a Catholic journal of those days, and certified to be his by
Father Prout, who said nobody else would have dared put it in."

BOOT AND SADDLE (originally *My Wife Gertrude*). See *Cavalier Tunes.*

BY THE FIRESIDE.

First appeared in *Men and Women*, 1855, Vol. i. pp. 63-80.
Reprinted, *Poems*, 1863, Vol. i. pp. 98–110.
Ditto   ditto, 1868, Vol. iii. pp. 170-182.
Ditto, *Poetical Works*, 1889, Vol. vi. pp. 126-141.

CALIBAN UPON SETEBOS; OR, NATURAL THEOLOGY IN THE ISLAND.

First appeared in *Dramatis Personæ*, 1864, pp. 121–135.
Reprinted, *Poems*, 1868, Vol. vi. pp. 136–147.
Ditto, *Poetical Works*, 1889, Vol. vii. pp. 149–161.

In the first edition of this poem there was a motto prefixed, which gave a clear indication of the drift of the argument: " Thou thoughtedst that I was altogether such a one as thyself." When the poem was reprinted in the collected edition of 1868, this motto was, strangely enough, omitted. On Mr. Browning's attention being called to this, he at once saw the gravity of the omission, and remarked that it must have been due to the carelessness of the printer, who had possibly mislaid the printed leaf of copy : he, however, said he would take care it was restored in any subsequent edition.

Concerning the character of *Setebos*, the following quotation from the Hükluyt Society's Englishing of *Magellan's Voyage*, and from *Purchas his Pilgrimes* (from which we get a reference to the origin of Shakspere's Setebos), may be of interest : He comes from Patagonia, from among the people whom the captain Magellan named " Pataghom," on account of their big feet. In 1519, the captain put irons upon the feet of two giants, and " when they saw the trick which had been played them, they began to be enraged and to foam like bulls, crying out very loud ' *Setebos*,' that is to say, the great devil, that he should help them." And " when one of them dies, ten or twelve devils áppear, and dance all round the dead man. It seems that these are painted, and one of these enemies is taller than the others, and makes a greater noise, and more mirth than the others : that is whence these people have taken the custom of painting their faces and bodies, as has been said. The greatest of these devils is called in their language *Setebos*, and the others *Cheleule*." Again, Purchas says of the surviving giant, " On a time as one made a Crosse before him and kissed it, shewing it unto him, hee suddenly cried *Setebos*, and declared by signes that if they made any more Crosses, *Setebos* would enter into his body, and make him burst. But when in fine hee saw no hurt came thereof, hee tooke the Crosse, and embraced and kissed it oftentimes, desiring that hee might be a Christian before his death. Hee was therefore baptized, and named Paul." This, Dr. Furnivall points out, was the original Setebos ; and he infers that Shakespere, " fifteen years before *Purchas* was in print (1636), had got hold of the name from some sailor, and had put *Setebos* into the *Tempest* : Shakespere's conception of Setebos being that he is the god of Caliban's dam, yet such a poor god, that *Prospero*, who was powerful only in his books, could subdue *Setebos* and make him his vassal." Concerning the character of *Caliban*, Mr. Cotter Morison remarks that it was quite natural " that Browning's attention should be drawn to the strange figure of Caliban—one of the most singular creations of Shakespere's fancy. What an opportunity was offered by ' the freckled whelp, hag-born,' for subtle analysis and grotesque humour ! ' The poisonous slave got by the devil himself upon his wicked dam ' is a monster indeed ; but he has a human element within his monsterhood. But there is nothing very complex and subtle in Shakespere's conception of Caliban. His physical form apart, he is little more than a depraved, brutish and malicious man. One cannot say that Shakespere has taken much pains with the character ; we see little more than the surface of such mind as he has ; his sulky anger, his fear of cramps and side stitches ' that shall pen his breath up,' his vindictive rage against the enchanter. This deficiency has been supplied by Browning in the most magnificent grotesque work of his poem. The proper province of grotesque would seem to be the exhibition of fanciful power by the artist ; not beauty or truth in the literal sense, but inventive affluence of unreal yet absurdly comic forms, with just a flavour of the terrible added, to give a grim dignity, and save from the triviality of caricature. Our best grotesques belong to the art of the sculptor or modeller, as in mediæval and oriental work. In literature the grotesque does not seem to rise with the same spontaneity ; the tendency there is either to broad farce or delicate comedy. Browning, however, has produced in this poem a grotesque in language which is as solid and sharp in

record,' as Landor calls Cenci, would probably have perished before his daughter had been set in the dire necessity of compassing his death. How far Aldobrandino may have been interested in extinguishing the family, of whom only the innocent Bernardo escaped with difficulty, it were hazardous to surmise ; but probably his enormous influence with the Pope would be against them. The story of Onofrio and this diabolical dignitary of the Church is within every one's reach, and should be read by all who are interested in those by-paths of history which have fed the imaginations of our greatest poets."

" Having occasion," continues Mr. Buxton Forman, " to write to Mr. Browning, I asked him the precise value we were to attach to the terminal *aja* in the title of his poem, and I received the following answer from the poet : ' "*Aia* " is generally an accumulative yet depreciative termination : " Cenciaja "—a bundle of rags—a trifle. The proverb means " Every poor creature will be pressing into the company of his betters," and I used it to deprecate the notion that I intended anything of the kind. Is it any contribution to " all connected with Shelley," if I mention that my " Book " (*The Ring and the Book*[1]) has a reference to the reason given by Farinacci, the advocate of the Cenci, of his failure in the defence of Beatrice ? " Fuise punitam Beatricem " (he declares), " pœnâ ultimi supplicii, non quia ex intervallo occidi mandavit insidiantem suo honori, sed quia ejus exceptionem non probavitibi. *Prout, et idem firmiter sperabatur de sorore Beatrice si propositam excusationem probasset, prout non probavit.*" That is, she was expected to avow the main outrage, and did not : in conformity with her words, " That which I ought to confess, that will I confess ; that to which I ought to assent, to that I assent ; and that which I ought to deny, that will I deny." " Here is another Cenciaja ! ' "

CHERRIES.

First appeared in *Ferishtah's Fancies*, 1884, pp. 78-85.
Reprinted, *Poetical Works*, 1889, Vol. xvi. pp. 53-57.

[1] Of course, says Mr. Forman, this reference is to the "old square yellow book," giving the actual details of the tragedy—not to Mr. Browning's poem.

"Childe Roland to the Dark Tower came."

First appeared in *Men and Women*, Vol. i. pp. 135–148.
Reprinted, *Poems*, 1863, Vol. i, pp. 312–320.
Ditto   ditto   1868, Vol. iv. pp. 301–310.
Ditto, *Poetical Works*, 1889, Vol. v. pp. 194–205.

This poem, Mr. Browning tells us, was "only a *fantaisie*," written "because it pleased his fancy." The incident of the horse, "his every bone a-stare," was imagined from a red horse with a glaring eye standing behind a dun one, on the right hand of a large tapestry that used to hang in his drawing-room.

Christmas-Eve and Easter-Day.

First appeared in 1850, pp. 1–142.
Reprinted, *Poems*, 1863, Vol. iii. pp. 163–251.
Ditto   ditto   1868, Vol. v. pp. 115–204.
Ditto, *Poetical Works*, 1889, Vol. v. pp. 209–307.

This poem was written in Florence in 1850, and published in London the same year. It is probably unnecessary to remark that the curious would search in vain for the identity of the "little chapel"—for (as Mr. Browning once said in conversation with Mr. W. G. Kingsland), "all the incidents are imaginary— save the lunar rainbow : I saw that."

Various alterations have been made in the text of this poem ; those in *Christmas Eve* being for the most part verbal. In *Easter Day*, however, the deviations from the first edition are more numerous. For instance—in the original edition, section v. commences :

> "I see !
> You would grow smoothly as a tree,
> Soar heavenward, straightly up like fire—
> God bless you—there's your world entire
> Needing no faith, if you think fit ;"

This passage now reads—

> "I see !
> You would grow as a natural tree,
> Stand as a rock, soar up like fire.
> The world's so perfect and entire,
> Quite above faith, so right and fit !'

Again, in section xiii, lines 11 to 15 in the original edition—

> Seeing that as I carry through
> My purpose, if my words in you
> Find veritable listeners,
> My story, reason's self avers
> Must needs be false—the happy chance !—

Now read :

> Seeing that if I carry through
> My purpose, if my words in you
> Find a live actual listener,
> My story, reason must aver
> False after all—the happy chance !

In some cases the alterations appear to be distinctly for the better—as, for instance, in section xiv, lines 69-70, which, originally reading

> Your progressing is slower—right
> We deal with progressing, not flight,

Now stand :

> Your progressing is slower—right !
> We deal with progress and not flight.

The alterations in punctuation are numerous, and in many cases the capital letters are changed to lower case.

CLEON.

> Printed in London, in pamphlet form, privately, 1855.
> First appeared in *Men and Women*, 1855, Vol. ii. pp. 171-189.
> Reprinted, *Poems*, 1863, Vol. i. pp. 410-423.
> Ditto   ditto   1868, Vol. v. pp. 299-311.
> Ditto, *Poetical Works*, 1889, Vol. iv. pp. 279-293.

CLIVE.

> First appeared in *Dramatic Idylls* II., 1880, pp. 9-42.
> Reprinted, *Poetical Works*, 1889, Vol. xv. pp. 88-107.

COLOMBE'S BIRTHDAY.

> First appeared in *Bells and Pomegranates*, 1844, No. vi.
> Reprinted, *Poems*, 1849, Vol. i. pp. 303-385.

Reprinted, *Poems*, 1863, Vol. ii. pp. 275–356.
Ditto   ditto   1868, Vol. iv. pp. 61-143.
Ditto, *Poetical Works*, 1889, Vol. iv. pp. 71-169.

Writing to Mr. C. Dowson, March 10, 1844, Mr. Browning says : "Yesterday I read my play [*Colombe's Birthday*] to him [Charles Kean] and his charming wife, who is to take the principal part. All went off *au mieux*—but—he wants to keep it till 'Easter next year,' and unpublished all the time ! His engagement at the Haymarket, next May, is merely for twelve nights, he says. . . . . My play will take him two months at least to study, he being a special slow head, and after the Haymarket engagement nothing is to be done till this time next year. Of all which notable pieces of information I was apprised for the first time after the play was read and approved of, for it certainly never entered into my head that anybody, even an actor, could need a couple of months to study a part, only, in a piece, which I could match with such another in less time by a good deal. But though I could do such a thing, I have a head—that aches oftener now than of old—to take care of ; and, therefore, will do no such thing as let this new work lie stifled for a year and odd, and work double tides to bring out something as likely to be popular this present season. For something I must print, or risk the hold, such as it is, I have at present on my public—and, on consideration of the two other productions I have by me in a state of forwardness, neither seems nearly so proper for the requirements of the moment as this play ; and two or three hundred pounds will pay me but indifferently for hazarding the good fortune which appears slowly but not unmistakably setting in upon me just now. You will not wonder therefore that— though I was so far taken by surprise as to promise Kean a copy for Scotland and a fortnight's grace to come to terms in before I either published the play or accepted any other party's offer—I say, you will not wonder if I have determined to print it directly. Acting on the best advice I sent it to press yesterday, and merely put the right of the acting at his disposal—if he will purchase it with such a drawback as Macready would ; for I fear the only other alternative I shall allow—that of his getting up the part for next May—is quite beyond his power.

The poorest man of letters (if really of letters) I ever knew is of far higher talent than the best actor I ever expect to know ; nor is there one spangle too many, one rouge-smutch too much on their outside man, for the inward. Can't study a speech in a month ! God help them, and bless you !"—[*Letters from Robert Browning*, edited by T. J. Wise. Vol. i. pp. 7–11.]

So printed *Colombe's Birthday* accordingly was—and for "acting" had to await an interval of nine years : when, on the 25th of April, 1853, it was produced at the Haymarket Theatre, and aroused considerable interest in literary circles. Miss Helen Faucit (now Lady Martin) undertook the character of *Colombe*, Mr. Barry Sullivan impersonating *Valence*. "It was feared," says the *Athenæum* (April 25th, 1853), "that on performance, this fine poem would scarcely be intelligible to a mixed audience. Miss Faucit, however, by her skill, made them perfectly understand it, ... and we can record its apparent perfect success on the first night." The play evidently excited considerable admiration and sympathy ; but, as in the case of other of Mr. Browning's plays, the "acting" (with the one exception of Miss Faucit) seems to have been somewhat dubious. Indeed, it would appear that to this cause is to be traced the apparent failure of Mr. Browning's plays as "acting" dramas. On this point, the *Literary Gazette* (April 30th, 1853) says that if *Colombe's Birthday* does not succeed upon the stage, "it is from no fault in itself, but partly from want of power in the actors. . . . . The play demands performers of a higher stamp than are now upon the stage. . . . . Speeches which are full of broken emotion, and where a great actor would electrify the house, fall cold and meaningless from Mr. Sullivan's lips." The *Colombe* of Miss Helen Faucit, however, "is a portraiture in which Mr. Browning's conception receives all the completeness and enrichment which a great actress is able to bestow. . . . Through the finished delicacy of the details, the traces of great latent power are evident, which, while they help to elevate our impression of the character of *Colombe*, increase our admiration of the powers of the actress who so skilfully subordinates her genius to perfect harmony with the Poet's idea. Her clear and melodious enunciation of the dialogue and delicate phases of emotion seem

reading " 'twas with full strength," now reads " with all his strength." In stanza viii. line 4, instead of

> "The victor with his . . . there, 'twill last,"

we now have

> " The victor's crown, but . . . there 'twill last."

Again, in stanza xvi. line 2, originally reading

> " Was finished, there lay prone the Knight,"

now reads—

> " Was finished, prone lay the false knight."

And in line 4, in lieu of " My Knight flew at him," we now read, " Gismond flew at him."

Count Guido Franceschini. See *The Ring and the Book.*

Cristina.

First appeared in *Bells and Pomegranates,* 1842, No. iii. p. 12, under the heading, *Queen Worship, II. Cristina.*
Reprinted, *Poems,* 1849, Vol. i. pp. 297–299.
Ditto   ditto   1863, Vol. i. pp. 27–30.
Ditto   ditto   1868, Vol. iii. pp. 101–104.
Ditto, *Poetical Works,* 1889, Vol. vi. pp. 39–42.

In this poem there are to be duly noted some variations between the earlier and later readings. For instance, in the earlier version, the last lines of the last stanza were as follows :—

> That just holds out the proving
>   Our powers, alone and blended—
> And then, come next life quickly,
>   This life will have been ended !

They now read—

> Life will just hold out the proving
>   Both our powers, alone and blended :
> And then, come next life quickly !
>   This world's use will have been ended.

CRISTINA AND MONALDESCHI.

First appeared in *Jocoseria*, 1883, pp. 33-44.
Reprinted, *Poetical Works*, 1889, Vol. xv. pp. 188-194.

In Lord Malmesbury's *Memoirs of an Ex-Minister* (1884, Vol. i. p. 30) we read as follows : " Mr. Hill presented me at Court before I left Naples [in 1829]. . . . The Queen [Maria Isabella, second wife of Francis I., King of the two Sicilies] and the young and handsome Princess Cristina, afterwards Queen of Spain, were present. The latter was said at the time to be the cause of more than one inflammable victim languishing in prison for having too openly admired this royal coquette, whose manners with men foretold her future life after her marriage to old Ferdinand [VII., King of Spain]. When she came up to me in the circle, walking behind her mother, she stopped, and took hold of one of the buttons of my uniform, to see, as she said, the inscription upon it, the Queen indignantly calling upon her to come on."

In her own Memoirs, Cristina gives a striking account of the Marquis Monaldeschi. She describes him as "a gentleman of most handsome person and fine manners, who from the first moment reigned exclusively over my heart." " Italy," she says, " was a scene of enchantment to me when I met him there. The beautiful, proud Monaldeschi opened a new world to me." Monaldeschi, however, after having taken every advantage of his position, reaping riches and honours to himself, wearied of his royal mistress and sought new attractions. It is, in fact, the closing scene of Queen Cristina's *liason* with her Grand Equerry which inspired Browning to give us his fine poem. The poet chooses the moment when Cristina's eyes were opened to the treachery of her lover ; how her passion for him had been his " stock in trade " to amuse and interest a younger mistress in Rome. On learning this treachery, the maddened Queen arranged an interview with the Marquis in the picture gallery in the Palace of Fontainebleau. She was accompanied by an official of her Court, and had at hand a priest from the neighbouring Convent of the Maturins, armed with copies of Monaldeschi's letters to the Roman lady (which had come into the Queen's possession through a certain Cardinal Azzolino), and which were to serve as his death-warrant. The *originals* she had on her own person. Added to this, she had in the background her Captain of the Guard, Sentinelli, with two other officers. It is from this point that Browning's poem opens. In the Galerie des Cerfs was a picture of Henri II. and Diane de Poictiers.[1] To this picture the Queen leads the Marquis, pointing out the motto on the frame—" Quis separabit ?" [" The crescent," writes Mrs. Ireland, " was the natural sign of Diane, but the salamander of François I. needs some explanation. As a bold, brave, and imperious youth, his father, to restrain his ardent nature, placed him at the age of thirteen in the care of a wise governor, Le Chevalier de Boissy, who, to express his tender and watchful care of his fiery-minded pupil, gave him for his device or crest the salamander, with the legend ' Nutrisco et extinguo (Je le nourris et je l'éteins).' This device of the salamander still exists on some of the old carvings and paintings at Fontainebleau."] Cristina renews her attack. " Stand, Sir ! Read ! *Quis separabit ?*" It was true one vow had bound them. In the little church of Avon (a village on the east side of the park at Fontainebleau) they had stood, "on a memorable evening, close to the *bénitier* in a supreme moment. Before them lay an ancient tombstone : and here, pointing to the marble slab at their feet, the Marquis had vowed that as that grave kept a silence over the corpse which lay beneath, so would his love and trust hold fast the secret of Cristina's love to all eternity. Now she was scorned, her pride outraged, and she felt she must assert her dignity. But the Marquis was ' silent ' —and the priest and assassins approaching, she granted herself the bitter pleasure of such personal revenge as was possible." It is curious to note that in October, 1657, Cristina, suspicious of Monaldeschi, had led him on to a conversation touching a similar unfaithfulness. " What," said the queen, " does a man deserve who should so have betrayed a woman ?" " Instant death," replied Monaldeschi. " It is well," said she ; " I will

[1] Mr. Browning made a curious slip in this poem, making Francis I. the lover of Diane de Poictiers, whereas it was his son, Henri II., who was for a time infatuated with her.

remember your words." A word as to the rival painters mentioned in the poem may be interpolated here. François Primaticcio, who died in 1570 at Bologna, was the rival of Maître Roux or "Le Roux"; but Primaticcio was first in the field, and a terrible jealousy arose between the two painters. Primaticcio was the pet pupil of Giulio Romano. Rosso, who died in 1541, was a pupil of Michael Angelo. Both were patronised by François I., añd both largely contributed to the magnificent decorations of the palace. Primaticcio had been sent to Italy by the King, nominally to collect works of art; and it was only after Rosso's untimely death that he returned. Rosso had ill-luck; he was only forty-five at the time of his death, and poisoned himself from bitter remorse at having falsely accused his friend Pellegrini. [*Browning Society's Papers*, Part xiii. p. 103.]

"DANCE, YELLOWS AND WHITES AND REDS!"

First appeared in *The New Amphion*, 1886, p. 1.
Reprinted in *Parleyings*, vi., "Gerard de Lairesse," p. 189.

These lines were printed as *A Spring Song* in *The New Amphion* ("The Book of the Edinburgh University Union Fancy Fair"), 1886, and were accompanied with a full-page illustration by Elizabeth Gulland. They were subsequently inserted at the close of the *Parleying* with "Gerard de Lairesse."

DEAF AND DUMB: A GROUP BY WOOLNER.

First appeared in *Poems*, 1868, Vol. vi. p. 151.
Reprinted, *Poetical Works*, 1889, Vol. vii. p. 167.

These lines were written in 1862 for Woolner's partly-draped group of Constance and Arthur (the deaf and dumb children of Sir Thomas Fairbairn), which was exhibited in the International Exhibition of 1862.

"DE GUSTIBUS —"

First appeared in *Men and Women*, 1855, Vol. ii. pp. 147–149.
Reprinted, *Poems*, 1863, Vol. i. pp. 70–72.
Ditto   ditto   1868, Vol. iii. pp. 143–144.
Ditto, *Poetical Works*, 1889, Vol. vi. pp. 92–93.

DEVELOPMENT.

> First appeared in *Asolando*, 1889, pp. 123-130.
> Reprinted, *Poetical Works*, 1894, Vol. xvii. pp. 102-108.

DÎS ALITER VISUM ; OR, LE BYRON DE NOS JOURS.

> First appeared in *Dramatis Personæ*, 1864, pp. 45-54.
> Reprinted, *Poems*, 1868, Vol. vi. pp. 77-84.
> Ditto, *Poetical Works*, 1889, Vol. vii. pp. 85-93.

DOCTOR ——.

> First appeared in *Dramatic Idyls* II. 1880, pp. 113-136.
> Reprinted, *Poetical Works*, 1889, Vol. xv. pp. 146-158.

DODINGTON, GEORGE BUBB, PARLEYING WITH.

> First appeared in *Parleyings*, 1887, pp. 97-119.
> Reprinted, *Poetical Works*, 1889, Vol. xvi. pp. 160-174.
>
> George Bubb Dodington, who was born in 1691, was " the son
> of a gentleman of good fortune named Bubb." He was edu-
> cated at Oxford, and in 1715 was elected member of Parlia-
> ment for Winchelsea, and not long after this he was sent as
> envoy to Madrid. In 1720 he inherited the estate of Eastbury,
> in Dorsetshire, and took the name of Dodington. His career
> was full of political vicissitudes of a discreditable kind—by
> which he obtained a large share of the prizes in the political
> world. He held various offices—mostly in connexion with the
> navy, to which he was more than once treasurer. He was a
> great favourite with Lord Bute, from whom he received the
> title of Lord Melcombe. He was fond of surrounding himself
> with the noted men of the day, whom he entertained at his
> country seat. Both Pope and Churchill wrote in abuse of him,
> and Hogarth has immortalised his wig in his *Orders of
> Periwigs*. He died in 1726.

DOMINUS HYACINTHUS DE ARCHANGELIS, PAUPERUM
PROCURATOR. See *The Ring and the Book.*

DONALD.

First appeared in *Jocoseria*, 1883, pp. 5–22.
Reprinted, *Poetical Works*, 1889, Vol. xv. pp. 169–181.

In *The Keepsake* for 1832 will be found an interesting narrative from the pen of Sir Walter Scott, which bears so striking a resemblance to this poem that the following brief summary is appended :

" The story," writes Sir Walter, " is an old one : the actor and sufferer not being a very aged man, when I heard the anecdote in my early youth. Duncan, for so I shall call him, had been engaged in the affair of 1746, with others of his clan. On the one side of his body he retained the proportions and firmness of an active mountaineer ; on the other, he was a disabled cripple, scarce able to limp along the streets. The cause which reduced him to this state of infirmity was singular. Twenty years or more before I knew Duncan, he assisted his brothers in farming a large grazing in the Highlands. It chanced that a sheep or goat was missed from the flock, and Duncan went himself in quest of the fugitive. In the course of his researches he was induced to ascend a small and narrow path, leading to the top of a high precipice. It was not much more than two feet broad, so rugged and difficult, and, at the same time, so terrible, that it would have been impracticable to any but the light step and steady brain of the Highlander. The precipice on the right rose like a wall, and on the left sunk to a depth which it was giddy to look down upon. He had more than half ascended the precipice, when in midway he encountered a buck of the red-deer species coming down the cliff by the same path in an opposite direction. Neither party had the power of retreating, for the stag had not room to turn himself in the narrow path, and if Duncan had turned his back to go down, he knew enough of the creature's habits to be certain that he would rush upon him while engaged in the difficulties of the retreat. They stood therefore perfectly still, and looked at each other in mutual embarrassment for some space. At length the deer, which was one of the largest size, began to lower his formidable antlers, as they do when they are brought to bay. Duncan saw the danger, and, as a last resource, stretched himself on the little ledge of rock, not making the least motion for fear of alarming the animal. They remained in this posture for three or four hours. At length the buck approached towards Duncan very slowly; he came close to the Highlander, when the devil, or the untamable love of sport, began to overcome Duncan's fears. Seeing the animal proceed so gently, he totally forgot not only the dangers of his position, but the implicit compact which certainly might have been inferred from the circumstances of the situation. With one hand Duncan seized the deer's horn, whilst with the other he drew his dirk. But in the same instant the buck bounded over the precipice, carrying the Highlander along with him. Fortune ordered that the deer should fall undermost, and be killed on the spot, while Duncan escaped with life, but with the fracture of a leg, an arm, and three ribs. I never could approve of Duncan's conduct towards the deer in a moral point of view, but I have given you the story exactly as I recollect it."

"DON JUAN, MIGHT YOU PLEASE TO HELP ONE GIVE A GUESS."

First appeared in *Fifine at the Fair*, 1872, p. vi.
Reprinted, *Poetical Works*, 1889, Vol. xi. p. 214.

These lines form a motto to *Fifine at the Fair*, and were translated from *Molière*.

DRAMATIC IDYLS: FIRST SERIES.

First appeared (1879) in one Vol. See *ante*, p. 387, No. 22.
Reprinted, *Poetical Works*, 1889, Vol. xv. pp. 1–80.

DRAMATIC IDYLS: SECOND SERIES.

First appeared (1880) in one Vol. See *ante*, p. 388, No. 23.
Reprinted, *Poetical Works*, 1889, xv. pp. 81–163.

DRAMATIC LYRICS.

This was the title given to No. iii. (1842) of *Bells and Pomegranates*, which consisted of sixteen poems ; afterwards rearranged in separate sections of the various collected editions of the *Poems*.

DRAMATIC ROMANCES AND LYRICS.

This was the title given to No. vii. of *Bells and Pomegranates* (1845), which consisted of twenty poems ; these were afterwards rearranged in separate sections of the various collected editions of the *Poems*.

DRAMATIS PERSONÆ.

First appeared (1864) in one Vol. See *ante*, p. 378, No. 11.
Reprinted, *Poems*, 1868, Vol. vi. pp. 41-222.
Ditto, *Poetical Works*, 1889, Vol. vii. pp. 43-255.

DUBIETY.

First appeared in *Asolando*, 1889, pp. 8-9.
Reprinted, *Poetical Works*, 1894, Vol. xvii. pp. 6-7.

EARTH'S IMMORTALITIES.

First appeared in *Bells and Pomegranates*, 1845, No. vii. p. 19.
Reprinted, *Poems*, 1849, Vol. ii. pp. 393-394.
Ditto   ditto   1863, Vol. i. pp. 31-32.
Ditto   ditto   1868, Vol. iii. pp. 105-106.
Ditto, *Poetical Works*, 1889, Vol. vi. p. 45.

EASTER DAY. See *Christmas Eve and Easter Day*.

ECHETLOS.

First appeared in *Dramatic Idyls* II. 1880, pp. 1-7.
Reprinted, *Poetical Works*, 1889, Vol. xv. pp. 85-87.

EPILOGUES.

"At the midnight, in the silence of the sleep-time"—see *Asolando*.
" First Speaker, as David ; " " Second Speaker, as Renan ; "
" Third Speaker "—see *Dramatis Personæ*.
Fust and his Friends—see *Parleyings*.
" Good to Forgive " (" Pisgah Sights, 3 ")—see *La Saisiaz*.
" Oh, Love—no, Love ! "—see *Ferishtah's Fancies*.
The Householder—see *Fifine at the Fair*.
" The poets pour us wine "—see *Pacchiarotto*.
" Touch him ne'er so lightly "—see *Dramatic Idyls* II.
" What a pretty tale you told me "—see *The Two Poets of Croisic*.

EURIPIDES: TRANSCRIPTS FROM. See *Balaustion's Adventure* and *Aristophanes' Apology.*

EURYDICE TO ORPHEUS.

First appeared in the Royal Academy Catalogue, 1864, p. 13, under the title *Orpheus and Eurydice.*
Reprinted, *Selections,* 1865, p. 215.
Ditto, *Poems,* 1868, Vol. vi. p. 153.
Ditto, *Poetical Works,* 1889, Vol. vii. p. 170.

These lines were interpretive of a picture by Sir Frederick Leighton, representing Orpheus leading Eurydice from Hades. So charmed were the nether gods with the music of Orpheus, that they consented to restore Eurydice to him on condition that he would refrain from looking at her till they had passed out of the nether world. To this Orpheus agreed ; but desire proved too strong for him, and, like Lot's wife, he looked—and lost. Mrs. Orr says, in her invaluable *Handbook* : " The face of Leighton's Eurydice wears an intensity of longing which seems to challenge the forbidden look, and make her responsible for it. The poem thus interprets the expression, and translates it into words."

EVELYN HOPE.

First appeared in *Men and Women,* 1855, Vol. i. p. 19.
Reprinted, *Poems,* 1863, Vol. i. pp. 36–38.
Ditto   ditto   1868, Vol. iii. pp. 110–112.
Ditto, *Poetical Works,* 1889, Vol. vi. pp. 51–53.

EYES, CALM BESIDE THEE, (LADY COULD'ST THOU KNOW !).

First appeared in *The Monthly Repository,* Vol. viii. p. 712.
Reprinted in *The Browning Society's Papers,* Part xii. p. 36*

When published in *The Monthly Repository,* this sonnet appeared under the signature " Z." It was not included by Mr. Browning in the final, seventeen vol., edition of his Works : it is therefore quoted here.

Eyes, calm beside thee, (Lady could'st thou know !)
　May turn away thick with fast-gathering tears :
I glance not where all gaze : thrilling and low
　Their passionate praises reach thee—my cheek wears
Alone no wonder when thou passest by ;
Thy tremulous lids bent and suffused reply
To the irrepressible homage which doth glow
　On every lip but mine : if in thine ears
Their accents linger—and thou dost recall
　Me as I stood, still, guarded, very pale,
Beside each votarist whose lighted brow
Wore worship like an aureole, " O'er them all
　My beauty," thou wilt murmur, " did prevail
Save that one only : "—Lady couldst thou know !

FEARS AND SCRUPLES.

First appeared in *Pacchiarotto*, 1876, pp. 83-87.

Reprinted, *Poetical Works*, 1889, Vol. xiv. pp. 54-57.

In a letter (addressed to Mr. W. G. Kingsland) Mr. Browning has made the following remarks regarding *Fears and Scruples* :—

" *Where there is a genuine love of the ' letters' and ' actions' of the invisible 'friend,'—however these may be disadvantaged by an inability to meet the objections to their authenticity or historical value urged by ' experts' who assume the privilege of learning over ignorance,—it would indeed be a wrong to the wisdom and goodness of the ' friend' if he were supposed capable of overlooking the actual ' love' and only considering the ' ignorance' which, failing to in any degree affect ' love,' is really the highest evidence that ' love' exists.*"

FERISHTAH'S FANCIES.

First appeared (1884) in one Vol.　See *ante*, p. 390, No. 25.

Reprinted, *Poetical Works*, 1889, Vol. xvi. pp. 1-92.

Writing to a correspondent in October 1884, Mr. Browning says : " I hope and believe that one or two careful readings of the poem [*Ferishtah*] will make its sense clear enough.　Above all, pray allow for the poet's inventiveness in any case, and do not suppose there is more than a thin disguise of a few Persian names and allusions. There was no such person as Ferishtah ; and the stories are all inventions. The Hebrew quotations are put in for a purpose, as a direct acknowledgment that certain doctrines may be found in the Old Book which the Concocters of Novel Schemes of Morality put forth as discoveries of their own."

Confirmatory of the "inventiveness" mentioned here, the following mottoes are given on the blank reverse of the half-title page of this volume :—

' His genius was jocular, but, when disposed, he could be very serious.' —Article ' Shakespear,' Jeremy Collier's *Historical &c. Dictionary,* second edition, 1701.

' You, Sir, I entertain you for one of my Hundred ; only, I do not like the fashion of your garments : you will say they are Persian ; but let them be changed.'—*King Lear,* Act iii., sc. 6.

FIFINE AT THE FAIR.

First appeared (1872) in one Vol. See *ante,* p. 382, No. 15. Reprinted, *Poetical Works,* 1889, Vol. xi. pp. 211-343.

It is interesting to note that " Fifine " had an " original "—being sketched from the recollection of a certain Gipsy whom the poet once saw at Pornic.

' FIFTY YEARS' FLIGHT ! WHEREIN SHOULD HE REJOICE."

First appeared in *The Pall Mall Gazette.*

Reprinted in W. G. Kingsland's *Robert Browning: Chief Poet of the Age,* p. 31.

These lines were written, by request, for a memorial window, commemorative of the Queen's Jubilee, placed in St. Margaret's Church, Westminster. They have not been reprinted in any edition of Mr. Browning's works ; and are as follows—

> " Fifty years' flight ! wherein should he rejoice
> Who hailed their birth, who as they die decays !
> This—England echoes his attesting voice ;
> Wondrous and well—thanks Ancient Thou of days."

FILIPPO BALDINUCCI ON THE PRIVILEGE OF BURIAL.

First appeared in *Pacchiarotto*, 1876, pp. 184–222.
Reprinted, *Poetical Works*, 1889, Vol. xiv. pp. 117–140.

"FIRE IS IN THE FLINT: TRUE, ONCE A SPARK ESCAPES."

First appeared in *Ferishtah's Fancies*, 1884, p. 45.
Reprinted, *Poetical Works*, Vol. xvi. p. 31.

FLUTE-MUSIC, WITH AN ACCOMPANIMENT.

First appeared in *Asolando*, 1889, pp. 99–111.
Reprinted, *Poetical Works*, 1894, Vol. xvii. pp. 82–92.

FRA LIPPO LIPPI.

First appeared in *Men and Women*, 1855, Vol. i. pp. 35–55.
Reprinted, *Poems*, 1863, Vol. i. p. 346–359.
Ditto   ditto   1868, Vol. v. pp. 234–248.
Ditto, *Poetical Works*, 1889, Vol. iv. pp. 205–220.

Apropos of the brief lyric breaks in this blank-verse poem, Miss Helen Clarke writes: "These little love-songs are called *stornelli*, and consist of three lines: the first, of five syllables, usually contains the name of a flower, which sets the rhyme ; then the love theme is told in two lines of eleven syllables, each agreeing by rhyme, assonance, or repetition with the first. The address to the flower usually has no connection with the sentiment expressed in the following lines."

Concerning the reference to the Prior's niece (line 387), it may be interesting to compare Landor's view in his *Imaginary Conversation* between *Fra Filippo Lippi and Pope Eugenius the Fourth* :—

Filippo.   In fact, there were only two genuine abbates, the third was Donna Lisetta, the good canonico's pretty niece, who looks so archly at your Holiness when you bend your knees before her at bed time.

Eugenius.   How? Where?

Filippo.   She is the angel on the right hand side of the Holy

Family, with a tip of amethyst-coloured wing over a basket of figs and pomegranates. I painted her from memory; she was then only fifteen, and worthy to be the niece of an archbishop. . . .

Eugenius. Poor soul! So this is the angel with the amethyst-coloured wing? I thought she looked wanton.

FURINI, FRANCIS, PARLEYING WITH.

First appeared in *Parleyings*, 1887, pp. 121–159.
Reprinted, *Poetical Works*, 1889, Vol. xvi. pp. 175–200.

Francis Furini was born at Florence, in the year 1600. He took orders at the age of 40, and remained an exemplary parish priest until his death in 1649. In his earlier career he was especially famous for his painting of the nude figure. It is, indeed, complained by one of his French biographers that he painted the nude too well to be quite proper—pointing to the *Adam and Eve* in the Pitti Palace in proof of this assertion. The painter may have thought so too—for it is said that on his death-bed he desired all his pictures of the nude to be collected and destroyed. If this was so, his wishes were thwarted; for most private galleries in Florence have specimens of his art.

FUST AND HIS FRIENDS.

First appeared in *Parleyings*, 1887, pp. 221–268.
Reprinted, *Poetical Works*, 1889, Vol. xvi. pp. 241–275.

This poem forms the Epilogue to *Parleyings with certain People of Importance in their Day.*

GARDEN FANCIES.

First appeared in *Hood's Magazine*, Vol. ii. (July 1844), pp. 45–48.
Reprinted in *Bells and Pomegranates*, 1845, No. vii. p. 10.
Ditto, *Poems*, 1849, Vol. ii. pp. 349–354.
Ditto ditto 1863, Vol. i. pp. 13–18.
Ditto ditto 1868, Vol. iii. pp. 87–92.
Ditto, *Poetical Works*, 1889, Vol. vi. pp. 19–25.

GIUSEPPE CAPONSACCHI.   See *The Ring and the Book.*

In explanation of lines 1666, 1667 of this monologue—

> "Verse, quotha ?   Bembo's verse !   When Saint John wrote
> The tract, ' *De* Tribus,' I wrote this to match "—

Dr. Berdoe in his most useful 'Browning Cyclopædia'
(p. 421) says that " Caponsacchi refers to the three heavenly
witnesses, a verse held by all commentators to be an
interpolated passage—as much as to say, I wrote these
verses when St. John wrote the surrendered verse—that is,
I did not write them at all." In contradistinction to this, Dr.
Hiram Corson writes that the professor of Romance Languages
in Cornell University (Mr. T. F. Crane) suggests that the tract
referred to is the legendary work known as the *De Tribus
Impostoribus*, the three impostors being Moses, Christ, and
Mohammed.   "Such a work abundantly satisfies the idea
involved in the Canon's speech ; and I am quite assured, after
looking into the extensive material on the subject, contained in
the White historical library of the University, that the Canon
refers to this legendary work.   It was whispered through three
or four centuries, that such a blasphemous work existed somewhere, nobody knew where, or by whom ; the result being
finally that several works appeared, each pretending to be the
original work, where there may have been no original."

GIVE A ROUSE.   See *Cavalier Tunes.*

GOLD HAIR : A STORY OF PORNIC.

First appeared in *The Atlantic Monthly* for *May* 1864.
Also printed in London, in Pamphlet form, privately, 1864.
Reprinted in *Dramatis Personæ*, 1864, pp. 25–34.
Ditto, *Dramatis Personæ*, second edition, 1864.
Ditto, *Poems*, 1868, Vol. vi. pp. 62–69.
Ditto, *Poetical Works*, 1889, Vol. vii. pp. 69–77.

In *The Atlantic Monthly*, the pamphlet of 1864, and the first
edition of *Dramatis Personæ*, this poem consisted of twenty-

seven stanzas; but in the second edition of *Dramatis Personæ* three fresh stanzas were added—the poem thus consisting of thirty stanzas. The fresh stanzas are those now numbered 21, 22, and 23.

" GOLDONI,—GOOD, GAY, SUNNIEST OF SOULS."

First appeared in *The Pall Mall Gazette*, Dec. 8, 1883.
Reprinted in *The Browning Society's Papers*, Part v. p. 98*.
Ditto, W. G. Kingsland's *Robert Browning : Chief Poet of the Age*, p. 30.

This sonnet was written for the " Album " of the Committee of the Goldoni monument at Venice. Not having been reprinted in any edition of Mr. Browning's works, the lines are here given as they appear on the first page of the " Album " :—

> Goldoni,—good, gay, sunniest of souls,—
>> Glassing half Venice in that verse of thine,—
>> What though it just reflect the shade and shine
> Of common life, nor render, as it rolls,
> Grandeur and gloom? Sufficient for thy shoals
>> Was Carnival : Parini's depths enshrine
>> Secrets unsuited to that opaline
> Surface of things which laughs along thy scrolls.
> There throng the People : how they come and go,
>> Lisp the soft language, flaunt the bright garb—see—
> On Piazza, Calle, under Portico
>> And over Bridge ! Dear King of Comedy,
> Be honoured ! Thou that didst love Venice so,
>> Venice and we who love her, all love thee !

" GONE NOW! ALL GONE ACROSS THE DARK SO FAR."

First appeared in *Dramatis Personæ*, 1864, pp. 246-248.
Reprinted, *Poems*, 1868, Vol. vi. pp. 223-224.
Ditto, *Poetical Works*, 1889, Vol. vii. pp. 251-253.

This poem is the " SECOND SPEAKER, *as Renan*," of the Epilogue to *Dramatis Personæ*.

"GOOD TO FORGIVE."

First appeared in *La Saisiaz*, 1878, pp. 3-4.
Reprinted, *Poetical Works*, 1889, Vol. xiv. pp. 155-156.

This poem is the proem to *La Saisaiz*. It is printed in the second series of *Selections* as *Pisgah Sights*, 3.

GUIDO.   See *The Ring and the Book*.

HALBERT AND HOB.

First appeared in *Dramatic Idyls* I. 1879, pp. 45-55.
Reprinted, *Poetical Works*, 1889, Vol. xv. pp. 26-31.

HALF-ROME.   See *The Ring and the Book*.

HELEN'S TOWER.

First appeared in *The Pall Mall Gazette*, Dec. 28, 1883.
Reprinted in *The Browning Society's Papers*, Part v. p. 97*.
Ditto, W. G. Kingsland's *Robert Browning: Chief Poet of the Age*, p. 28.

This fine sonnet was written *apropos* of the Tower erected by the Earl of Dufferin to the memory of his mother, Helen, Countess of Gifford, at Clandeboye, Ireland. The sonnet is dated 1870, but it was not publicly acknowledged until 1883: Mr. Browning consenting to its publication on learning that Lord Tennyson had published the lines he had written on the same subject. As the sonnet is not included in the collected edition of Mr. Browning's *Poems* it is quoted here :—

> Who hears of Helen's Tower, may dream perchance
> How the Greek Beauty from the Scæan Gate
> Gazed on old friends unanimous in hate,
> Death-doom'd because of her fair countenance.
> Hearts would leap otherwise at thy advance,
> Lady, to whom this Tower, is consecrate !
> Like hers, thy face once made all eyes elate,
> Yet, unlike hers, was blessed by every glance.

 The Tower of Hate is outworn, far and strange :
  A transitory shame of long ago,
  It dies into the sand from which it sprang ;
 But thine, Love's rock-built Tower, shalt fear no change :
  God's self laid stable earth's foundations so,
  When all the morning stars together sang.

" HERE'S TO NELSON'S MEMORY."   See *Nationality in Drinks*.

HERVÉ RIEL.

 First appeared in *The Cornhill Magazine*, March, 1871, pp. 257–260.

 Reprinted in *Pacchiarotto*, 1876, pp. 117–130.

 Ditto, *Poetical Works*, 1889, Vol. xiv. pp. 77–85.

This poem was written in 1867—although not published till 1871. It appeared—against Mr. Browning's usual custom—in the *Cornhill* because he desired to give a subscription to the Fund on behalf of the French after the siege of Paris by the Germans in 1870–71 : he accordingly sent the £100 given by Mr. Smith for the poem to that fund. When the poem appeared the facts of the story seem to have been forgotten, and were denied at St. Malo ; but on the reports to the French Admiralty of the time being looked up, they were found to be correct. It seems, however, that Browning was mistaken in stating that Hervé Riel was granted but one day's holiday in which to see his wife, " La Belle Aurore "—that is, if the *Notes sur le Croisic* (par Caillo Jeune) are correct : "Ce brave homme ne demanda pour récompense d'un service aussi signalé, qu'un congé absolu pour rejoindre sa femme, qu'il nommait la Belle Aurore." Under date December 16th, 1881, Mr. Browning writes to Dr. Furnivall : "Where do you find that the holiday of *Hervé Riel* was for more than a day—his whole life-time ? If it is to be found I have strangely overlooked it." That he had overlooked it is evident from a further letter, dated December 20th, 1881, when he again writes to Dr. Furnivall : "You are undoubtedly right, and I have mistaken the meaning of the phrase—I suppose through thinking that, if the coasting-pilot's business ended with reaching land, he might claim as a right to be let go : otherwise an absolute discharge seems to approach in importance a substantial reward.   Still—truth above all things ; so treat the matter as you please."

HOLY-CROSS DAY.

First appeared in *Men and Women*, 1855, Vol. ii. pp. 158–166.
Reprinted, *Poems*, 1863, Vol. i. pp. 291–296.
Ditto   ditto   1868, Vol. iv. pp. 280–285.
Ditto, *Poetical Works*, 1889, Vol. v. pp. 167-174

HOME-THOUGHTS, FROM ABROAD.

First appeared in *Bells and Pomegranates*, No. vii. p. 8.
Reprinted, *Poems*, 1849, Vol. ii. pp. 343–344.
Ditto   ditto   1863, Vol. i. pp. 72–73.
Ditto   ditto   1868, Vol. iii. pp. 145.
Ditto, *Poetical Works*, 1889, Vol. vi. pp. 95–96.

In *Bells and Pomegranates*, No. vii. p. 8, under the heading *Home Thoughts, from Abroad*, are included three poems : the poem now so-called being No. 1 ; *Here's to Nelson's memory* (now printed under the title *Nationality in Drinks*) as No. 2 ; and the poem now called *Home Thoughts, from the Sea*, as No. 3.

HOME-THOUGHTS FROM THE SEA.

First appeared in *Bells and Pomegranates*, 1845, No. vii. p. 8.
Reprinted, *Poems*, 1849, Vol. ii. p. 344.
Ditto   ditto   1863, Vol. i. p. 73.
Ditto   ditto   1868, Vol. iii. p. 146.
Ditto, *Poetical Works*, 1889, Vol. vi. p. 97.

HOUSE.

First appeared in *Pacchiarotto*, 1876, pp. 60–63.
Reprinted, *Poetical Works*, 1889, Vol. xiv. pp. 39-41.

HOW IT STRIKES A CONTEMPORARY.

First appeared in *Men and Women*, 1855, Vol. i. pp. 177–183.
Reprinted, *Poems*, 1863, Vol. i. pp. 323–327.
Ditto   ditto   1868, Vol. v. pp. 209–212.
Ditto, *Poetical Works*, 1889, Vol. iv. pp. 176-180.

"How they brought the Good News from Ghent to Aix."

First appeared in *Bells and Pomegranates*, No. vii. p. 3.
Reprinted, *Poems*, 1849, Vol. ii. pp. 318–320.
Ditto   ditto   1863, Vol. i. pp. 6–9.
Ditto   ditto   1868, Vol. iii. pp. 80–83.
Ditto, *Poetical Works*, 1889, Vol. vi. pp. 9–12.

"There is no sort of historical foundation," writes Browning, "about *Good News from Ghent* : I wrote it under the bulwark of a vessel off the African coast, after I had been at sea long enough to appreciate even the fancy of a gallop on the back of a certain good horse ' York,' then in my stable at home. It was written in pencil on the fly-leaf of Bartoli's *Simboli*, I remember." For the towns on the route the poet may have referred to an atlas on board the vessel ; but the riders evidently went by the longest route.   Dr. W. J. Rolfe (*Poet Lore*, Vol. iv. pp. 379-380) thus describes the " course " : " Aix-la-Chapelle is a little south of east from Ghent, and the distance in a straight line, as I measure it on four different maps, no two of which are on the same scale, is about 105 miles.   It is a level country for most of the way ; but if Browning had tried to gallop over it at one stretch, his good steed ' York ' would probably have given out sooner than Dirck's did in the poem.   The riders at the start take a course a little *north* of east to *Lokeren*, twelve miles distant, and thence due east to *Boom*, sixteen miles further.   The next town mentioned is Düffeld, or Duffel, about twelve miles east of Boom.   It is six miles north of *Mecheln*, or Mechlin, the ' half-chime ' from the lofty cathedral tower of which the riders are said to hear.   We are not to suppose that they pass through Mechlin, which would be quite out of the course they are taking ; but if Browning had had a better map, he would probably have made them steer directly to that city from Ghent.   From Duffel they pass on to *Aerschot*, fifteen miles more ; and thence, twenty-four miles, to *Hasselt*, the capital of the province of Limbourg.   From Hasselt we should expect them to make for Maastricht, or Maestricht ; but they turn almost at a right angle and go seven or eight miles due *south* to *Loos*.   Thence they aim for Aix again, and proceed to *Tongres* (the French form of the Flemish *Tongeren*), six and a-half miles further. From Tongres to Aix it is about twenty-seven miles in a straight course ; but the only landmark the poem gives us for this stretch is in the line, ' Till over by Dalhem a dome-spire sprang white " —that is, the cupola of the ' octagon' of the Cathedral at Aix. Dalhem is to be found on no map that I have seen, nor is it mentioned in the guide-books or gazetteers. It would seem to be a village near Aix, but I can learn of none such. On one of Bartholomew's maps I find a *Daelheim*, some five miles south of the line from Tongres to Aix, and about seventeen miles from the latter. Charlemagne's ' dome-spire' cannot be visible from this place, but I suspect that it is the *Dalhem* of the poem. It will be seen that by the route described it is at least 120 miles from Ghent to Aix, if a straight line is taken from Tongres to the latter city. One hundred and twenty-five miles would probably be nearer the true total. The more direct course from Hasselt to Aix through Maastricht would have been about seven miles shorter."

HUMILITY.

First appeared in *Asolando*, 1889, p. 11.
Reprinted, *Poetical Works*, 1894, Vol. xvii. p. 9.

" IMPERANTE AUGUSTO NATUS EST—"

First appeared in *Asolando*, 1889, pp. 112-122.
Reprinted, *Poetical Works*, 1894, Vol. xvii. pp. 93-101.

IN A BALCONY.

First appeared in *Men and Women*, 1855, Vol. ii. pp. 49-110.
Reprinted, *Poems*, 1863, Vol. ii. pp. 468-502.
Ditto   ditto   1868, Vol. vi. pp. 1-40.
Ditto, *Poetical Works*, 1889, Vol. vii. pp. 1-41.

On the evening of Friday, November 28, 1884, *In a Balcony* was, for the first time, put upon the stage. The performance took place at the Princes' Hall, and was given under the auspices of the Browning Society. *Constance* was portrayed by Miss Alma Murray (Mrs. Alfred Forman); the *Queen* by Miss Nora Gerstenberg; and *Norbert* by Mr. Philip Beck. Mr. Frederick Wedmore, writing in *The Academy* of December 6, 1884, says: "Miss Alma Murray's *Constance* was nothing less than a great performance, instinct with intelligence, grace, and fire. The more exacting was the situation, the more evident became the capacity of the actress to grapple with it. It was the performance of an artist who had thought of all the part contained, and had understood it—who knew how to compose a *rôle* as a whole, and how to execute it, alike in its least and its most important detail. It is long since our stage has seen an interpretation more picturesque or more moving."

In a Gondola.

First appeared in *Bells and Pomegranates*, 1842, No. iii. pp. 6–9.
Reprinted, *Poems*, 1849, Vol. ii. pp. 271–280.
Ditto   ditto 1863, Vol. i. pp. 205–214.
Ditto   ditto 1868, Vol. iv. pp. 196–205.
Ditto, *Poetical Works*, 1889, Vol. v. pp. 66–77.

The opening stanza of this poem was originally written to illustrate a picture by Maclise. Charles Dickens, writing to Maclise in 1844, says: "In a certain picture called *The Serenade*, for which Browning wrote that verse in Lincoln's Inn Fields, you, O Mac, painted a sky." Browning, however, writing to Dr. Furnivall on September 15, 1881, gives the following details: "I wrote the Venice stanza to illustrate Maclise's picture, for which he was anxious to get some line or two. I had not seen it, but, from Forster's description, gave it to him, in his room, *impromptu*. Maclise (a friend of my own) painted the whole thing, not the sky merely. When I did see it I thought the serenader too jolly, somewhat, for the notion I got from Forster, and I took up the subject in my own way." This poem has been considerably revised since it first appeared in *Bells and Pomegranates*. For instance, in line 87, where in the original version we have

"Lie back; could I improve you?"

we now read

> " Lie back ; could thought of mine improve you ? "

and in line 104, in place of

> " He and the Couple catch at last,"

we now have

> " What if the Three should catch at last."

But in lines 171–177 a still more extensive revision has been made.   In place of the original reading—

> " Breathes slumbrously as if some elf
> Went in and out tall chords his wings
> Get murmurs from whene'er they graze
> As may an angel thro' the maze
> Of pillars on God's quest have gone
> At guilty glorious Babylon "—

the passage now reads :

> " Breathes slumberously, as if some elf
> Went in and out the chords, his wings
> Make murmur, wheresoe'er they graze,
> As an angel may, between the maze
> Of midnight palace-pillars, on
> And on, to sow God's plagues, have gone
> Through guilty glorious Babylon."

IN A YEAR.

First appeared in *Men and Women*, 1855, Vol. ii. p. 24.
Reprinted, *Poems*, 1863, Vol. i. pp. 133–137.
Ditto   ditto   1868, Vol. iii. pp. 205–208.
Ditto, *Poetical Works*, 1889, Vol. vi. pp. 175–179.

IN THREE DAYS.

First appeared in *Men and Women*, 1855, Vol. ii. p. 21.
Reprinted, *Poems*, 1863, Vol. i. pp. 132–133.
Ditto   ditto   1868, Vol. iii. pp. 204–205.
Ditto, *Poetical Works*, 1889, Vol. vi. 172–174.

INCIDENT OF THE FRENCH CAMP.

First appeared in *Bells and Pomegranates*, No. iii. p. 5, under
the heading of *Camp and Cloister*, 1, *Camp*.

Dramatic Romances.

Incident of the French Camp.

I.

You know, we French stormed Ratisbon:
    A mile or so away
On a little mound, Napoleon
    Stood on our storming-day;
With neck out-thrust, you fancy how,
    Legs wide, arms locked behind,
As if to balance the prone brow
    Oppressive with its mind.

INCIDENT OF THE FRENCH CAMP: FIRST STANZA.

FAC-SIMILE OF BROWNING'S ORIGINAL MANUSCRIPT.

Reprinted, *Poems,* 1849, Vol. i. pp. 266–267.
Ditto   ditto 1863, Vol. i. pp. 156–157.
Ditto   ditto 1868, Vol. iv. pp. 147–148.
Ditto, *Poetical Works,* 1889, Vol. v. pp. 3–5.

INSTANS TYRANNUS.

First appeared in *Men and Women,* 1855, Vol. i. p. 123.
Reprinted, *Poems,* 1863, Vol. i. pp. 171–173.
Ditto   ditto 1868, Vol. iv. pp. 162–164.
Ditto, *Poetical Works,* 1889, Vol. v. pp. 24–27.

INTRODUCTORY ESSAY TO " LETTERS OF PERCY BYSSHE SHELLEY."

First appeared in 1852.
Reprinted in the *Browning Society's Papers,* Part i. 1881.
Ditto, in Pamphlet form, 1888.

IVÀN IVÀNOVITCH.

First appeared in *Dramatic Idyls* I. 1879, pp. 59–100.
Reprinted, *Poetical Works,* 1889, Vol. xv. pp. 32–56.

IXION.

First appeared in *Jocoseria,* 1883, pp. 55–69.
Reprinted, *Poetical Works,* 1889, Vol. xv. pp. 199–208.

It has been pointed out by Mrs. Orr (*Handbook to the Works of Robert Browning,* p. 13) that the alternative hexameter and pentameter is employed by Mr. Browning for the only time in this poem : the measure cleverly " imitating the turning of the wheel on which Ixion is bound."

JAMES LEE'S WIFE.

First appeared in *Dramatis Personæ,* 1864, pp. 1–24.
Reprinted, *Poems,* 1868, Vol. vi. pp. 41–61.
Ditto, *Poetical Works,* 1889, Vol. vii. pp. 45–68.

When issued originally in *Dramatis Personæ* this Poem was

entitled *James Lee*: but four years later, in the collected edition of his works, Mr. Browning changed it to *James Lee's Wife*. There are some alterations in the punctuation, and also in the capitaling, of the 1868 edition; but the only alteration of real importance is the long addition to the eighth section of the Poem. In the original edition this section consisted of the first subsection as it now stands, beginning

"As like as a Hand to another Hand : "

And ending

"Still from one's soulless finger tips."

Then followed two lines as subsection 2—

" Go, little girl, with the poor coarse hand !
I have my lesson, shall understand."

In the edition of 1868, two new subsections were added: the one consisting of twenty-two lines, now forming subsection 2 :

II.

'Tis a clay cast, the perfect thing,
    From Hand live once, dead long ago :
Princess-like it wears the ring
    To fancy's eye, by which we know
That here at length a master found
    His match, a proud lone soul its mate,
As soaring genius sank to ground
    And pencil could not emulate
The beauty in this,—how free, how fine
To fear almost !—of the limit-line.
Long ago the god, like me
The worm, learned, each in our degree :
Looked and loved, learned and drew,
    Drew and learned and loved again,
While fast the happy minutes flew,
    Till beauty mounted into his brain
And on the finger which outvied
    His art he placed the ring that's there,
Still by fancy's eye descried,
    In token of a marriage rare :
For him on earth, his art's despair,
For him in heaven, his soul's fit bride.

The other of thirty-nine lines, forming subsection 3 :

III.

Little girl with the poor coarse hand
   I turned from to a cold clay cast—
I have my lesson, understand
   The worth of flesh and blood at last !
Nothing but beauty in a Hand?
   Because he could not change the hue,
   Mend the lines and make them true
To this which met his soul's demand,—
   Would Da Vinci turn from you?
I hear him laugh my woes to scorn—
" The fool forsooth is all forlorn
" Because the beauty, she thinks best
" Lived long ago or was never born,—
" Because no beauty bears the test.
" In this rough peasant Hand !   Confessed
" 'Art is null and study void !'
" So sayest thou ?   So said not I,
" Who threw the faulty pencil by,
" And years instead of hours employed,
" Learning the veritable use
" Of flesh and bone and nerve beneath
" Lines and hue of the outer sheath,
" If haply I might reproduce
" One motive of the mechanism,
" Flesh and bone and nerve that make
" The poorest coarsest human hand
" An object worthy to be scanned
" A whole life long for their sole sake.
" Shall earth and the cramped moment-space
" Yield the heavenly crowning grace ?
" Now the parts and then the whole !
" Who art thou, with stinted soul
"And stunted body, thus to cry
"   I love,—shall that be life's strait dole ?
" 'I must live beloved or die !'
" This peasant hand that spins the wool
" And bakes the bread, why lives it on,
" Poor and coarse with beauty gone,—
" What use survives the beauty?   Fool ! "

closing with the two lines originally forming subsection 2 :

> " Go, little girl with the poor coarse hand !
> I have my lesson, shall understand."

The poem is, as all readers of Browning are aware, descriptive, by a series of lyrical verses, of an unhappy married life, as far as it has its effect on the mood, and at last on the critical conduct, of the wife. The husband, it would seem, we are meant to know little about—and to this is of course attributable the subsequent change of title. The poem is the more noteworthy as containing specimens of Browning's work of three different kinds and times—that is, so far as we can judge, of 1836, 1864, and 1868.

JOCHANAN HAKKADOSH.

First appeared in *Jocoseria*, 1883, pp. 71–131.
Reprinted, *Poetical Works*, 1889, Vol. xv. pp. 209-255.

The scene of this poem, writes Miss Cohen (*Jewish Messenger*, March 4, 1887) is laid at Schiphas (probably Sheeraz, on the Bendimir, as Browning writes it, no doubt Bundemeer, one of the chief rivers in the province of Farsiztan, in Persia). Mr. Browning writes concerning it : " This story can have no better authority than that of the treatise, existing dispersedly in fragments of rabbinical writing. The two Hebrew quotations—put in to give a grave look to what is mere fun and invention—being translated amount to, first, 'A collection of many lies,' and the second an old saying 'From Moses to Moses arose none like Moses.' " This, Miss Cohen points out, refers, of course, to the Moses of the Bible and to the distinguished Maimonides of the twelfth century.

JOCOSERIA.

First appeared (1883) in one Vol.   See *ante*, p. 389, No. 24.
Reprinted, *Poetical Works*, 1889, Vol. xv. pp. 165–260.

JOHANNES AGRICOLA IN MEDITATION.

First appeared in the *Monthly Repository*, 1836, Vol. x. p. 45.
Reprinted, *Bells and Pomegranates*, 1842, No. ii. p. 13.

Reprinted, *Poems*, 1849, Vol. ii. pp. 300–302.
Ditto   ditto 1863, Vol. i. pp. 284–286.
Ditto   ditto 1868, Vol. v. pp. 229–230.
Ditto, *Poetical Works*, 1889, Vol. iv. pp. 199–201.

Following the heading of this poem as it originally appeared in *The Monthly Repository* [where the poem was called *Madhouse Cells.* 1] was the following quotation from the *Dictionary of all Religions* (1704) : "Antinomians, so denominated for rejecting the law as a thing of no use under the gospel dispensation : they say that good works do not further, nor evil works hinder salvation ; that the child of God cannot sin, that God never chastiseth him, that murder, drunkenness, &c., are sins in the wicked but not in him, that the child of grace being once assured of salvation, afterwards never doubteth . . . . that God doth not love any man for his holiness, that sanctification is no evidence of justification, &c. Pontanus, in his Catalogue of Heresies, says John Agricola was the author of this sect, A.D. 1535."
In the reprint of 1849, the title was given as 1.—*Madhouse Cell* ; the sub-title being *Johannes Agricola in Meditation.* In the 1863 edition, however, the heading of the poem was given as *Johannes Agricola in Meditation.*

JURIS DOCTOR JOHANNES - BAPTISTA BOTTINIUS, FISCI ET REV. CAM. APOSTOL. ADVOCATUS. See *The Ring and the Book.*

KING VICTOR AND KING CHARLES.

First appeared in *Bells and Pomegranates*, 1842, No. ii. pp. 5–20.
Reprinted, *Poems*, 1849, Vol. i. pp. 231–302.
Ditto   ditto 1863, Vol. ii. pp. 68–139.
Ditto   ditto 1868, Vol. iii. pp. 1–72.
Ditto, *Poetical Works*, 1889, Vol. iii. 81–165.

KENTISH SIR BYNG. See *Cavalier Tunes.*

Lairesse, Gerard de, Parleying with.

First appeared in *Parleyings*, 1887, pp. 161–189.
Reprinted, *Poetical Works*, 1889, Vol. xvi. pp. 201–220.

Gerard de Lairesse, a Flemish painter, was born at Liége in 1640. At the age of fifteen he produced portraits and historical pictures. Notwithstanding that he was of deformed figure, he was very fond of dress, and was of dissipated life. The Dutch called him their "second Raphael"—Hemskirk being the first. For many years he painted at Amsterdam, and towards the end of his career was much troubled by his eyesight —at times being quite blind. Exceedingly fond of teaching, he was always willing to communicate his method of work to students.

His name is generally associated with a *Treatise on the Art of Painting*; but there appears to be some doubt as to whether he actually wrote it. He was very eccentric in his method of work : having prepared his canvas, he would take his violin, and, sitting down before it, play for some time, then, putting down the instrument, would rapidly sketch in the picture—resuming his fiddle when needing fresh inspiration for his work. He died in 1711.

La Saisiaz.

First appeared (1878), with *The Two Poets of Croisic*, in one Vol. See *ante*, p. 387, No. 21.
Reprinted, *Poetical Works*, 1889, Vol. xiv. pp. 153–204.

This poem was inspired by the sudden death of Miss Anne Egerton Smith (the Proprietress of the *Liverpool Mercury*), at La Saisiaz, September 14, 1877—where she had been enjoying the companionship of Mr. Browning and his sister : the poem being so called, Mrs. Orr tells us, from the name of the villa ("La Saisiaz") in which they had resided.

Life in a Love.

First appeared in *Men and Women*, 1855, Vol. i. p. 90.
Reprinted, *Poems*, 1863, Vol. i. p. 131.
Ditto   ditto   1868, Vol. iii. p. 203.
Ditto, *Poetical Works*, 1889, Vol. vi. p. 171.

LINES ADDRESSED TO LEVI LINCOLN THAXTER.

First appeared in *Poet Lore*, Vol. i. p. 398.

Not included in any edition of Robert Browning's collected works.

LOVE AMONG THE RUINS.

First appeared in *Men and Women*, 1855, Vol. i. pp. 1–6.

Reprinted, *Poems*, 1863, Vol. i. pp. 38–42.

Ditto   ditto   1868, Vol. iii. pp. 112–115.

Ditto, *Poetical Works*, 1889, Vol. vi. pp. 54–57.

LOVE IN A LIFE.

First appeared in *Men and Women*, 1855, Vol. i. pp. 173–174.

Reprinted, *Poems*, 1863, Vol. i. p. 130.

Ditto   ditto   1868, Vol. iii. p. 202.

Ditto, *Poetical Works*, 1889, Vol. vi. p. 170.

LURIA.

First appeared in *Bells and Pomegranates*, 1845, No. viii. pp. 1–20.

Reprinted, *Poems*, 1849, Vol. ii. pp. 139–210.

Ditto   ditto   1863, Vol. ii. pp. 357–427.

Ditto   ditto   1868, Vol. v. pp. 43–114.

Ditto, *Poetical Works*, 1889, Vol. vi. pp. 205–289.

This tragedy deals with one of many hereditary outbreaks of feud between Florence and Pisa. Mr. Browning appears to have in mind the struggle between the two cities, which took place almost at the beginning of the fifteenth century, although he does not hamper himself by too strict an observance of actual facts. At the beginning of the fifteenth century, the early death of Galeazzo Visconti had put an end for a time to the power of that ambitious and dangerous family in Florence. But Pisa, the old enemy of the Florentines, had fallen under the tyrannous supremacy of a member of the hated house of Visconti,—Gabriello Maria, a son of Gian Galeazzo. Florence had thus a new cause of grievance against Pisa; she detested not only the city, but its ruler. In 1404 she fitted out an expedition against Pisa, and two years later captured the city after a long and cruel siege. This is, apparently, the bare historical foundation of the play.

Luria—"the last attempt for the present at dramatic poetry "—
was dedicated to Walter Savage Landor—who replied in his
characteristic yet kindly fashion : "Accept my thanks for the
richest of Easter offerings made to any one for many years.   I
staid at home last evening on purpose to read Luria, and if I
lost any good music (as I certainly did) I was well compensated
in kind.   To day I intend to devote the rainy hours entirely to
The Soul's Tragedy. . . . Go on and pass us poor devils ! If
you do not go far ahead of me, I will crack my whip at you and
make you spring forward."

In another letter, Landor takes up *Luria* again, remarking : " I
have written to Browning, a great poet, a very great poet
indeed, as the world will have to agree with us in thinking.
The sudden close of *Luria* is very grand ; but preceding it, I
fear there is rather too much of argumentation and reflection.
It is continued too long after the Moor has taken poison.   I
may be wrong, but if it is so you will see him and tell him.
God grant that he may live to be much greater than he is, high
as he stands above most of the living."

The key-note of this play would seem to be struck in the fine
parallel between the people of Florence led to the field by Luria
and the unfinished Cathedral—the pride of the people, "joined
to a Moorish front " (Act i. lines 121–126).   On this matter, Mr.
Ernest Radford makes the following interesting observations
(*vide Browning Society's Papers*, Part ii. pp. 251–252) : "The
reader who does not know Florence, who has not indeed some
knowledge of its architecture, will hardly perceive how apt is
the parallel : he will not realise how fine an instance it affords
of Browning's searching intelligence in every matter of art.   At
Florence, in the small and hardly visited Museum called ' Opera
del Duomo,' one may see models and plans relating to the
Cathedral of all dates, from the time of Arnolfo (its original
designer) until now.   The building, it is well known, has
remained unfinished.   For more than 500 years the art-loving
Florentines impatiently expected its completion, and Florentine
artists throughout that time have had it for their highest hope
to be found worthy of the work.   And, curiously enough, there
is, amongst many designs in the Museum which bear witness

to this honourable ambition and diligent effort, one which accords with the poet's thought

> "——a fancy, how a *Moorish front*
> Might join to, and complete, the body."

It is a design which dwells in the memory. It is imaginative, and more poetical perhaps than any of those which a stricter taste prefers. It is not quite compatible, yet it is not wholly incongruous. The influence of the East was strong upon Arnolfo when, in the late 13th century, he made his plan. The architect has realised also an idea of Browning's (*see Old Pictures in Florence*), that the spire which formed part of its original design should be added to the Campanile of Giotto. The Campanile is detached, but its west side is flush with the façade, and practically, where alterations are in question, it must be considered as part of the Cathedral. The tower with the short spire added, small pinnacles or minarets on the shoulders of the façade, and the great dome with its sub-domes in the rear, have an appearance almost Eastern. Few, I have said, would realise that the work might so be treated, yet one architect at least has done so, and Browning has realised it too. For it is an interesting fact that Browning has not seen the design I have just described, which embodies so precisely the ideas expressed in his verse."

MAGICAL NATURE.

First appeared in *Pacchiarotto*, 1876, p. 90.
Reprinted, *Poetical Works*, 1889, Vol. xiv. p. 60.

MANDEVILLE, BERNARD DE, PARLEYING WITH.

First appeared in *Parleyings*, 1887, pp. 29–50.
Reprinted, *Poetical Works*, 1889, Vol. xvi. pp. 117–131.

Bernard de Mandeville was born at Dort, in Holland, in the year 1670. He became a student of medicine, and eventually took up his residence in London. In 1714 he issued *The Grumbling Hive, or Knaves Turned Honest*—a work which was subsequently (1723) enlarged into *The Fable of the Bees, or Private Vices, Public Benefits.* It is this latter work by which Mandeville is now best known. It was, however, condemned as of pernicious tendency by the grand jury of Middlesex. A second part of the *Fable* was afterwards published by Mandeville—who claimed an ironical meaning for his arguments in favour of vice. He wrote other treatises on questions of social polity, etc.; but his personal character, says *The Pall Mall Gazette* (Jan. 18, 1887), is reported to have been by no means worthy of respect. For instance—it is stated that he was paid by distillers to write in different periodicals in favour of the custom of indulging in spirituous liquors; while it is reported by Sir John Hawkins that he was "a great flatterer of certain vulgar Dutch merchants," from whom he received a pension. The first Earl of Macclesfield was his chief patron; and it was as his guest that Mandeville met Addison, whom he afterwards described as "a parson in a tye wig." He died in 1733.

MAN I AM AND MAN WOULD BE, LOVE.

First appeared in *Ferishtah's Fancies*, 1884, pp. 31–32.
Reprinted, *Poetical Works*, 1889, Vol. xvi. pp. 22-23.

MARCHING ALONG. See *Cavalier Tunes.*

MARTIN RELPH.

First appeared in *Dramatic Idyls* I. pp 1–26
Reprinted, *Poetical Works*, 1889, Vol. xv. pp. 3-16.

MARY WOLLSTONECRAFT AND FUSELI.

First appeared in *Jocoseria*, 1883, pp. 45–49.
Reprinted, *Poetical Works*, 1889, Vol. xv. pp. 195–196.

MASTER HUGUES OF SAXE-GOTHA.

First appeared in *Men and Women*, 1855, Vol. i. p. 194-204.
Reprinted, *Poems*, 1863, Vol. i. pp. 149-155.
Ditto   ditto 1868, Vol. iii. pp. 221-227.
Ditto, *Poetical Works*, 1889, Vol. vi. pp. 196-204.

MAY AND DEATH.

First appeared in *The Keepsake*, 1857.
Reprinted, *Dramatis Personæ*, 1864, pp. 143 146.
Ditto, *Poems*, 1868, Vol. vi. pp. 150-151.
Ditto, *Poetical Works*, 1889, Vol. vii. pp. 165-166.

When reprinted in *Dramatis Personæ*, some new readings were substituted—as for instance (line 15) "save a sole streak," in place of "except a streak."

The "plant" alluded to in stanza 4 of this poem is doubtless the *Polygonum Persicaria*, or Spotted Persicaria. It is a common weed, with purple stains on its rather large leaves—these spots varying in size and vividness of colour according to the nature of the soil where it grows. A legend attached to the plant attributes these stains to the blood of Christ having fallen on the leaves growing below the cross.

MEETING AT NIGHT.

First appeared in *Bells and Pomegranates*, 1845, No. vii. p. 20.
Reprinted, *Poems*, 1849, Vol. ii. p. 399.
Ditto   ditto   1863, Vol. i. p. 32.
Ditto   ditto   1868, Vol. iii. p. 106.
Ditto, *Poetical Works*, 1889, Vol. vi. p. 46.

MEMORABILIA.

First appeared in *Men and Women*, 1855, Vol. i. p. 259.
Reprinted, *Poems*, 1863, Vol. i. p. 145.
Ditto   ditto   1868, Vol. iii. p. 217.
Ditto, *Poetical Works*, 1889, Vol. vi. pp. 190-191.

Mr. W. G. Kingsland writes : " I remember on one occasion Browning narrating the incident that inspired these stanzas. He was in the shop of a then well-known London bookseller, when a stranger to himself entered, and commenced a conversation with the bookseller on Shelley—stating, *inter alia*, that he had both seen and spoken to him. While thus conversing, the stranger suddenly turned round, and burst into a laugh on observing how Browning was 'staring at him' with blanched face : 'and,' said the poet, 'I have not yet forgotten how strangely the sight of one who had spoken with Shelley affected me.'" (*Poet Lore*, Vol. ii., 1890, p. 131.)

MEN AND WOMEN.

First appeared (1855) in Two Vols. See *ante*, p. 373, No. 7.

In these volumes the title belongs to fifty poems then published, with an Epilogue addressed to Mrs. Browning, entitled *One Word More*. The poems are mainly monologues—utterances each of a single speaker : but in some the lyric note predominates more distinctly than in others ; and one (*In a Balcony*) is a drama. In the collected editions, the title *Men and Women* is given to a comparatively small number of poems, not, of course, including *In a Balcony* ; the rest are distributed under the two headings *Dramatic Lyrics* and *Dramatic Romances*.

MESMERISM.

First appeared in *Men and Women*, 1855, Vol. i. pp. 107–116.
Reprinted, *Poems*, 1863, Vol. i. pp. 174–180.
Ditto   ditto   1868, Vol. iv. pp. 165–171.
Ditto, *Poetical Works*, 1889, Vol. v. pp. 28–35.

MIHRAB SHAH.

First appeared in *Ferishtah's Fancies*, 1884, pp. 46–56.
Reprinted, *Poetical Works*, 1889, Vol. xvi. pp. 32–38.

MISCONCEPTIONS.

First appeared in *Men and Women*, 1855, Vol. ii. p. 227–228.
Reprinted, *Poems*, 1863, Vol. i. p. 119.
Ditto   ditto   1868, Vol. iii. p. 191.
Ditto, *Poetical Works*, 1889, Vol. vi. p. 154.

MR. SLUDGE, "THE MEDIUM."

First appeared in *Dramatis Personæ*, 1864, pp. 169–236.
Reprinted, *Poems*, 1868, Vol vi. pp. 162–218.
Ditto, *Poetical Works*, 1889, Vol. vii. pp. 182–245.

MUCKLE-MOUTH MEG.

> First appeared in *Asolando*, 1889, pp. 52-55.
> Reprinted, *Poetical Works*, 1894, Vol. xvii. pp. 44-46.

MULÉYKEH.

> First appeared in *Dramatic Idyls* II., 1880, pp. 43-59.
> Reprinted, *Poetical Works*, 1889, Vol. xv. pp. 108-116.

"MY HEART SANK WITH OUR CLARET-FLASK." See *Nationality in Drinks*.

MY LAST DUCHESS.

> First appeared in *Bells and Pomegranates* (under the heading *Italy and France*), 1842, No. iii.
> Reprinted, *Poems*, 1849, Vol. ii. pp. 258-260.
> Ditto   ditto   1863, Vol. i. pp. 159-161.
> Ditto   ditto   1868, Vol. iv. pp. 150-152.
> Ditto, *Poetical Works*, 1889, Vol. v. pp. 8-10.
>
> In this poem, Fra Pandolf and his picture, Claus of Innsbruck, and the bronze Neptune taming a sea horse, are all imaginary. The Duke's avowed design when he "said Fra Pandolf," was to call attention to the bright smile portrayed by the artist on his Last Duchess's countenance, and in reply to an anticipated look of inquiry, to impress on the Envoy and on the Count his master the necessity for dignity of demeanour and obedience on the part of the future Duchess.

MY STAR.

> First appeared in *Men and Women*, 1855, Vol. i. p. 122.
> Reprinted, *Poems*, 1863, Vol. i. p. 98.
> Ditto   ditto   1868, Vol. iii. p. 170.
> Ditto, *Poetical Works*, 1889, Vol. vi. p. 125.

NATIONALITY IN DRINKS.

> First appeared in *Hood's Magazine, June* 1844, Vol. i. p. 525.
> Reprinted, *Poems*, 1863, Vol i. pp. 11-12.
> Ditto   ditto   1868, Vol. iii. pp. 85-86.
> Ditto, *Poetical Works*, 1889, Vol. vi. pp. 16-18.

NATURAL MAGIC.

First appeared in *Pacchiarotto*, 1876, pp. 88–89.
Reprinted, *Poetical Works*, 1889, Vol. xiv. pp. 58–59.

NED BRATTS.

First appeared in *Dramatic Idyls* I. 1879, pp. 107–143.
Reprinted, *Poetical Works*, 1889, Vol. xv. pp. 60–80.

The original of *Ned Bratts* is doubtless to be found in the story
of "old Tod," narrated in John Bunyan's *Life and Death of
Mr. Badman* [1680]. Indeed, Dr. Furnivall says this story,
which Browning had read in his boyhood, "was distinctly in
the poet's mind" when he wrote the poem at the Splugen, far
from books. Bunyan's narrative takes the form of a dialogue
between Mr. Wiseman and Mr. Attentive, and the former relates
the "story concerning one old *Tod*, that was hanged about
Twenty years or more, at *Hartford*." Here is the story : "At
a Summer Assizes holden at *Hartford*, while the Judge was sitting upon the Bench, comes this old Tod into the Court, cloathed
in a green Suit, with his Leathern Girdle in his hand, his bosom
open, and all in a dung sweat, as if he had run for his Life ; and
being come in, he spake aloud as follows : *My Lord*, said he,
*Here is the veryest Rogue that breaths upon the face of the
earth. I have been a Thief from a Child: When I was but a
little one, I gave my self to rob Orchards, and to do other such
like wicked things, and I have continued a Thief ever since.
My Lord, there has not been a Robbery committed thus many
years, within so many miles of this place, but I have either been
at it or privy to it.*
"The Judge thought the fellow was mad, but after some confer-
ence with some of the Justices, they agreed to Indict him ; and
so they did, of several felonious Actions ; to all of which he
heartily confessed Guilty, and so was hanged with his Wife at
the same time. . . . As for the truth of this Story, the Relator
told me that he was at the same time himself in the Court, and
stood within less than two yards of old *Tod*, when he heard
him aloud to utter the words,"

NEVER THE TIME AND THE PLACE.

First appeared in *Jocoseria*, 1883, pp. 133–136.
Reprinted, *Poetical Works*, 1889, Vol. xv. pp. 256–257.

"NOT WITH MY SOUL, LOVE."

First appeared in *Ferishtah's Fancies*, 1884, pp. 91–92.
Reprinted, *Poetical Works*, 1889, Vol. xvi. pp. 61–62.

NOW.

First appeared in *Asolando*, 1889, p. 10.
Reprinted, *Poetical Works*, 1894, Vol. xvii. p. 8.

NUMPHOLEPTOS.

First appeared in *Pacchiarotto*, 1876, pp. 95–105.
Reprinted, *Poetical Works*, 1889, Vol. xiv. pp. 63–69.

Concerning this poem, Mr. Browning (in a letter addressed to
Dr. Furnivall) writes as follows : " Is not the key to the meaning of the poem in its title—νυμφόληπτος [caught or entranced by
a Nymph], not γυναικεραστής [a woman-lover]?   An allegory,
that is, of an impossible ideal object of love, accepted conven-
tionally as such by a man who, all the while, cannot quite blind
himself to the demonstrable fact that the possessor of knowledge
and purity obtained without the natural consequences of obtain-
ing them by achievement—not inheritance—such a being is
imaginary, not real, a nymph and no woman : and only such an
one would be ignorant of and surprised at the results of a
lover's endeavour to emulate the qualities which the beloved is
entitled to consider as pre-existent to earthly experience, and
independent of its inevitable results.
" I had no particular woman in my mind ; certainly never
intended to personify wisdom, philosophy, or any other abstrac-
tion; and the orb, raying colour out of whiteness, was altogether
a fancy of my own.   The ' seven spirits ' are in the Apocalypse,
also in Coleridge and Byron : a common image."

"O THE OLD WALL HERE."

First appeared in *Pacchiarotto*, 1876, pp. 1–2.
Reprinted, *Poetical Works*, 1889, Vol. xiv. pp. 3–4.

This poem forms the Prologue to *Pacchiarotto and how he Worked in Distemper: with other Poems*. It is printed in the second series of *Selections* under the title of *A Wall*.

OH LOVE, LOVE!

First appeared in Mahaffy's *Euripides*,[1] 1879.
Reprinted, *Browning Society's Papers*, Part i. p. 69.
This was a rendering into English of two stanzas of Euripides' *Hippolytus*, and has not been reprinted in any edition of Mr. Browning's Poems. The lines are as follows:—

I.

Oh Love, Love, thou that from the eyes diffusest
Yearning, and on the soul sweet grace inducest—
Souls against whom thy hostile march is made—
Never to me be manifest in ire,
Nor, out of time and tune, my peace invade!
Since neither from the fire—
No, nor the stars—is launched a bolt more mighty
Than that of Aphrodité
Hurled from the hands of Love, the boy with Zeus for sire.

II.

Idly, how idly, by the Alpheian river
And in the Pythian shrines of Phœbus, quiver
Blood-offerings from the bull, which Hellas heaps:
While Love we worship not—the Lord of men!
Worship not him, the very key who keeps
Of Aphrodité, when
She closes up her dearest chamber-portals:
—— Love, when he comes to mortals,
Wide-wasting, through those deeps of woes beyond the deep!

OH, LOVE—NO, LOVE! ALL THE NOISE BELOW, LOVE."

First appeared in *Ferishtah's Fancies*, 1884, pp. 140–143.
Reprinted, *Poetical Works*, 1889, Vol. xvi. pp. 90–92.
This poem is the Epilogue to *Ferishtah's Fancies*.

---

[1] Macmillan's Classical Writers: Euripides, by Prof. Mahaffy. Macmillan and Co.

OLD PICTURES IN FLORENCE.

First appeared in *Men and Women*, 1855, Vol. ii. pp. 30–48.
Reprinted, *Poems*, 1863, Vol. i. pp. 58–70.
Ditto   ditto   1868, Vol. iii. pp. 131–142.
Ditto, *Poetical Works*, 1889, Vol. vi. pp. 77–91.

In the Second Series of *Selections* (1880), Mr. Browning appended a note to this poem replying to Professor Colvin's "condemnation" of the line

" You're wroth—can you slay your snake like Apollo?"

A fierce controversy has for many a day raged about Apollo's attitude in this statue. Has he just shot his arrow (the view adopted by Browning, and supported in the "Note")? Is he about to shoot, or is he grasping the Ægis in battle? Since the date of the Poet's Note, the controversy has been briskly continued—the witness both for and against the ægis theory having been the Stroganoff statuette, first noticed by Stephani in 1860, as proving that Apollo held the ægis. In 1882, Furtwängler declared that an examination of the Stroganoff Apollo convinced him that the god held whatever he may have held far too daintily for it to be the ægis. This opinion for a time seemed to have petrified the gorgon, but that it was ineffectual appears by the later advocacy of Kieseritzky, who says that *his* examination of the statuette convinced *him* that the ægis theory is correct. The whole history of the controversy will be found summarised in Mrs. Mitchell's *History of Ancient Sculpture* (London, 1883, pp. 621–626). It is pointed out by " K," in " Browning Notes and Queries " (*Browning Society's Papers*, part vii., p. 10*) that " Mrs. Mitchell is evidently, at heart, with Furtwängler (and Browning) and not with Colvin and Kieseritzky, but she ventures only to call the ægis theory ' unpleasant.' "

" ON THE FIRST OF THE FEAST OF FEASTS."

First appeared in *Dramatis Personæ*, 1864, pp. 245–246
Reprinted, *Poems*, 1868, Vol. vi. pp. 222–223.
Ditto, *Poetical Works*, 1889, Vol. vii. pp. 250–251.

This poem is the " FIRST SPEAKER, *as David*," in the Epilogue to *Dramatis Personæ*.

"ONCE I SAW A CHEMIST TAKE A PINCH OF POWDER."

First appeared in *Ferishtah's Fancies*, 1884, pp. 76–77.
Reprinted, *Poetical Works*, 1889, Vol. xvi. pp. 51–52.

ONE WAY OF LOVE.

First appeared in *Men and Women*, 1855, Vol. ii. p. 30.
Reprinted, *Poems*, 1863, Vol. i. pp. 122–123.
Ditto   ditto   1868, Vol. iii. pp. 194–195.
Ditto, *Poetical Works*, 1889, Vol. vi. pp. 159–160.

ONE WORD MORE. TO E. B. B.

First appeared in *Men and Women*, 1855, Vol. ii. p. 229.
Reprinted, *Poems*, 1863, Vol. i. pp. 425–432.
Ditto   ditto   1868, Vol. v. pp. 313–321.
Ditto, *Poetical Works*, 1889, Vol. iv. pp. 296–305.

This poem forms the Epilogue to *Men and Women*, and is, in effect, the dedication of the fifty poems originally appearing under this title, to Mrs. Browning.

Concerning the Dante allusions in this poem, Mr. W. M. Rossetti writes in the *Academy* (1891) : " I understand the allusions, but Browning is far from accurate in them.

1. Towards the end of the *Vita Nuova*, Dante says that, on the first anniversary of the death of Beatrice, he began drawing an angel, but was interrupted by certain people of distinction, who entered on a visit. Browning is, therefore, wrong in intimating that the angel was painted to please Beatrice.

2. Then Browning says that the pen with which Dante drew the angel was, perhaps, corroded by the hot ink in which it had previously been dipped for the purpose of denouncing a certain wretch,—*i.e.*, one of the persons named in his *Inferno*. This about the ink, as such, is Browning's own figure of speech, not got out of Dante.

3. Then Browning speaks of Dante's having his 'left hand i' the hair o' the wicked,' etc. This refers to *Inferno*, Canto 32, where Dante meets (among the traitors to their country) a

certain Bocca degli Abati, a notorious Florentine traitor, dead some years back, and Dante clutches and tears at Bocca's hair to compel him to name himself, which Bocca would much rather not do.

4. Next Browning speak of this Bocca as being a 'live man.' Here Browning confounds two separate incidents. Bocca is not only damned, but also dead ; but, further on—Canto 33—Dante meets another man, a traitor against his familiar friend. This traitor is Frate Alberigo, one of the Manfredi family, of Faenza. This Frate Alberigo was, though damned, not, in fact, dead ; he was still alive, and Dante makes it out that traitors of this sort are liable to have their souls sent to hell before the death of their bodies. A certain Branca d'Oria, Genoese, is in like case,—damned, but not dead.

5. Browning proceeds to speak of the wretch going 'festering through Florence.' This is a relapse into his mistake,—the confounding of the dead Florentine Bocca degli Abati with the living (though damned) Faentine and Genoese traitors, Frate Alberigo and Branca d'Oria, who had nothing to do with Florence."

PACCHIAROTTO, AND HOW HE WORKED IN DISTEMPER.

First appeared (1876) in one Vol. See *ante*, p. 384, No. 19.
Reprinted, *Poetical Works*, 1889, Vol. xiv. pp. 1–241.

PAMBO.

First appeared in *Jocoseria*, 1883, pp. 137–143.
Reprinted, *Poetical Works*, 1889, Vol. xv. pp. 258–260.

PAN AND LUNA.

First appeared in *Dramatic Idyls II.* 1880, pp. 137–147.
Reprinted, *Poetical Works*, 1889, Vol. xv. pp. 159–163.

PARACELSUS.

First appeared (1835) in one Vol. See *ante*, p. 363, No. 2.
Reprinted, *Poems*, 1849, Vol. i. pp. 1–162.
Ditto   ditto   1863, Vol. iii. pp. 1–162.
Ditto   ditto   1868, Vol. i. pp. 43–206.
Ditto   *Poetical Works*, 1889, Vol. ii. pp. 1–186.

For the edition of 1863, this poem underwent considerable revision—several lines being omitted, fresh ones inserted, and many verbal changes made in the text. For instance—in the edition of 1835, p. 13 :

> As you had your own soul : accordingly
> I could go further back, and trace each bough
> Of this wide branching tree even to its birth ;
> Each full-grown passion to its outspring faint ;
> But I shall only dwell upon the intents—

appears in the edition of 1863 (p. 10) as one line only.

> " As you had your own soul and those intents."

Mr. Browning always held he had been true to the real character of Paracelsus in his poem ; he was likewise well versed in the works of this pioneer of modern chemists. In this connection it may be well to give here the following summary from the *Encyclopædia Britannica* (9th ed., 1875, i., p. 465—467) : " Paracelsus is the prophet of a revolution in general science. ' Madman, charlatan, impostor,' no name is too bad for him with the historians, and yet they are forced to confess that this impudent adventurer brought about a necessary revolution. Thomas Thompson is very severe . . . . He would have wished, forsooth, the revolutionist of Basle to have delivered before his young and enthusiastic audience '.the sober lectures of a professor of a university.' Dryasdusts are fond of falling into such anachronisms : a far truer estimate of Paracelsus has been given us by Mr. Browning in the drama which bears his name. There are souls of fire always enveloped in clouds, from which ever and anon the lightnings of genius flash forth, who bear humanity towards a goal, foreseen rather than seen by themselves, by a rough and rugged road with endless turns and windings. Such a nature was Paracelsus. He was the greatest traveller in that age of scientific travellers ; he practised medicine as the doctor of the poor, and inaugurated lectures in the vulgar tongue. . . . Nature, as he views it, is not a clear and intelligible system of which the form declares the essence ; no, it is mysterious. There is a spirit at work beneath the outside shell. What is written on this shell, no one can read but the initiated who have learned to separate the real and the apparent. By making the viscera the seat of diseases, Paracelsus claims to be the founder of the organicists ; by his chemistry of the blood—mercury which evaporates, sulphur which burns, salt which is constant—he is answerable for the blunderings of Maître Purgon ; by his *archeus*, the grand motor and regulator of the astrology of the body, he is the ancestor in a direct line of animism, and collaterally of modern Hippocratism or vitalism of the Montpelier school. In short, it is hard to name anything that cannot be found in the works of this mad genius, who, in spite of the jars and jolts of his wild career, still manages to keep the road without upsetting either at Paris or Montpelier. What, we may ask, would modern therapeutics be without the opium and mercury of Paracelsus— without the laudanum of his disciple Quercetan, physician to Henry IV. ? When this charlatan had substituted for astrological influence a simple parallelism, it was easy for Van Helmont to rid modern science of this simple parallelism. Besides all this, Paracelsus was a real doctor. . . . a patient was dining with him ninety-nine days after he had been pronounced *in extremis* . . . those strange bodies which escaped from the retorts of the masters of the sacred art were called by them 'souls' ; their successors, on a closer acquaintance, called them 'spirits.' Basil Vatentin and Paracelsus, recognising their importance in the transmutation of bodies, gave to them the name of mercury. Van Helmont studied them more minutely, and invented the name 'gas.' Hence modern chemistry was born."

In a note to *Paracelsus*, Browning says that " Bombast his proper name, probably acquired, from the characteristic phraseology of his lectures, that unlucky signification which it has ever since retained." Professor W. J. Rolfe, however, points out that Bombast has really no connexion whatever with Paracelsus, as one may see by reference to any standard English dictionary. The word was originally applied to the soft down of the cotton-plant, or " cotton-wool " as it is popularly called. Gerard, in his *Herbal* (1597) says that this is " called in English and French, Cotton, Bombaste, and Bombace," and Sandys, in his *Travels* (1615), referring to the cotton-plant, says : " The head, ripening, breaks, and is delivered of a white, soft Bombast." Cotton and certain stuffs made of cotton being often used as padding for clothes, bombast came to be applied to padding and stuffing in both a literal and a figurative sense, and hence to inflated and turgid language. The verb (to swell out, render turgid) is found as early as 1573, in Reginald Scot's *Hop Garden.* "Not bumbasting the same with the figures and flowers of rhetoric." Florio, in his *Montaigne* (1603) has the expression, "Bumbast his labours with high swelling and heaven—disembowelling words." Every student of Shakespeare is familar with the use of the word in Robert Greene's famous fling at the dramatist (1594): "An upstart Crow, beautified with our feathers, that, with his Tyger's heart wrapt in a Player's hide, supposes he is as well able to bumbast out a blank verse as the best of you." The noun in the figurative sense is used by Nashe (dedication to Greene's *Menaphon*) in (1589): "To outbrave better pens with the swelling bumbast of a bragging blanke verse." Shake-speare has the word, literally, in *I. Henry IV.* (ii. 4, 359) where Hal calls Falstaff "my sweet creature of bombast" ("a stuffed man," as Beatrice puts it); figuratively in *Othello* (i. 1, 13),

> with a bombast circumstance,
> Horribly stuff'd with epithets of war ;

and with a punning double sense in *Love's Labour's Lost,* (v. 2, 791) :

> At courtship, pleasant jest, and courtesy,
> As bombast and as lining to the time.

[*Poet Lore*, Vol. iii. p. 104.]

PARLEYINGS WITH CERTAIN PEOPLE OF IMPORTANCE IN THEIR DAY.

To wit : BERNARD DE MANDEVILLE,
   DANIEL BARTOLI,
   CHRISTOPHER SMART,
   GEORGE BUBB DODINGTON,
   FRANCIS FURINI,
   GERARD DE LAIRESSE,
and CHARLES AVISON.

Introduced by

A DIALOGUE BETWEEN APOLLO AND THE FATES.

Concluded by

ANOTHER BETWEEN JOHN FUST AND HIS FRIENDS.

First appeared (1887) in one Vol. See *ante*, p. 390, No. 26.

Reprinted, *Poetical Works*, 1889, Vol. xvi. pp. 1-275.

PARTING AT MORNING.

First appeared in *Bells and Pomegranates* (under the title "Morning"), 1845, No. vii. p. 20.

Reprinted, *Poems*, 1849, Vol. ii. p. 399.

Ditto   ditto   1863, Vol. i. p. 33.

Ditto   ditto   1868, Vol. iii. p. 107.

Ditto, *Poetical Works*, 1889, Vol. vi. p. 46.

PAULINE ; A FRAGMENT OF A CONFESSION.

First appeared (1833) in one Vol. See *ante*, p. 361, No. 1.

Reprinted, *Poems*, 1868, Vol. i. pp. 1-42.

Ditto   1886, a facsimile of the original edition of 1833. Edited by Thos. J. Wise.

Ditto, *Poetical Works*, 1889, Vol. i. pp. 1-45.

Pauline was not accorded a place among Mr. Browning's collected works till it appeared in the edition of 1868—when it was reprinted for the first time : the poet evidently deploring the necessity (owing to the probable publication of surreptitious editions) which led to the re-issue.

On a fly-leaf of an original edition of *Pauline*, Browning (according to Mr. R. N. Shepherd) wrote (under date December 14, 1838) : " *Pauline* written in pursuance of a foolish plan I forget, or have no wish to remember ; involving the assumption of several distinct characters : the world was never to guess that such an opera, such a comedy, such a speech proceeded from the same notable person. Mr. V. A. (see page second) was Poet of the party, and predestined to cut no inconsiderable figure. 'Only this crab' (I find set down in my copy) remains of the shapely Tree of Life in my Fool's Paradise."

The following " pretty conceit " (from the *Monthly Repository*) regarding the genesis of *Pauline*, had its "foundation in fact," Mr. Browning having lent his copy of *Rosalind and Helen* to Miss Flower, and which she lost in a wood: "Last autumn L—— dropped a poem of Shelley's down there in the wood ; amongst the thick, damp, rotting leaves, and this spring someone found a delicate exotic-looking plant, growing wild on the very spot, with *Pauline* hanging from its slender stalk. Unripe fruit it may be, but of pleasant flavour and promise, and a mellower produce, it may be hoped, will follow."

The whole of the pretty "huitain" of Marot's, the first two lines of which form the motto to *Pauline*, reads thus :—

> "Plus ne suis ce que j'ay esté,
> Et ne le saurois jamais estre :
> Mon beau printemps et mon esté
> Ont faict le saut par la fenestre.
> Amour, tu as esté mon maistre,
> Je t'ay servy sur tous les dieux,
> O si je povois deux fois naistre,
> Comme je te servirois mieulx ! "

PHEIDIPPIDES.

First appeared in *Dramatic Idyls*, 1, pp. 27–44.

Reprinted, *Poetical Works*, 1889, Vol. xv. pp. 17–25.

This poem, Mrs. Orr tells us (*Handbook to the Works of Robert Browning*, p. 13), is written in a measure of Mr. Browning's own—being composed of dactyles and spondees, each line ending with a half-foot or pause. It is certainly well adapted to the character of the poem.

PICTOR IGNOTUS. FLORENCE, 15—

First appeared in *Bells and Pomegranates*, 1845, No. vii. p. 4.

Reprinted, *Poems*, 1849, Vol. ii. pp. 321–323.

Ditto   ditto   1863, Vol. i. pp. 343–345.

Ditto   ditto   1868, Vol. v. pp. 231–234.

Ditto, *Poetical Works*, 1889, Vol. iv. pp. 202–204.

In this poem as now printed will be found various deviations from its first form. In line 23, the first reading was

"Men, women, children, hath it spilt, my cup?"

This now reads—

> " O human faces, hath it spilt, my cup?"

And in lines 45 to 48, the first version was—

> " Mixed with my loving ones there trooped—for what?
> Who summoned those cold faces which begun
> To press on me and judge me? As asquat
> And shrinking from the soldiery a nun,—

This stands now—

> " Mixed with my loving trusting ones, there trooped
> . . . Who summoned those cold faces that begun
> To press on me and judge me? Though I stooped
> Shrinking, as from the soldiery a nun,"

PIETRO OF ABANO.

First appeared in *Dramatic Idyls II.* 1880, pp. 61-111.
Reprinted, *Poetical Works*, 1889, Vol. xv. pp. 117-145.

Peter of Ábano—*Petrus de Ápono* or *Petrus de Padua*—was an Italian physician and alchemist, born at Abano near Padua in 1246. It is related of him that he studied Greek at Constantinople, mathematics at Padua, and to have been made Doctor of Medicine and Philosophy at Paris. He then returned to Padua, where he was professor of medicine, and followed the Arabian physicians, especially Averroes. His reputation was great, and his fees enormous. Jealous of his wealth and renown, his enemies denounced him to the Inquisition as a magician ; and probably had he not in the meantime died a natural death (about 1320), he would have been burnt. However, his corpse was ordered to be burnt : but as that had been purloined by a friend, his portrait was publicly burnt by the executioner. In 1560 a Latin epitaph to his memory was put up in the church of St. Augustin. His best known work is his *Conciliator differentiarum quæ inter philosophos et medicos versantur* (Mantua, 1472, and Venice, 1476).

In Bishop Thirlwall's *Letters to a Friend* (1881, Vol. ii. pp. 77-79), there is a story somewhat resembling Peter's : "A young student calls on Don Manuel at Seville, and asks for a spell to get him along in life. Don Manuel calls to his housekeeper, ' Jacinta, roast the partridges. Don Diego will stay to dinner,'

The student makes a grand career : is Dean, Bishop, and then Pope soon after he is forty.   When Don Manuel calls on him in Rome, he threatens the magician, who has made him, with the prisons of the Holy Office : and then hears Don Manuel call out, ' Jacinta, you need *not* put down the partridges.   Don Diego will not stay to dinner.'   And, lo !   Diego found himself at Don Manuel's door,—with his way yet to make in the world."

Pippa Passes.

First appeared in *Bells and Pomegranates,* 1841, No. i. pp. 1–16.

Reprinted, *Poems*, 1849, Vol. i. pp. 163–230.

Ditto   ditto   1863, Vol. ii. pp. 1–67.

Ditto   ditto   1868, Vol. ii. pp. 219–287.

Ditto   ditto   1889, Vol. iii. pp. 1–79.

As noted above, *Pippa Passes* first appeared in 1841, in No. I. of *Bells and Pomegranates*, and was not reprinted until eight years later, when it was included in the two-volume edition of the *Poems* of 1849.   In the meantime it had undergone considerable revision, and had been greatly enlarged.   As the original series of *Bells and Pomegranates* is rendered practically inaccessible to the general reader by reason of its scarcity, it may be of more than ordinary interest to specify some of the more important variations.   These will also serve to illustrate the amount of revision to which several of Mr. Browning's works were submitted.

In the second section of the Prologue—after the line now reading " Then shame fall on Asolo, mischief on me "—the original version consists of the following twenty-seven lines :—

> But in turn, Day, treat me not
> As happy tribes—so happy tribes ! who live
> At hand—the common, other creatures' lot—
> Ready to take when thou wilt give,
> Prepared to pass what thou refusest ;
> Day, 'tis but Pippa thou ill-usest
> If thou prove sullen, me, whose old year's sorrow
> Who except thee can chase before to-morrow,
> Seest thou, my day ?   Pippa's—who mean to borrow
> Only of thee strength against new year's sorrow

Song from "Pippa passes".
The year's at the Spring,
The Day's at the morn;
Morning's at seven:
The hill-side's dew-pearled:
The bee's on the wing,
The snail's on the thorn:
God's in his Heaven —
All's right with the world.

Robert Browning.

Paris, October 17.ʳ '58.

FAC—SIMILE OF A SONG FROM PIPPA PASSES, IN
ROBERT BROWNING'S HAND WRITING.

> For let thy morning scowl on that superb
> Great haughty Ottima—can scowl disturb
> Her Sebald's homage? And if noon shed gloom
> O'er Jules and Phene—what care bride and groom
> Save for their dear selves? Then, obscure thy eve
> With mist—will Luigi and Madonna grieve
> —The mother and the child—unmatched, forsooth,
> She in her age as Luigi in his youth,
> For true content? And once again, outbreak
> In storm at night on Monsignor they make
> Such stir to-day about, who foregoes Rome
> To visit Asolo, his brother's home,
> And say there masses proper to release
> The soul from pain—what storm dares hurt that peace?
> But Pippa—just one such mischance would spoil,
> Bethink thee, utterly next twelvemonth's toil
> At wearisome silk-winding, coil on coil !

If the reader will compare this with the present version, he will find that it is not only altered almost past recognition, but that it now consists of fifty-one lines in place of the seven-and-twenty quoted above. In the next section—"Worship whom else ? for am I not this Day "—seven lines have been added to the original three ; while the following section, commencing in the original—

> Up the hill-side, thro' the morning,
> Love me as I love !
> I am Ottima, take warning !—

now reads :—

> See ! Up the Hill-side yonder, through the morning.
> Some one shall love me, as the world calls love :
> I am no less than Ottima, take warning !

It is interesting to note that the first of Pippa's songs—"All service ranks the same with God "—has only one or two merely verbal alterations ; but the section following has been extensively altered ; while seven lines have been deleted therefrom. The original stands thus :—

> And more of it, and more of it—oh, yes !
> So that my passing, and each happiness
> I pass, will be alike important—prove
> That true ! Oh yes—the brother,

The bride, the lover, and the mother,—
Only to pass whom will remove—
Whom a mere look at half will cure
The Past, and help me to endure
The Coming . . . I am just as great, no doubt,
As they!
A pretty thing to care about
So mightily—this single holiday!
Why repine?
With thee to lead me, Day of mine,
Down the grass path gray with dew,
'Neath the pine-wood, blind with boughs,
Where the swallow never flew
As yet, nor cicale dared carouse :
No, dared carouse!

For the purpose of more immediate reference it may be well to append the version as it now reads :—

And more of it, and more of it!—oh yes—
I will pass each, and see their happiness,
And envy none—being just as great, no doubt,
Useful to men, and dear to God, as they!
A pretty thing to care about
So mightily, this single holiday!
But let the sun shine! Wherefore repine?
—With thee to lead me, O Day of mine,
Down the grass-path grey with dew,
Under the pine-wood, blind with boughs,
Where the swallow never flew
Nor yet cicala dared carouse—
No, dared carouse!

In scene 2 (noon) the additions and alterations are equally extensive. As one specimen—and perhaps the most interesting —out of many, we will subjoin the original version of the Allegory commencing "I am a painter who cannot paint." It is printed in the ordinary Roman type, and not (as now) in italics : and the reader will not fail to note, in comparing it with the present version, how immeasurably for the better Browning's alterations were :—

The Bard said, do one thing I can—
Love a man and hate a man

Supremely : thus my love began.
Thro' the Valley of Love I went,
In its lovingest spot to abide ;
And just on the verge where I pitched my tent
Dwelt Hate beside—
(And the bridegroom asked what the bard's smile meant
Of his bride.)
Next Hate I traversed, the Grove,
In its hatefullest nook to dwell—
And lo, where I flung myself prone, couched Love
Next cell.
(For not I, said the bard, but those black bride's eyes above
Should tell !)
(Then Lutwyche said you probably would ask,
" You have black eyes, love,—you are sure enough
My beautiful bride—do you, as he sings, tell
What needs some exposition—what is this ? "
. . . And I am to go on, without a word,)
Once when I loved I would enlace
Breast, eyelids, hands, feet, form and face
Of her I loved in one embrace—
And, when I hated, I would plunge
My sword, and wipe with the first lunge
My foe's whole life out like a spunge :
—But if I would love and hate more
Than ever man hated or loved before—
Would seek in the Valley of Love
The spot, or in Hatred's grove
The spot where my soul may reach
The essence, nought less, of each . . .
(Here he said, if you interrupted me
With, " There must be some error,—who induced you
To speak this jargon ? "—I was to reply
Simply—" Await till . . . until . . " I must say
Last rhyme again—)
. . The essence, nought less, of each—
The Hate of all Hates, or the Love
Of all Loves in its glen or its grove,
—I find them the very warders
Each of the other's borders.
So most I love when Love's disguised
In Hate's garb—'tis when Hate's surprised
In Love's weed that I hate most ; ask

How Love can smile thro' Hate's barred iron casque,
Hate grin thro' Love's rose-braided mask,
   Of thy bride, Giulio !
                (Then you, " Oh, not mine—
Preserve the real name of the foolish song ! "
But I must answer, "Giulio—Jules—'tis Jules !)
      Thus, I, Jules, hating thee
      Sought long and painfully. . .
                              [JULES *interposes.*

There are likewise many variations in scene 3, together with
many additions.   In Pippa's song, however (" A King lived long
ago "), the following lines (immediately after " At his wondrous
forest rites ") are omitted from the present version :—

      But which the God's self granted him
      For setting free each felon limb
      Because of earthly murder done
      Faded till other hope was none.

Concerning the word " twats " in line 95 of the epilogue of this
poem—

      Then, owl and bats, cowls and twats,—

Mr. W. J. Rolfe says : " ' Twats ' is in no dictionary.   We now
have it from the poet (through Dr. Furnivall) that he got the
word from the Royalist rhymes entitled ' Vanity of Vanities,' on
Sir Harry Vane's picture.   Vane is charged with being a
Jesuit :—

      'Tis said they will give him a cardinal's hat :
      They sooner will give him an old nun's twat.

' The word struck me,' says Browning, ' as a distinctive part
of a nun's attire that might fitly pair off with the cowl appro-
priated to a monk."   It has been pointed out, however, that the
poet is altogether wrong in his surmise—the word being a
mere vulgarism.

Writing in 1870, Sir John Kaye says : " What a story it [*Pippa
Passes*] is—or rather what a sheaf of stories !   It quite settled
the question as to whether Robert Browning was a great
dramatic poet— not a playwright, but a dramatic poet.   *Strafford*
had been written and acted before this, but the question was
still an open one, when that magnificent scene in the garden-
house between Sebald and Ottima—the very concentrated

essence of Tragedy, than which there is nothing more terrible in any Greek drama extant—settled the question for ever. But such a scene would be no more fit for theatrical representation in these days than the *Agamemnon.*"

PISGAH-SIGHTS, 1, 2.

First appeared in *Pacchiarotto*, 1876, pp. 75–82.
Reprinted, *Poetical Works*, 1889, Vol. xiv. pp. 49–53.
In the collected edition of 1889, the Proem to *La Saisiaz* (" Good to forgive ") was printed as " Pisgah-Sights, 3."

PLOT-CULTURE.

First appeared in *Ferishtah's Fancies*, 1884, pp. 87–91.
Reprinted, *Poetical Works*, 1889, Vol. xvi. pp. 58–61.

POETICS.

First appeared in *Asolando*, 1889, p. 12.
Reprinted, *Poetical Works*, 1894, Vol. xvii. p. 10.

POMPILIA. See *The Ring and the Book.*

PONTE DELL' ANGELO, VENICE.

First appeared in *Asolando*, 1889, pp. 61–75.
Reprinted, *Poetical Works*, 1894, Vol. xvii. pp. 50–61.

POPULARITY.

First appeared in *Men and Women*, 1855, Vol. ii. p. 193–197.
Reprinted, *Poems*, 1863, Vol. i. pp. 146-148.
Ditto   ditto   1868, Vol. iii. pp. 218–220.
Ditto, *Poetical Works*, 1889, Vol. vi. pp. 192–195.

PORPHYRIA'S LOVER.

First appeared in *The Monthly Repository*, Vol. x. pp. 43-46.
Reprinted in *Bells and Pomegranates*, No. iii. p. 13.
Ditto   *Poems*, 1849, pp. 302-303.
Ditto   ditto   1863, Vol. i. pp. 310-312.
Ditto   ditto   1868, Vol. iv. pp. 299-300.
Ditto, *Poetical Works*, 1889, Vol. v. pp. 191-193.

This poem was originally called *Porphyria;* in *Bells and Pomegranates* it was called *Madhouse Cells,* 2 ; in the edition of 1849, 2. *Madhouse Cells,* with *Porphyria's Lover* as a subtitle ; but in the 1863 and subsequent editions it is given as above.

Prince   Hohenstiel-Schwangau :   Saviour   of Society.

First appeared (1871) in one Vol.   See *ante,* p. 382, No. 14.
Reprinted, *Poetical Works,* 1889, Vol. xi. p. 123–210.

Louis Napoleon, who is depicted under the pseudonym *Hohenstiel Schwangau,* was, says Mr. C. H. Herford, no unpromising subject for Mr. Browning.   " He had ruled France for twenty years with as much iron as he dared and as much show of liberalism as he had face for—not escaping however to be regarded by a majority of thinking persons as a renegade to the cause of which he had been the most influencial advocate. The poem is a subtle study of the insidious intellectual influences which lie in wait for the Radical on his accession to power, and allure him in the name of principle, of human sympathy, nay of democratic fellow-feeling itself, to tread the primrose path of official conservatism, with a glib *Non possumus* ready on his lips for all his ardent and enterprising comrades of old."
It may be interesting to note that " the grim guardian of this Square," referred to on page 14 of this poem, was an equestrian statue of George I., erected in Leicester Square, and which had, during the sixties, from its dilapidated condition, &c., been the occasion of much merriment : so much so, that certain wags set themselves to the task of calling public attention to the Square's "guardian" by a practical joke: and one morning the "horse" was found to have been " pieballed" during the night, while the effigy of the king clasped a broom-handle.   The statue was removed soon after this.

Pray, Reader, have you eaten Ortolans ?

First appeared in *Ferishtah's Fancies,* 1884, pp. 1-4.
Reprinted, *Poetical Works,* 1889, Vol. xvi. pp. 3–5.

This poem is the prologue to *Ferishtah's Fancies.* It is interesting to note that in *Pippa Passes* there is also a reference to "ortolans"—in the scene (iii.) where the "poor girls" are gossiping "on the steps"; one of whom says :—

> " Do you pretend you ever tasted lampreys
> And ortolans? Giovita, of the palace,
> Engaged (but there's no trusting him) to slice me
> Polenta with a knife that had cut up
> An ortolan."

PROLOGUES.

Amphibian (" The Fancy I had to-day ")—see *Fifine at the Fair*
Apollo and the Fates—see *Parleyings.*
" Good to forgive"—see *La Saisiaz.*
" O the old wall here "—see *Pacchiarotto.*
" Pray, Reader, have you ever eaten ortolans ? "—see *Ferishtah's Fancies.*
" Such a starved bank of moss "—see *The Two Poets of Croisic.*
" The Poet's age is sad : for why ? "—see *Asolando.*
" You are sick, that's sure—they say : "—see *Dramatic Idyls II.*
" Wanting is—what ? "—see *Jocoseria.*

PROSPICE.

First appeared in the *Atlantic Monthly*, Vol. xiii. p. 694.
Also printed in London, in Pamphlet form, privately, 1864.
Reprinted in *Dramatis Personæ*, 1864, pp. 149–150.
Ditto   *Poems*, 1868, Vol. vi. pp. 152–153.
Ditto, *Poetical Works*, 1889, Vol. vii. pp. 168–169.
No separate edition of "Prospice," printed as a " leaflet" or " half-sheetlet," was ever printed, though Mr. William Sharp incorrectly states that such exist. See his " Life of Browning," 1890, p. 173.

PROTUS.

First appeared in *Men and Women*, 1855, Vol. ii. pp. 154-157.
Reprinted, *Poems*, 1863, Vol. i. pp. 297-299.
Ditto   ditto   1868, Vol. iv. pp. 286-288.
Ditto, *Poetical Works*, 1889, Vol. v. pp. 175-177.

RABBI BEN-EZRA.

First appeared in *Dramatis Personæ*, 1864, pp. 75-109.
Reprinted, *Poems*, 1868, Vol. vi. pp. 99-109.
Ditto, *Poetical Works*, 1889, Vol. vii. pp. 109-119.

Rabbi Ben Ezra (or Ibn Ezra) was a learned Jew ; of whom M. Friedländer (in an Introduction to a translation of the Rabbi's Commentary on Isaiah) gives some interesting particulars. He was born at Toledo, in Spain, about 1092 or 1093 (according to Graetz, 1088). He was poor, but was nevertheless a hard student, and composed poems wherewith to "adorn his own, his Hebrew nation." He wrote many treatises—on Hebrew grammar, astronomy, mathematics, &c., as also commentaries on the books of the Bible ; and two pamphlets in England "for a certain Salomon of London." He died in 1167, at the age of 75. It was evident Ibn Ezra believed in a future life,—for he says : "Your soul shall live for ever after the death of the body, or you will receive new life through Messiah, when you will return to the Divine Law." Dr. Furnivall remarks that of the potter's clay passage he has only a translation, "shall man be esteemed as the potter's clay," and "no comment that could have given Browning a hint for the use of the metaphor in his poem, even if he had seen Ibn Ezra's commentary."

RED COTTON NIGHT-CAP COUNTRY, OR TURF AND TOWERS.

First appeared (1873) in one Vol. See *ante*, p. 383, No. 16.
Reprinted, *Poetical Works*, 1889, Vol. xii. pp. 1-177.

This poem embodies the story of Mellerio, the Paris jeweller, and was studied at St. Aubyn, in Normandy, from the documents used in the law-suit concerning his will. Dr. Furnivall writes · "It was put in type with all the true names of persons and things ; but on a proof being submitted by Browning to his friend Lord Coleridge [the late Lord Chief Justice], then Attorney-General, the latter thought that an action for libel might lie for what was said in the poem, however unlikely it was that such procedure would be taken. Thereupon fictitious names were substituted for the real ones in every case. Next year, the appeal against the judgment in favour of the will was dismissed, and, I suppose, the matter set at rest in accordance with the ethics of the poem. I believe that Browning means to restore the names in the next edition of his poem." These names were duly made public by the poet.

The poem was dedicated to Miss Anne Thackeray—who, in a measure, was also responsible for the title. In the summer of 1872, Mr. Browning and Miss Thackeray happened to meet at St. Aubin : and she, in humorous banter, termed the district " White Cotton Nightcap Country "—as much from its somnolent appearance as from the universal white cap of the women. Mr. Browning, however, with the awful tragedy of Clairvaux in mind, considered *Red* Cotton Nightcap Country the juster appellation—and at once hit upon it as the title of his poem.

REPHAN.

First appeared in *Asolando*, 1889, pp. 131–140.

Reprinted, *Poetical Works*, 1894, Vol. xvii. pp. 109–116.

In a work entitled *The Contributions of Q. Q.*, by Jane Taylor, is a prose sketch called " How it Strikes a Stranger," and it was the recollection of this that suggested *Rephan* to Browning. Jane Taylor was one of the earliest writers of books for children, and especially of religious books. She was the second sister of Isaac Taylor, the author of *The Natural History of Enthusiasm*, *The Physical Theory of Another Life*, *The Spirit of Hebrew Poetry*, and other works. The greater part of her life was spent at Ongar,[1] and with her sister Ann she wrote *Hymns for Infant Minds*. She also wrote *Display*, a novel ; *Essays in Rhyme ; Morals and Manners*, and *The Contributions of Q. Q.* Her *Twinkle, Twinkle, Little Star*, and *My Mother*, are now the best known of her poems. She died in 1824, at the age of forty, her " Memoirs " being written

---

[1] In a note to *Rephan*, Browning says the poem was suggested by the recollection of a story by Jane Taylor, of Norwich : this was evidently a slip of the pen for *Ongar*.

by her brother Isaac, and published in connexion with her correspondence.

RESPECTABILITY.

First appeared in *Men and Women*, 1855, Vol. i. pp. 149-150.
Reprinted, *Poems*, 1863, Vol. i. p. 129.
Ditto   ditto   1868, Vol. iii. p. 201.
Ditto, *Poetical Works*, 1889, Vol. vi. p. 168.

REVERIE.

First appeared in *Asolando*, 1889, pp. 141-155.
Reprinted, *Poetical Works*, 1894, Vol. xvii. pp. 117-129.

ROSNY.

First appeared in *Asolando*, 1889, pp. 5-7.
Reprinted, *Poetical Works*, 1894, Vol. xvii. pp. 4-5.

"ROUND US THE WILD CREATURES, OVERHEAD THE TREES."

First appeared in *Ferishtah's Fancies*, 1884, p. 8.
Reprinted, *Poetical Works*, 1889, Vol. xvi. p. 7-8.

RUDEL TO THE LADY OF TRIPOLI.

First appeared in *Bells and Pomegranates*, 1842, No. iii. p. 12.
Reprinted, *Poems*, 1849, Vol. ii. pp. 295-296.
Ditto   ditto   1863, Vol. i. pp. 423-424.
Ditto   ditto   1868, Vol. v. pp. 311-313.
Ditto, *Poetical Works*, 1889, Vol. iv. pp. 294-295.

In the first version of this poem the opening lines read as follows :—

> " I know a Mount the Sun perceives
> First when he visits, last, too, when he leaves
> The world ; and it repays
> The day-long glory of his gaze
> By no change of its large calm steadfast front of snow
> A Flower I know,— "

In the edition of 1868, they were thus printed :—

> " I know a Mount, the gracious Sun perceives
> First, when he visits, last, too, when he leaves
> The world ; and, vainly favoured, it repays
> The day-long glory of his steadfast gaze
> By no change of its large calm front of snow,
> And underneath the Mount, a Flower I know."

SAUL.

First appeared—sections 1–9—in *Bells and Pomegranates*, No
vii. p. 21 ; sections 10–19 being added to the poem on its
appearance in *Men and Women*, 1855 (Vol. ii. pp. 111–146).
Reprinted, *Poems*, 1849, pp. 400–406.
Ditto   *Men and Women*, 1855, Vol. ii. pp. 111–146.
Ditto   *Poems*, 1863, Vol. i. pp. 74–97.
Ditto   ditto   1868, Vol. iii. pp. 146–169.
Ditto, *Poetical Works*, 1889, Vol. vi. pp. 98–124.

The first nine sections or strophes of *Saul* were as stated above
issued in No. vii of the *Bells and Pomegranates* series, in 1845 :
the last ten sections being added when the poem was re-issued
in *Men and Women*. The first version was printed in short
lines—three feet in one and two in the next. When revising it,
however, Mr. Browning printed it in what we now feel to be
the more suitable and dignified pentameter. In finally revising the poem, Mr. Browning made various alterations : the
scope of which may be noted by appending the last few lines
of Section ix., as given in the original version :

> " On one head the joy and the pride,
> Even rage like the throe
> That opes the rock, helps its glad labour,
> And lets the gold go—
> And ambition that sees a sun lead it—
> Oh, all of these—all
> Combine to unite in one creature—
> Saul ! "

The present version reading—

> " On one head, all the beauty and strength, love and rage (like the throe
> That, a-work in the rock, helps its labour and lets the gold go),
> High ambition and deeds which surpass it, fame crowning it,—all
> Brought to blaze on the head of one creature—King Saul ! "

Selections from the Poetical Works of Robert Browning, 1863.

A Selection from the Works of Robert Browning, 1865.

Selections from the Poetical Works of Robert Browning First Series, 1872.

Selections from the Poetical Works of Robert Browning, Second Series, 1880.

SHAH ABBAS.

First appeared in *Ferishtah's Fancies*, 1884, pp. 13–23.
Reprinted, *Poetical Works*, 1889, Vol. xvi. pp. 12–18.

SHOP.

First appeared in *Pacchiarotto*, 1876, pp. 64–74.
Reprinted, *Poetical Works*, 1889, Vol. xiv. pp. 42–48.

SIBRANDUS SCHAFNABURGENSIS. See *Garden Fancies*, 2.

SIGHED RAWDON BROWN : " YES, I'M DEPARTING, TONI ! "

First appeared in *The Century Magazine*, February 1884.
Reprinted in the *Browning Society's Papers*, Part v. p. 132*.

This sonnet has not been reprinted in any edition of Mr. Browning's poems. Mr. Rawdon Brown was an Englishman of much culture, and well known to visitors in Venice. He originally went there on a short visit, with a definite object in view,—and ended by staying there for forty years : in fact, till his death in the summer of 1883. So great was his love for Venice, that some one invented an " apocryphal story " about him—which was related by Mr. Browning in the sonnet—which is as follows :

"Tutti ga i so gusti, e mi go i mii "[1] (*Venetian saying*)
Sighed Rawdon Brown : "Yes, I'm departing, Toni !
    I needs must, just this once before I die,
    Revisit England : *Anglus* Brown am I,
Although my heart's Venetian. Yes, old crony—

---

[1] " Everybody follows his taste, and I follow mine."

Venice and London—London's ' Death the bony '
  Compared with Life—that's Venice !   What a sky,
  A sea, this morning !   One last look !   Good-bye,
Cà Pesaro !   No, lion—I'm a coney
To weep !   I'm dazzled ; 'tis that sun I view
  Rippling the . . . the . . . *Cospetto*, Toni !   Down
  With carpet-bag, and off with valise-straps !
" Bella Venezia, non ti lascio più ! "
Nor did Brown ever leave her : well, perhaps
Browning, next week, may find himself quite Brown !

SMART, CHRISTOPHER, PARLEYING WITH.

First appeared in *Parleyings*, 1887, pp. 77–95.
Reprinted, *Poetical Works*, 1889, Vol. xvi. pp. 148–159.

It was at the village of Shipbourne, in Kent, on April 11, 1722, that Christopher Smart was born.   He early displayed poetical talent, and at the age of eleven is said to have written a remarkable poem.   He was about this age when he went to Durham ; and in his eighteenth year was admitted of Pembroke Hall.   His allowance from home was scanty, but he fortunately found powerful protectors in Lord Barnard and the Duchess of Cleveland : the latter allowing him £40 a year until her death in 1742.   He did well at college, becoming a Fellow of Pembroke ; and gaining the Seatonian prize poem on five occasions.   He seems to have imbibed an unfortunate tendency for dissipation ; while his recklessness in money matters and tendency to convivial excess caused him to be in constant distress.   Otherwise his conduct appears to have been blameless, and his principles strict. He was very popular among his friends ; but was a shy man, somewhat vain, and sensitive regarding his personal appearance, which was rather ill-favoured.   From Cambridge he came to London, mixing in the literary society which was adorned by Dr. Johnson, Dr. Burney, Garrick, and Dr. James—all of whom helped him in his frequent pecuniary troubles.   He married Miss Carnan, a step-daughter of Mr. John Newbery, the publisher.   In 1752, Smart published a collection of his poems, which were attacked in the *Monthly*

Review by Dr. (afterwards Sir John) Hill. The poet avenged this in 1753 in the *Hilliard*—a most bitter satire. Meanwhile, Smart had suffered from more than one attack of insanity, and the year 1761 found him again shut up in Bedlam. In 1763, soon after his release from the Asylum, Smart issued, in a separate quarto, his celebrated *Song to David.* In 1765, Smart published a translation of the *Psalms of David*, with Hymns and spiritual songs for the feasts and festivals of the Church of England, together with a reprint of the *Songs to David* (4to, pp. 194.) Soon after this his powers began to fail; he got hopelessly into debt, and died in 1770, in the forty-eighth year of his age.

"SO, THE HEAD ACHES AND THE LIMBS ARE FAINT!"

> First appeared in *Ferishtah's Fancies*, 1884, pp. 57–58.
> Reprinted, *Poetical Works*, 1889, Vol. xvi. pp. 38–39.

SOLILOQUY OF THE SPANISH CLOISTER.

> First appeared in *Bells and Pomegranates*, 1842, No. iii. p. 6, under the title of *Cloister (Spanish)*.
> Reprinted, *Poems*, 1849, Vol. ii. p. 268–271.
> Ditto   ditto   1863, Vol. i. p. 18-21.
> Ditto   ditto   1868, Vol. iii. p. 92–95.
> Ditto, *Poetical Works*, 1889, Vol. vi. p. 26–29.

SOLOMON AND BALKIS.

> First appeared in *Jocoseria*, 1883, pp. 21–32.
> Reprinted, *Poetical Works*, 1889, Vol. xv. pp. 182-187.

SONG (" Nay, but you who do not love her ").

> First appeared in *Bells and Pomegranates*, 1845, No. vii. p. 19.
> Reprinted, *Poems*, 1849, Vol. ii. p. 394.
> Ditto   ditto   1863, Vol. i. p. 33.
> Ditto   ditto   1868, Vol. iii. p. 107.
> Ditto, *Poetical Works*, 1889, Vol. vi. p. 47.

SORDELLO.

> First appeared (1840) in one Vol.   See *ante*, p. 364, No. 4.
> Reprinted, *Poems*, 1863, Vol. iii. pp. 251-464.

Reprinted, *Poems*, 1868, Vol. ii. pp. 1–218.
Ditto, *Poetical Works*, 1889, Vol. i. pp. 47–289.

Writing in 1838 to Miss Haworth, Mr. Browning thus refers to *Sordello* : " You will see *Sordello* in a trice if the fagging fit holds. I did not write six lines while absent (except a scene in a play, jotted down as we sailed thro' the Straits of Gibraltar)— but I did hammer out some four, two of which are addressed to you, two to the Queen—the whole to go in Book III.— perhaps. I called you ' Eyebright'—meaning a simple and sad sort of translation of ' Euphrasia ' into my own language : folks would know who Euphrasia, or Fanny, was—and I should not know Ianthe or Clemanthe."

Sordello, issued as here stated in 1840, was not republished till 1863—when it was included in the three-volume edition of the Poems, forming the last poem in the third volume. Strangely enough, it was omitted in the two-volume edition of 1849. In a letter to one of his correspondents a few years since, Mr. Browning says : " I did certainly at one time intend to re- write much of it, but changed my mind,—and the edition which I reprinted was the same in all respects as its predecessor— only with an elucidatory heading to each page, and some few alterations, presumably for the better, in the text, such as occur in most of my works."

The " few alterations," however, were fairly numerous—several fresh lines being added, while in many cases the rhymes were changed.

SPECULATIVE.

First appeared in *Asolando*, 1889, p. 16.
Reprinted, *Poetical Works*, 1894, Vol. xvii. p. 13.

" STILL AILING, WIND ? WILT BE APPEASED OR NO ? "

First appeared in *The Monthly Repository*, Vol. x. New Series, 1836, pp. 270–271.
Reprinted in *The Atlantic Monthly*, Vol. xiii. *July*, 1864, pp. 737–738.

These lines were subsequently included in *Dramatis Personæ*, 1864, forming the first six stanzas of Section vi of *James Lee*.

St. Martin's Summer.

First appeared in *Pacchiarotto*, 1876, pp. 108–116.
Reprinted, *Poetical Works*, 1889, Vol. xiv. pp. 71–76.

Strafford.

First appeared (1837) in one Vol.   See *ante*, p. 363, No. 3.
Reprinted, *Poems*, 1863, Vol. ii. pp. 503–605.
Ditto   ditto   1868, Vol. i. pp. 207–310.
Ditto   "Acting Edition," 1881, and "School Edition," 1884.
See *ante*, p. 364.
Ditto, *Poetical Works*, 1889, Vol. ii. pp. 187–307.

On the 26th of May, 1836, Robert Browning—in the company of
Landor, Wordsworth, Macready, and others—had been dining
with Mr. Serjeant Talfourd, the author of *Ion*. As they were
leaving the house, Macready overtook Browning, and said to
him : "Write a play, Browning, and keep me from going to
America." The poet took the great actor at his word, and at
once queried—"Shall it be historical and English? What do
you say to a drama on Strafford?"   Such was the genesis of
Robert Browning's first play. On the 3rd of the following
August, Macready writes in his journal : "Forster told me that
Browning had fixed on *Strafford* for the subject of a tragedy ;
he could not have hit upon one that I could more readily have
concurred in." The subject of Strafford was doubtless in the
poet's mind when Macready asked him to write a tragedy, for
he had been not long before revising the manuscript of a life of
Strafford for his friend Forster (who had been overtaken by
illness) ; and the subject was therefore ready to hand.

It was produced on the 1st of May, 1837, at the Theatre-Royal,
Covent Garden. The part of *Strafford* was taken by Macready
—whose acting is said to have been most forcible and striking.
Miss Helen Faucit (now Lady Martin) represented *Lady
Carlisle*—playing, the *Literary Gazette* (May 6, 1837) says,
"with great taste and effect." *Pym* was entrusted to Mr.
Vandenhoff's hands, Mr. Webster taking the part of the young
Vane. As to the success of the play opinion seems to be equally
divided ; though the *Examiner* (May 14, 1837) strikes an
optimistic note : "*Strafford* was winning its way into even

greater success than we had ventured to hope for it ; but Mr.
Vandenhoff's secession from the theatre has caused its temporary withdrawal. It will be only temporary, we trust ; no
less in justice to the great genius of the author, than to the
fervid applause with which its last performance was received
by an admirably filled house." Despite this praise, the tragedy
does not seem to have had fair play—for in the preceding issue
of the *Examiner* we are told that it "was most infamously got
up," and that even Mr. Macready was not "so fine as he is
wont to be." Then, too, we learn that "the rest of the
performers, with the exception of Miss Faucit, they were a barn
wonder to look at ! Mr. Vandenhoff was positively nauseous,
with his whining, drawling, and slouching, in *Pym ;* and Mr.
Webster whimpered in somewhat too juvenile a fashion through
Young Vane. Some one should have stepped out of the pit,
and thrust Mr. Dale [the *King*] from the stage. Any thing
should have been done, rather than that such exhibitions should
be allowed to disgrace the stage of a ' national' theatre." This
is strong, but then the writer (John Forster) speaks with some
semblance of authority : and he also arrives at the conclusion
that, although he does not think it will take a permanent hold of
the stage, it "was produced . . . with all the evidences of a
decided success."

That *Strafford* did not take a permanent hold of the stage may
be evidenced from the fact that it was not until the 21st of
December, 1886, that it was again put upon the boards : it
being on this occasion revived by the Browning Society, at the
Strand Theatre. There was an excellent caste, and the performance seems to have been in every way successful.

Strafford was again performed on February 12, 1890, at the
Oxford Theatre, by members of the University Dramatic
Society. The acting version was prepared by Mr. W. Courtney,
and Mr. Alma Tadema designed the various scenes. It was, on
the whole, decidedly successful—and seven performances in all
were given.

Browning himself has told us that his *Lady Carlisle* is purely
imaginary : " I at first sketched her singular likeness roughly
in, as suggested by Matthews and the memoir writers—but it
was too artificial, and the substituted outline is exclusively from

Voiture and Waller." Keeping this in mind, the following translation from the French of Voiture is of especial interest. The letter is addressed "To Mr. Gordon, London," and is numbered xlix. in *Letters and other Works of Voiture* (1709): "The pleasantest thoughts I had, have been of you or of the things I saw through your kindness. You will easily guess that I do not mean by this the Tower, or the lions you showed me. In one human being you let me see more treasures than there are there, and even more lions and leopards. It will not be difficult for you to guess after this that I speak of the Countess of Carlisle. For there is nobody else of whom this good and evil can be said. No matter how dangerous it is to let the memory dwell upon her, I have not, so far, been able to keep mine from it, and quite honestly, I would not give the picture of her that lingers in my mind, for all the loveliest things I have seen in my life. I must confess that she is an enchanting personality, and there would not be a woman under heaven so worthy of affection, if she only knew what it was, and if she had as sensitive a nature as she has a reasonable mind. But with the temperament we know she possesses, there is nothing to be said except that she is the most lovable of all things not good, and the most delightful poison that Nature ever concocted. My dread of her wit nearly decided me not to send you these verses, for I know she is a judge in all things of the good, and the bad, and all the kindness that ought to reside in the will, with her is concentrated in the judgment. Still it hardly matters to me if she condemn them. I do not even wish them better, since I composed them before I had the honor of meeting her, and I should be very sorry to have praised or blamed anything to perfection until that occasion, for I reserve perfect praise and perfect blame for herself."

"SUCH A STARVED BANK OF MOSS."

First appeared in the *La Saisiaz* volume, 1878, pp. 85–86, where it forms the proem to the *Two Poets of Croisic*
Reprinted, *Poetical Works*, 1889, Vol. xiv. pp. 207–208.
No alteration in text. In the *Selections* (second series) this poem is called *Apparitions*.

Summum Bonum.

> First appeared in *Asolando*, 1889, p. 13.
> Reprinted, *Poetical Works*, 1894, Vol. xvii. p. 11.

Tertium Quid. See *The Ring and the Book.*

The Agamemnon of Æschylus.

> First appeared (1877) in one Vol. See, *ante*, p. 386, No. 20.
> Reprinted, *Poetical Works*, 1889, Vol. xiii. p. 259-357.
>
> Writing in 1877 Mr. Browning says : " My work, I hope, is closer to the original than any 'crib,' and wants no praise for anything of my own."

The Bean-Feast.

> First appeared in *Asolando*, 1889, pp. 46-51.
> Reprinted, *Poetical Works*, 1894, Vol. xvii. pp. 39-43.

The Bishop orders his Tomb at Saint Praxed's Church.

> First appeared in *Hood's Magazine*, Vol. iii. p. 237.
> Reprinted, *Poems*, 1849, Vol. ii. pp. 345-349.
> Ditto   ditto   1863, Vol. i. pp. 369-373.
> Ditto   ditto   1868, Vol. v. pp. 257-262.
> Ditto, *Poetical Works*, 1889, Vol. iv. pp. 232-237.
>
> This now celebrated " tomb " is, it need hardly be said, entirely imaginary—nevertheless, the curious in such matters have, on due inquiry accompanied with befitting " fee," had duly pointed out to them the tomb beneath which the remains of the fastidious bishop were said to repose.
> Referring to a line in this poem, Mr. Browning wrote to Dante Gabriel Rossetti (May 29, 1856) as follows : " I remember you asked me some questions of which one comes to mind of a sudden—'elucesco' is dog-latin rather—the true word would be 'eluceo'—and Ulpian, the golden Jurist, is a copper latinist —see about him in any Biographical Dictionary."

"THE BLIND MAN TO THE MAIDEN SAID."

First appeared in *The Hour will Come*, 1879, Vol. ii. p. 174.
Reprinted, *Whitehall Review*, March 1, 1883.
Ditto, *Browning Society's Papers*, Part iv. p. 410.

These lines were Englished by Mr. Browning for Mrs. Clara Bell, and appear in her translation of Wilhelmine von Hillern's tale *The Hour will Come*.[1] A note is appended to the verses, " The translator is indebted for these verses to the kindness of a friend." They are as follows :

> The blind man to the maiden said :
>   ' O thou of hearts the truest,
> Thy countenance is hid from me,
> Let not my questions anger thee !
>   Speak, though in words the fewest !
>
> ' Tell me what kind of eyes are thine ?
>   Dark eyes, or light ones rather ? '
> ' My eyes are a decided brown
> So much at least—by looking down—
>   From the brook's glass I gather.'
>
> ' And is it red—thy little mouth ?
>   That too the blind must care for ! '
> ' Ah, I would tell that soon to thee,
> Only—none yet has told it me.
>   I cannot answer therefore ! '
>
> ' But dost thou ask what heart I have
>   There hesitate I never !
> In thine own breast 'tis borne, and so
> 'Tis thine in weal and thine in woe,
>   For life, for death,—thine ever ! '

THE BOOK AND THE RING. See *The Ring and the Book.*

[1] *The Hour will Come. A Tale of an Alpine Cloister.* By Wilhelmine von Hillern. From the German by Clara Bell. In two volumes. Leipzig 1879]. London : Sampson Low, Marston, and Co.

The Boy and the Angel.

First appeared in *Hood's Magazine*, August 1844, Vol. ii. pp. 140-142.

Reprinted, *Poems*, 1849, Vol. ii. pp. 395-398.

Ditto   ditto   1863, Vol. i. pp. 167-170.

Ditto   ditto   1868, Vol. iv. pp. 158-161.

Ditto, *Poetical Works*, 1889, Vol. v. pp. 19-23.

Several changes have been made in this poem since its first publication. In the *Bells and Pomegranates* of 1845, five fresh couplets were inserted, and one was substituted for an old one, several minor changes also being effected. One fresh couplet was also inserted in the edition of 1863, namely (inserted after " and ever lived on earth content "),—

> (" He did God's will ; to him, all one
> If on the earth or in the sun.)

As illustrative of the alterations, we may note that the lines

> " Be again the boy all curl'd ;
> I will finish with the world,"

appearing in *Hood's Magazine* were changed to the more euphonious

> " Back to the cell and poor employ,
> Resume the craftsman and the boy ! "

The Cardinal and the Dog.

First appeared in *Asolando*, 1889, pp. 40-41.

Reprinted, *Poetical Works*, 1894, Vol. xvii. pp. 34-35.

The incident related in this poem is put by Browning in the year 1522, and he tells us the Legate was Crescenzio. Moreri, in his *Dictionnaire Historique*, gives an account of Crescenzio, which has been thus Englished : " Marcel Crescentio, Cardinal Bishop of Marsico, in the kingdom of Naples, was born in Rome, of one of the most noble and ancient families. From his youth he made great progress in letters, particularly in civil and canon law. He had a canonship in the Church of St. Mary Major, and was also given the office of the auditor of the Rota. Then Pope Clement VII. named him for the bishopric of Marsico, and Paul III. made him Cardinal (June 2, 1542). Crescentio was Protector of the Order of Citeaux, perpetual Legate at Bologna, Bishop of Conserans, etc. Julius III. made him Legate to preside at the Council of Trent, and he presided there at the eleventh, twelfth, thirteenth, fourteenth, and fifteenth sessions. The latter ended in 1552, and the Cardinal Crescentio, who was ill, remained in Trent. Rumour said that his malady came upon him in this way : After working almost the whole of the night of March 20, to write to the Pope, as he arose from his seat he imagined that he saw a dog that opened its jaws frightfully, and appeared to him with its flaming eyes and low-hanging ears as if mad, and about to attack him. Crescentio called his servants at once, and made them bring lights, but the dog could not be found. The Cardinal, terrified by this spectre, fell into a deep melancholy, and then immediately into a sickness which made him despair of recovery, although his friends and physicians assured him there was nothing to fear. This is the story about the end of Cardinal Crescentio, who died at Verona the 1st of June, 1552. It could have been invented only by ill-meaning people, who lacked respect for the council."

THE CONFESSIONAL.

First appeared in *Bells and Pomegranates*, 1845, No. vii. p. 11.
Reprinted, *Poems*, 1849, Vol. i. pp. 357–360.
Ditto   ditto 1863, Vol. i. pp. 24–27.
Ditto   ditto 1868, Vol. iii. pp. 98–101.
Ditto, *Poetical Works*, 1889, Vol. vi. pp. 34–38.

THE EAGLE.

First appeared in *Ferishtah's Fancies*, 1884, pp. 5–7.
Reprinted, *Poetical Works*, 1889, Vol. xvi. pp. 6–8.

THE ENGLISHMAN IN ITALY.

First appeared in *Bells and Pomegranates*, 1845, No. vii. p. 5 under the title of *England in Italy*.

Reprinted, *Poems*, 1849, Vol. ii. pp. 330–340.
Ditto   ditto 1863, Vol. i. pp. 195–205.
Ditto   ditto 1868, Vol. iv. pp. 186–196.
Ditto, *Poetical Works*, 1889, Vol. v. pp. 54–65.

THE FAMILY.

First appeared in *Ferishtah's Fancies*, 1884, pp. 25–30.
Reprinted, *Poetical Works*, 1889, Vol. xvi. pp. 19–23.

THE FLIGHT OF THE DUCHESS.

First appearance in *Hood's Magazine*, 1845, Vol. iii. p. 313.
Reprinted (with additional sections), *Bells and Pomegranates*,
No. vii. p. 13.
Reprinted, *Poems*, 1849, Vol. ii. pp. 360–393.
Ditto   ditto 1863, Vol. i. pp. 246–278.
Ditto   ditto 1868, Vol. iv. pp. 237–269.
Ditto, *Poetical Works*, 1889, Vol. v. pp. 116–153.

THE FLOWER'S NAME. See *Garden Fancies.*

THE FOUNDER OF THE FEAST.

First appeared in *The World*, April 16, 1884.
Reprinted in *Browning Society's Papers*, Part vii. p. 18*.
Ditto W. G. Kingsland's *Robert Browning : Chief Poet of the
Age*, p. 30.
This sonnet was inscribed by Mr. Browning in the Album presented to Mr. Arthur Chappell (so well and worthily known in connexion with the St. James' Hall Saturday and Monday Popular Concerts). It has not been printed in any edition of Mr. Browning's poems ; and is as follows :

"Enter my palace," if a prince should say—
  "Feast with the Painters ! See, in bounteous row,
  They range from Titian up to Angelo ! "
Could we be silent at the rich survey?
A host so kindly, in as great a way
  Invites to banquet, substitutes for show
  Sound that's diviner still, and bids us know
Bach like Beethoven ; are we thankless, pray?

> Thanks, then, to Arthur Chappell,—thanks to him
> Whose every guest henceforth not idly vaunts,
> "Sense has received the utmost Nature grants,
> My cup was filled with rapture to the brim,
> When, night by night—ah, memory, how it haunts!—
> Music was poured by perfect ministrants,
> By Halle, Schumann, Piatti, Joachim."

The Glove.

First appearance in *Bells and Pomegranates*, 1845, No. vii. p. 23.

Reprinted, *Poems*, 1849, Vol. ii. pp. 409–416.

Ditto   ditto   1863, Vol. i. pp. 180–187.

Ditto   ditto   1868, Vol. iv. pp. 171–178.

Ditto, *Poetical Works*, 1889, Vol. v. pp. 36–43.

This poem—the story of which has also been told by Schiller and Leigh Hunt—is of especial interest on account of the wide departure taken by Mr. Browning from the facts as narrated in the commonly accepted version.

The Guardian Angel : a Picture at Fano.

First appeared in *Men and Women*, 1855, Vol. ii. pp. 167–170.

Reprinted, *Poems*, 1863, Vol. i. pp. 142–145.

Ditto   ditto   1868, Vol. iii. pp. 214–216.

Ditto, *Poetical Works*, 1889, Vol. vi. pp. 187–189.

This poem was suggested to Mr. Browning by a picture in the church of St. Augustine, at Fano, attributed to Guercino. An angel is represented, standing, with wings outstretched, by a little child—whose hands the angel is joining in the attitude of prayer: while its gaze is directed skyward—whence cherubs are looking down. The " Alfred, dear friend," of stanza vi. was Mr. Alfred Domett, some time Prime Minister of New Zealand. [See *Waring*, p. 226.]

The Heretic's Tragedy ; a Middle-Age Interlude.

First appeared in *Men and Women*, 1855, Vol. ii. pp. 198–204.

Reprinted, *Poems*, 1863, Vol. i. pp. 286–290.

Ditto   ditto   1868, Vol. iv. pp. 275–279.

Ditto, *Poetical Works*, 1889, Vol. v. pp. 161–166.

THE HOUSEHOLDER.

First appeared in *Fifine at the Fair*, 1872, pp. 169–171.
Reprinted, *Poetical Works*, 1889, Vol. xii. pp. 342–343.

THE INN ALBUM.

First appeared (1875) in one Vol. See *ante*, p. 384, No. 18.
Reprinted, *Poetical Works*, 1889, Vol. xii. pp. 181–311.

Writing in *Notes and Queries* (March 25, 1876), Dr. Furnivall
says : " The story told by Mr. Browning in this poem is, in its
main outlines, a real one, that of Lord ——, once a friend
of the great Duke of Wellington, and about whom there is much
in the Greville *Memoirs.* The original story was, of course,
too repulsive to be adhered to in all its details of, first, the
gambling lord producing the portrait of the lady he had seduced
and abandoned, and offering his expected dupe, but real beater,
an introduction to the lady, as a bribe to induce him to wait for
payment of the money he had won ; secondly, the eager acceptance of the bribe by the young gambler, and the suicide of
the lady from horror at the base proposal of her old seducer.
(The story made a great sensation in London over thirty years
ago.)   Readers know how Mr. Browning has lifted the base
young gambler, through the renewal of that old love which the
poet has invented, into one of the most pathetic creations of
modern times, and has spared the baser old *roué* the degradation
of the attempt to sell the love which was once his delight."

THE ITALIAN IN ENGLAND.

First appeared in *Bells and Pomegranates* (under the title of
Italy in England, 1845, No. vii. p. 4.
Reprinted, *Poems*, 1849, Vol. ii. pp. 324–329.
Ditto   ditto   1863, Vol. i. pp. 189–195.
Ditto   ditto   1868, Vol. iv. pp. 180–186.
Ditto, *Poetical Works*, 1889, Vol. v. pp. 47–53.

Mrs. Orr remarks in her *Handbook* : " Mr. Browning is proud
to remember that Mazzini informed him he had read this
poem to certain of his fellow exiles in England, to show how an
Englishman could sympathise with them."

THE KING ("A King lived long ago ").

First appeared in *The Monthly Repository*, Vol. ix. New Series,
1835, pp. 707-708.
Reprinted, *Bells and Pomegranates*, No. i. 1841, p. 12.
When reprinted in *Bells and Pomegranates*, this poem was
incorporated (with considerable variations) in *Pippa Passes*,
where it is given as one of Pippa's songs.

THE LABORATORY.

First appeared in *Hood's Magazine*, Vol. i. p. 513.
Reprinted in *Bells and Pomegranates*, 1845, No. vii. p. 11.
Reprinted, *Poems*, 1849, Vol. ii. pp. 354-357.
Ditto   ditto   1863, Vol. i. pp. 21-23.
Ditto   ditto   1868, Vol. iii. pp. 95-97.
Ditto, *Poetical Works*, 1889, Vol. vi. pp. 30-33.

THE LADY AND THE PAINTER.

First appeared in *Asolando*, 1889, pp. 58-60.
Reprinted, *Poetical Works*, 1894, Vol. xvii. pp. 48-49.

THE LAST RIDE TOGETHER.

First appeared in *Men and Women*, 1855, vol. i. pp. 184-190.
Reprinted, *Poems*, 1863, Vol. i. pp. 229-234.
Ditto   ditto   1868, Vol. iv. pp. 220-224.
Ditto, *Poetical Works*, 1889, Vol. v. pp. 96-107.

THE LOST LEADER.

First appeared in *Bells and Pomegranates*, 1845, No. vii. p. 8.
Reprinted, *Poems*, 1849, Vol. ii. pp. 340-341.
Ditto   ditto   1863, Vol. i. pp. 4-5.
Ditto   ditto   1868, Vol. iii. pp. 78-79.
Ditto, *Poetical Works*, 1889, Vol. vi. pp. 7-8.

"*I did in my hasty youth presume to use the great and vene-
rated personality of Wordsworth as a sort of painter's model,
one from which this or the other particular feature may be
selected and turned to account : had I intended more, above
all, such a boldness as pourtraying the entire man, I should*

not have talked about ' handfuls of silver and bits of riband.'
These never influenced the change of politics in the great poet;
whose defection, nevertheless, accompanied as it was by a regular
face-about of his special party, was to my juvenile apprehension,
and even mature consideration, an event to deplore." [Letter to
Rev. A. B. Grosart. See *Letters from Robert Browning, Edited*
by T. J. Wise, Vol. i. pp. 28-29.]

THE LOST MISTRESS.

First appeared in *Bells and Pomegranates,* 1845, Vol. vii. p 8.
Reprinted, *Poems,* 1849, Vol. ii. pp. 342-343.
Ditto   ditto   1863, Vol. i. pp. 30-31.
Ditto   ditto   1868, Vol. iii. pp. 104-105.
Ditto, *Poetical Works,* 1889, Vol. vi. pp. 43-44.

THE MELON-SELLER.

First appeared in *Ferishtah's Fancies,* 1884, pp. 9-12.
Reprinted, *Poetical Works,* 1889, Vol. xvi. pp. 9-11.

THE NAMES.

First appeared in *The Shaksperean Show-Book,* 1884.
Reprinted in *The Pall Mall Gazette,* May 29, 1884.
Ditto in *The Browning Society's Papers,* Part v. p. 105*.
Ditto W. G. Kingsland's *Robert Browning : Chief Poet of the*
Age, p. 79.

This sonnet was contributed to the *Shakesperean Show-Book* of
the Shaksperean Show held at the Albert Hall, London, in
May 1884, on behalf of the Hospital for Women in the Fulham
Road, London. Not having been reprinted in any edition of
Mr. Browning's poems, it is here quoted :

Shakspeare !—to such name's sounding what succeeds,
   Fitly as silence?   Falter forth the spell,—
   Act follows word, the speaker knows full well,
Nor tampers with its magic more than needs.
Two names there are : That which the Hebrew reads
   With his soul only : if from lips it fell,
   Echo, back thundered by earth, heaven and hell,
Would own " Thou did'st create us ! "   Nought impedes.

We voice the other name, man's most of might,
Awesomely, lovingly : let awe and love
Mutely await their working, leave to sight
All of the issue as—below—above—
Shakspeare's creation rises : one remove,
Though dread—this finite from that infinite.

THE OTHER HALF-ROME. See *The Ring and the Book.*

THE PATRIOT : AN OLD STORY.

> First appeared in *Men and Women,* 1855, vol. i. pp. 191–193.
> Reprinted, *Poems,* 1863, Vol. i. pp. 158–159.
> Ditto   ditto   1868, Vol. iv. pp. 149–150.
> Ditto, *Poetical Works,* 1889, Vol. v. pp. 6–7.

THE PIED PIPER OF HAMELIN : A CHILD'S STORY.

> First appeared in *Bells and Pomegranates,* 1842, No. iii. pp. 14–16.
> Reprinted, *Poems,* 1849, Vol. ii. pp. 306–317.
> Ditto   ditto   1863, Vol. i. pp. 234–245.
> Ditto   ditto   1868, Vol. iv. pp. 225–236.
> Ditto, 1880, illustrated by Jane E. Cook.
> Ditto (*no date*), illustrated by Kate Greenaway.
> Ditto, 1884, in pamphlet form, to accompany Mr. Macbeth's etchings.
> [*For full particulars regarding the above three separate reprints of " The Pied Piper of Hamelin" see under Part VI. " Selections."*]
> Reprinted, *Poetical Works,* 1889, Vol. v. pp. 102–115.

This ever-delightful child's poem was written for, and inscribed to William Macready—the eldest son of the celebrated actor. The young Macready had evidently much talent for drawing, and on one occasion he asked Mr. Browning to give him some subject for illustration.   Mr. Browning thereupon wrote a short poem, founded upon an old account of the death of the Pope's Legate at the Council of Trent—which poem has never been printed.   It will be preferable, however, to give this interesting episode in Mr. Browning's own words. Writing to Dr. Furnivall in October 1881, the poet says :—" The ' W. M. the Younger' was poor William Macready's eldest boy—dead, a few years ago. He had a talent for drawing, and asked me to give him some little things to illustrate ; so I made a bit of a poem out of an old account of the death of the Pope's legate at the Council of Trent—which he made such clever drawings for, that I tried at a more picturesque subject, the Piper. I still possess the half-dozen of the designs he gave me. If you care to have the Legend of the Legate I am sure you are welcome to it, when I can transcribe it from the page of the old book it remains upon—unprinted hitherto."—[*Letters of Robert Browning*, edited by T. J. Wise, vol. i. pp. 76–77.]

The story of the " *Piper* " seems to have been taken from one of the " Familiar Letters " of James Howell [1] (Section vi. Letter xlvii.): " Hamelen, a Town in *Germany*, which I hop'd to have pass'd through when I was in *Hamburgh* (nor would I relate it unto you were there not there som ground of truth for it). The said Town of Hamelen was annoyed with Rats and Mice ; and it chanc'd, that a Pied-coated Piper came thither, who covenanted with the chief Burgers for such a reward, if he could free them quite from the said Vermin, nor would he demand it, till a twelvemonth and a day after : The agreement being made, he began to play on his Pipes, and all the Rats, and the Mice, followed him to a great Lough hard by, where they all perish'd ; so the Town was infested no more. At the end of the yeer, the Pied Piper return'd for his reward, the Burgers put him off with slightings, and neglect, offering him som small matter, which he refusing, and staying som dayes in the Town, one Sunday morning, at High-Masse, when most people were at Church, he fell to play on his Pipes, and all the children up and down, follow'd him out of the Town, to a great Hill not far off, which rent in two, and open'd, and let him and

---

[1] *Epistolæ Ho-Elianæ.* Familiar LETTERS *Domestic* and *Forren ;* Divided into Six Sections, Partly *Historicall, Politicall, Philosophicall,* Upon Emergent Occasions ; by *J. H.* Esq.; One of the Clerks of His Majesties most Honourable Privy Councell. *London,* Printed for *Humphrey Moseley ;* and are to be sold at his shop at the Prince's Arms in *S. Paul's* Churchyard, 1645.

the children in, and so clos'd up again : This happen'd a matter of two hundred and fifty years since ; and in that Town, they date their Bills and Bonds, and other Instruments of Law, to this day from the yeer of the going out of their children. Besides, ther is a great piller of stone at the foot of the said Hill, whereon this story is engraven."

" THE POET'S AGE IS SAD: FOR WHY ?"

First appeared in *Asolando*, 1889, pp. 1–4.
Reprinted, *Poetical Works*, 1894, Vol. xvii. pp. 1–3.

This poem is the Prologue to *Asolando*.

"THE POETS POUR US WINE."

First appeared in *Pacchiarotto, and other Poems*, 1876, pp. 223–241.
Reprinted, *Poetical Works*, 1889, Vol. xiv. pp. 141–152.

These lines form the Epilogue to *Pacchiarotto and other Poems* : the first line of the Epilogue being a quotation from Mrs. Browning's poem *Wine of Cyprus*.

THE POPE.   See *The Ring and the Book*.

THE POPE AND THE NET.

First appeared in *Asolando*, 1889, pp. 42–45.
Reprinted, *Poetical Works*, 1894, Vol. xvii. pp. 36–38.

THE RETURN OF THE DRUSES.

First appeared in *Bells and Pomegranates*, 1843, No. iv. pp. 1–19.
Reprinted, *Poems*, 1849, Vol. ii. pp. 61–137.
Ditto   ditto   1863, Vol. ii. pp. 140–215.
Ditto   ditto   1868, Vol. iii. pp. 229–305.
Ditto, *Poetical Works*, 1889, Vol. iii. pp. 167–255.

THE RING AND THE BOOK.

First appeared (1868–1869) in four volumes, each divided into
three monologues, separately headed with the speaker's names :
save the first and twelfth, in which Browning is himself the
speaker. These sub-titles are as follows :—

I. *The Ring and the Book* (Vol. i. pp. 1–74 ; *Poetical Works*,
1889, Vol. viii. pp. 1–57).

II. *Half-Rome* (Vol. i. pp. 75–155 ; *Poetical Works*, 1889, Vol.
viii. pp. 58–119).

III. *The Other Half-Rome* (Vol. i. pp. 157–245 ; *Poetical Works*,
1889, Vol. vii. pp. 120–187).

IV. *Tertium Quid* (Vol. ii. pp. 1–72 ; *Poetical Works*, 1889,
Vol. viii. pp. 188–253).

V. *Count Guido Franceschini* (Vol. ii. pp. 73–160 ; *Poetical
Works*, 1889, Vol. ix. pp. 1–82).

VI. *Giuseppe Caponsacchi* (Vol. ii. pp. 161–251 ; *Poetical Works*,
1889, Vol. ix. pp. 83–166).

VII. *Pompilia* (Vol. iii. pp. 1–89 ; *Poetical Works*, 1889, Vol.
ix. pp. 167–241).

VIII. *Dominus Hyacinthus de Archangelis, Pauperum Procurator*
(Vol. iii. pp. 90–174 ; *Poetical Works*, 1889, Vol. ix. pp.
242–313).

IX. *Juris Doctor Johannes-Baptista Bottinius, Fisci et Rev.
Cam. Apostol. Advocatus* (Vol. iii. pp. 175–249 ; *Poetical
Works*, 1889, Vol. x. pp. 1–63).

X. *The Pope* (Vol. iv. pp. 1–92 ; *Poetical Works*, 1889, Vol. x.
pp. 64–148).

XI. *Guido* (Vol. iv. pp. 93–195 ; *Poetical Works*, 1889, Vol. x.
pp. 149–279).

XII. *The Book and the Ring* (Vol. iv. pp. 197–235; *Poetical
Works*, Vol. x. pp. 244–279).

THE RING AND THE BOOK. See *The Ring and the
Book*—of which the first section is thus entitled.

In reference to a passage in this section of the *Ring and the
Book* (Vol. i. Part i. lines 679–772) George Eliot writes as follows
to Miss Hennell (February 15, 1869) : "I have looked back to the

verses in Browning's Poem about Elisha, and I find no mystery in them. The foregoing context for three pages describes that function of genius which revivifies the past. Man, says Browning (I am writing from recollection of his general meaning), cannot create, but he can restore : the poet gives forth of his own spirit, and reanimates the forms that lie breathless. His use of Elisha's story is manifestly symbolical, as his mention of *Faust* is —the illustration which he abandons the moment before, to take up that of the Hebrew seer. I presume you did not read the context yourself, but only had the two concluding verses pointed out or quoted to you by your friend. It is one of the afflictions of authorship to know that the brains which should be used in understanding a book are wasted in discussing the hastiest misconceptions about it ; and I am sure you will sympathise enough in this affliction to set any one right when you can about this quotation from Browning."

THE STATUE AND THE BUST.

First appeared in pamphlet form, 1855.
Reprinted, *Men and Women*, 1855, Vol. i. pp. 156–172.
Ditto, *Poems*, 1863, Vol. i. pp. 299–309.
Ditto ditto 1868, Vol. iv. pp. 288–298.
Ditto, *Poetical Works*, 1889, Vol. v. pp. 178–190.

In regard to this poem it has been pointed out that " the pile that the mighty shadow throws " across the Via Larga is the Medici Palace where Duke Ferdinand lived and gave his evening party, and not the Riccardi Palace in the Piazza dell' Annunziata, which the " statue watches from the square." Answering certain queries concerning this matter, Mr. Browning writes (Jan. 8th, 1887) : " The lady was the wife of Riccardi, and the Duke—Ferdinand, just as the poem says. As it was built by, and inhabited by the Medici till sold, long after, to the Riccardi,—it was not from the Duke's palace, but a ·vindow· in that of the Riccardi, that the lady gazed at her lover riding by. The statue is still in its place, looking at the window under which ' now is the empty shrine.' Can anything be clearer ? " On this point Dr. W. J. Rolfe writes : " By 'that of the Riccardi ' I think now that he meant the other palace, and not the one he has just mentioned as sold to the Riccardi by the Medici. If he had written 'that of the Riccardi in the Piazza dell' Annunziata,' his meaning would have been clear." Dr. Rolfe also points out that Browning is guilty of an anachronism in making the *bust* a product of " Robbia's craft." Luca della Robbia died in 1482, and Andrea in 1528. No doubt the poet had in mind one of these artists ; but the "bust must be supposed to be made at about the same time as the statue, which was in 1608. Giovanni, the son of Andrea, and the only other of the Robbia family worth mentioning, died about 1530." [*Poet Lore*, Vol. iii. p. 287.]

THE SUN.

First appeared in *Ferishtah's Fancies*, 1884, pp. 33–45.
Reprinted, *Poetical Works*, 1889, Vol. xvi. pp. 24–31.

THE TWINS.

First appeared in 1854, in " Two Poems by E. B. B. and R. B."
Reprinted in *Men and Women*, 1855, Vol. ii. p. 190.
Ditto, *Poems*, 1863, Vol. i. pp. 225–226.
Ditto ditto 1868, Vol. iv. pp. 216–217.
Ditto, *Poetical Works*, 1889, Vol. v. p. 90.

The pamphlet in which this poem first appeared is now excessively rare. It consisted of sixteen pages, comprising *The Twins* by Robert Browning, and *A Plea for the Ragged Schools of London*, by Elizabeth Barrett Browning. The Poems were printed by Miss Arabella Barrett (Mrs. Browning's sister) for sale at a Bazaar on behalf of the " Refuge for Young Destitute Girls," which she established in or about 1854. This Refuge was one of the first of its kind, and is still in existence.

THE TWO POETS OF CROISIC.

First appeared (1878), with *La Saisiaz*, in one vol. See *ante*,
p. 29, No. 21.
Reprinted, *Poetical Works*, 1889, Vol. xiv. pp. 205–273.

This poem is an episode in the biography of two French poets, whose respective " Poetical Work " enjoyed but a brief reputation. Mrs. Orr [*Handbook to the Works of Robert Browning,* p. 256] gives us a brief but succinct account of their career. The first, René Gentilhomme, was born in 1610, and becoming page to the Prince of Condé, occupied his leisure hours in the composition of complimentary verses. One day, while writing an ode, a storm broke over the place—the lightning shattering a marble crown which stood on a pedestal in the room. At this time, Condé was thought to be the future King of France— Louis XIII. being childless, as also his brother Gaston. This incident the poet took as an omen, and thereupon made his " ode" into a prophecy—declaring that the Prince's hopes were at an end, as a Dauphin would be born the next year, In the event, a Dauphin *was* born, and René received the title of Royal Poet. However, he wrote little after this, and his one volume of verse was soon forgotten.

The second Poet—Paul Desforges Maillard—was born some hundred years later, and occupied his early manhood in writing society verses. At length he competed for a prize offered by the Academy for the best poetical effusion commemorative of the progress of navigation during the last reign. His poem, however, was returned—to be afterwards submitted to the editor of a publication called *The Mercury.* The editor, La Roque, gave a due meed of praise to the poem, but declined to publish it—he not daring to offend the Academy. Paul thereupon charged the editor with cowardice—who retaliated by telling the Poet his work was execrable. Now it was that Paul's sister came upon the scene. She persuaded him to let her copy out some of the weakest of his poems or songs, and send them to La Roque as her own composition. This was done,—and as she was known by another name than her brother's, the stratagem succeeded. The fame of the lady grew apace—so much so, that La Roque (in writing) made love to her ; while the great Voltaire himself was smitten. At this juncture, Paul interposed—not caring to be kept in the background any longer. He therefore proceeded to Paris, and introduced himself as the much admired Poetess. La Roque pretended to enjoy the joke—but Voltaire waxed exceeding bitter : and the Poet was strongly advised to clear out of Paris. Paul reprinted the poems in his own name : but they fell flat this time—and he, too, was forgotten as speedily as René.

THE WORST OF IT.

First appeared in *Dramatis Personæ*, 1864, pp. 35–43.
Reprinted, *Poems*, 1868, Vol. vi. pp. 70–76.
Ditto, *Poetical Works*, 1889, Vol. vii. pp. 78–84.

THROUGH THE METIDJA TO ABD-EL-KADR.

First appeared in *Bells and Pomegranates*, 1842, No. iii. p. 14.
Reprinted, *Poems*, 1849, Vol. ii. pp. 304–306.
Ditto   ditto   1863, Vol. i. pp. 9–11.
Ditto   ditto   1868, Vol. iii. pp. 83–85.
Ditto, *Poetical Works*, 1889, Vol. vi. pp. 13–15.

"THUS I WROTE IN LONDON, MUSING ON MY BETTERS."

First appeared in *The Century*, Vol. xxv. 1882, pp. 159–160.
Reprinted in *The Browning Society's Papers* (first edition),
   Part iv. p. 48*.
These lines were printed in *The Century* as forming ten new lines to " Touch him ne'er so lightly " (*Dramatic Idyls*, Second Series, 1880, p. 149) ; they have not, however, been added to any reprint of the original verses, as they were not intended to form a permanent addition thereto—and were, indeed, printed in *The Century* without Mr. Browning's consent : at whose request the lines were cancelled from *The Browning Society's Papers*—only appearing in the first edition of Part iv.
As standing by themselves, and apart from the lines to which they were added in *The Century*, they are here quoted :

> " Thus I wrote in London, musing on my betters,
>   Poets dead and gone : and lo, the critics cried,
>   ' Out on such a boast !' as if I dreamed that fetters
>   Binding Dante, bind up—me ! as if true pride
>   Were not also humble !

> So I smiled and sighed
> As I oped your book in Venice this bright morning,
> Sweet new friend of mine! and felt the clay or sand,
> Whatsoe'er my soil be,—break—for praise or scorning—
> Out in grateful fancies—weeds; but weeds expand
> Almost into flowers—held by such a kindly hand!"

TIME'S REVENGES.

First appeared in *Bells and Pomegranates*, 1845, No. vii. p. 22
Reprinted, *Poems*, 1849, Vol. ii. pp. 407–409.
Ditto   ditto   1863, Vol. i. pp. 187–189.
Ditto   ditto   1868, Vol. iv. pp. 178–180.
Ditto, *Poetical Works*, 1886, Vol. v. pp. 44–46.

In the first edition of this poem, following line 54, we read—

> " As all my genius, all my learning
> Leave me, where there's no returning."

These lines are now omitted.

TO EDWARD FITZGERALD. (" I chanced upon a new book yesterday.")

First appeared in the *Athenæum*, July, 1889.
Reprinted in *The Browning Society's Papers*, Part xi. p. 347*.
Not included in any edition of Mr. Browning's *Poems*.

For full particulars concerning this sonnet see *ante*, pp. 53–54. As a matter of literary history, and to render this Bibliography as complete as possible, it is here reprinted from the *Browning Society's Papers*.

> I chanced upon a new book yesterday:
> I opened it, and, where my finger lay
>   'Twixt page and uncut page, these words I read—
> Some six or seven at most—and learned thereby
> That you, Fitzgerald, whom by ear and eye
>   She never knew, "thanked God my wife was dead."
>
> Ay, dead! and were yourself alive, good Fitz,
> How to return you thanks would task my wits;
>   Kicking you seems the common lot of curs—
> While more appropriate greeting lends you grace:
> Surely to spit there glorifies your face
>   Spitting—from lips once sanctified by Hers.

TOO LATE.

First appeared in *Dramatis Personæ*, 1864, pp. 55–63.
Reprinted, *Poems*, 1868, Vol. vi. pp. 85-91.
Ditto, *Poetical Works*, 1889, Vol. vii. pp. 94-100.

"TOUCH HIM NE'ER SO LIGHTLY, INTO SONG HE BROKE."

First appeared in *Dramatic Idyls* II., 1880, p. 149.
Reprinted, *Poetical Works*, 1889, Vol. xv. p. 164.
These lines appear as the Epilogue to the Second Series of *Dramatic Idyls*.

TRANSCENDENTALISM: A POEM IN TWELVE BOOKS.

First appeared in *Men and Women*, 1855, Vol. ii. pp. 223–226.
Reprinted, *Poems*, 1863, Vol. i. pp. 321-323.
Ditto   ditto   1868, Vol. v. pp. 207–209.
Ditto, *Poetical Works*, 1889, Vol. iv. pp. 173-175.

TRAY.

First appeared in *Dramatic Idyls* I., 1879, pp. 103-106.
Reprinted, *Poetical Works*, 1889, Vol. xv. pp. 57-59.

TWO CAMELS.

First appeared in *Ferishtah's Fancies*, 1884, pp. 69–76.
Reprinted, *Poetical Works*, 1889, Vol. xvi. pp. 47-52.

TWO IN THE CAMPAGNA.

First appeared in *Men and Women*, 1855, Vol. ii. pp. 205–209.
Reprinted, *Poems*, 1863, Vol. i. pp. 116-118.
Ditto   ditto   1868, Vol. iii. pp. 188-190.
Ditto, *Poetical Works*, 1889, Vol. vi. pp. 150-153.

UP AT A VILLA—DOWN IN THE CITY.

First appeared in *Men and Women*, 1855, Vol. i. pp. 23-30.
Reprinted, *Poems*, 1863, Vol. i. pp. 49-53.
Ditto   ditto   1868, Vol. iii. pp. 122-127.
Ditto, *Poetical Works*, 1889, Vol. vi. pp. 66-71.

"VERSE-MAKING WAS LEAST OF MY VIRTUES."

First appeared in *Ferishtah's Fancies*, 1884, pp. 85–86.
Reprinted, *Poetical Works*, 1889, Vol. xvi. p. 57.

"WANTING IS—WHAT ? "

First appeared in *Jocoseria*, 1883, p. 3.
Reprinted, *Poetical Works*, 1889, Vol. xv. p. 167.

WARING.

First appeared in *Bells and Pomegranates*, 1842, No. iii.
pp. 10–11.
Reprinted, *Poems*, 1849, Vol. ii. pp. 285-294.
Ditto   ditto   1863, Vol. i. pp. 215–224.
Ditto   ditto   1868, Vol. iv. pp. 206–215.
Ditto, *Poetical Works*, 1889, Vol. v. pp. 78–89.

The original of *Waring* was Mr. Alfred Domett, who was born
at Camberwell, May 20, 1811. In 1829 he matriculated at
Cambridge ; and in 1833 published a volume of poems. He was
called to the bar at the Middle Temple in 1841. For a time
he lingered in London Society, and is said to have been "one of
the handsomest and most attractive men there." In 1842 he
was induced to emigrate to New Zealand, and some interesting
particulars of his career in that colony will be found in Mr.
William Gisborne's *New Zealand Rulers and Statesmen*, 1840 *to*
1885 (London, 1886). Six years after his arrival in the colony
he was appointed Colonial Secretary for the province of New
Munster ; and in 1851 secretary for the whole of New Zealand.
He eventually became Premier of that Colony ; afterwards
holding other appointments ; and returning to England in
1871. In 1872 he published his chief poem—*Ranolf and
Amohia, a South Sea Day Dream*, a work descriptive of the
scenery of New Zealand, and of the legends, character and
habits of the Maori inhabitants. In this poem (Canto xix.
pp. 342-3) he paid the following warm tribute to the genius of
his old friend, Mr. Browning :

> ' Strange melodies '
> That lustrous Song-Child languished to impart,
> Breathing his boundless Love through boundless Art—

Impassioned Seraph, from his mint of gold
By our full-handed Master-Maker flung ;
By him, whose lays, like eagles, still upwheeling
To that shy Empyrean of high feeling,
Float steadiest in the luminous fold on fold
Of wonder-cloud around its sun-depths rolled.
Whether he paint, all patience and pure snow,
Pompilia's fluttering innocence unsoiled ;—
In verse, though fresh as dew, one lava flow
In fervour—with rich Titian-dyes aglow—
Paint Paracelsus to grand frenzy stung,
Quixotic dreams and fiery quackeries foiled ;—
Or—of Sordello's delicate Spirit unstrung
For action, in its vast Ideal's glare
Blasting the Real to its own dumb despair,—
On that Venetian water-lapped stair-flight,
In words condensed to diamond, indite
A lay dark—splendid as star-spangled Night :—
Still—though the pulses of the world-wide throng
He wields, with racy life-blood beat so strong
Subtlest Assertor of the Soul in song !

His other works were *Venice*, a poem (1839) ; *Narrative of the Wairoa Massacre* (1843) ; *Petition to the House of Commons for the Recall af Governor Fitzroy ; Ordinances of New Zealand, classified* (1850) ; and *Flotsam and Jetsom, Rhymes old and new* (1877). He died at Kensington, in November 1887

"What a Pretty Tale you told me."

These lines first appeared in *La Saisiaz* and *The Two Poets of Croisic*, 1878, pp. 193-201, and form the Epilogue to the volume.
Reprinted, *Poetical Works*, 1889, Vol. xiv. pp. 273-279.
No alteration in text. In the *Selections* of 1885 this poem is entitled "A Tale."

"When I vexed you and you chid me."

First appeared in *Ferishtah's Fancies*, 1884, p. 68.
Reprinted, *Poetical Works*, 1889, Vol. xvi. pp. 45-46.

WHICH ?

> First appeared in *Asolando*, 1889, pp. 37–39.
> Reprinted, *Poetical Works*, 1894, Vol. xvii. pp. 31–33.

WHITE WITCHCRAFT.

> First appeared in *Asolando*, 1889, pp. 17–18.
> Reprinted, *Poetical Works*, 1894, Vol. xvii. pp. 14–15.

"WHY FROM THE WORLD ?" FERISHTAH SMILED, "SHOULD THANKS."

> First appeared in *Ferishtah's Fancies*, 1884, p. 139.
> Reprinted, *Poetical Works*, 1889, Vol. xvi. p. 89.

WHY AM I A LIBERAL ?

> First appeared in a work entitled *Why am I a Liberal?* [1] 1885,
> p. 11.
> Reprinted in *The Browning Society's Papers*, Part viii. p. 92*.

This sonnet was written in answer to a request for the reason of the Poet's political faith. Not having been reprinted in any edition of Mr. Browning's Works, the lines are here quoted :

> " Why ? " Because all I haply can and do,
>   All that I am now, all I hope to be,—
>   Whence comes it save from fortune setting free
> Body and soul the purpose to pursue,
> God traced for both ? If fetters, not a few,
>   Of prejudice, convention, fall from me,
>   These shall I bid men—each in his degree
> Also God-guided—bear, and gaily too ?
>
> But little do or can the best of us :
>   That little is achieved through Liberty.
> Who, then, dares hold—emancipated thus—
>   His fellow shall continue bound ? Not I
> Who live, love, labour freely, nor discuss
>   A brother's right to freedom. That is " Why."

---

[1] *Why am I a Liberal?* Edited by Andrew Reid. London, Cassell and Co., 1885.

"WISH NO WORD UNSPOKEN, WANT NO LOOK AWAY!"

First appeared in *Ferishtah's Fancies*, 1884, p. 12.
Reprinted, *Poetical Works*, 1889, Vol. xvi. p. 11.

"WITLESS ALIKE OF WILL AND WAY DIVINE."

First appeared in *Dramatis Personæ*, 1864, pp. 248–250.
Reprinted, *Poems*, 1868, Vol. vi. pp. 225–227.
Ditto, *Poetical Works*, 1889, Vol. vii, pp. 253-255.

This poem is the "THIRD SPEAKER" in the Epilogue to *Dramatis Personæ*, and is representative of the attitude of Mr. Browning himself towards the views expressed by the two preceding Speakers (*David* and *Renan*).

WOMEN AND ROSES.

First appeared in *Men and Women*, 1855, Vol. ii. pp. 150–153.
Reprinted, *Poems*, 1863, Vol. i. pp. 137–138.
Ditto   ditto   1868, Vol. iii. pp. 209-211.
Ditto, *Poetical Works*, 1889, Vol. vi. pp. 180-182.

"YOU ARE SICK, THAT'S SURE," THEY SAY.

First appeared in *Dramatic Idyls* II., 1880, on unnumbered leaf, as a prologue.
Reprinted, *Poetical Works*, 1889, Vol. xv. p. 83.

"YOU GROPED YOUR WAY ACROSS MY ROOM."

First appeared in *Ferishtah's Fancies*, 1884, pp. 23–24.
Reprinted, *Poetical Works*, 1889, Vol. xvi. p. 18.

YOUTH AND ART.

First appeared in *Dramatis Personæ*, 1864, pp. 151–157.
Reprinted, *Poems*, 1868, Vol. vi. pp. 154-157.
Ditto, *Poetical Works*, 1889, Vol. vii. pp. 171-175.

PART VI.

COLLECTED EDITIONS.

PART VI.

COLLECTED EDITIONS.

(1.)

[*First Collected Edition :* 1849.]

Poems / By / Robert Browning. / In two Volumes.
Vol. I. [Vol. II.] / A New Edition. / London : / Chapman
& Hall, 186, Strand. / 1849.

Collation :—Post octavo. Vol. i, pp. vi + 385 ; Vol. ii, pp. viii + 416.
Issued in dark green cloth boards, gilt lettered.

P. v of Vol. i contains the following prefatory note :—

"*Many of these pieces were out of print, the rest had been withdrawn from circulation, when the corrected edition, now submitted
to the reader, was prepared. The various Poems and Dramas have
received the author's most careful revision. December,* 1848."

These two volumes contain only *Paracelsus* and *Bells and Pomegranates*—three poems (*Claret, Tokay,* and *Here's to Nelson's Memory*)
being omitted.

(2.)

[*Second Collected Edition :* 1863.]

The Poetical Works / of / Robert Browning. / Vol. i /
Lyrics, Romances, Men and Women. / [*Vol. ii, with Con-
tents ; Vol. iii, with Contents.*] Third Edition*. / London :
Chapman and Hall, 193, Piccadilly. / 1863.

* This "*Third Edition*" is somewhat misleading. It does not signify that
the present is the Third Edition of the three volumes, but that the poems
contained in them were now for the third time printed ; viz. 1st, in their
original editions—2nd, in the 2 vol. edition of 1849—and 3rd, in the present
3 vol. edition.

Collation :—Post octavo.   Vol. i, pp. xiv + 432 ; Vol. ii, pp. vi + 605 ; Vol. iii, pp. vi + 465.

Issued in dark brown cloth boards, gilt lettered.   Several of the poems included in these volumes underwent slight textual revision.

In addition to the General Titles as given above, each volume was supplied with a distinct title-page in order that, by the removal of the General Title, it might stand as a work complete in itself.   Thus rebound copies frequently occur having the individual titles only, and no General Title.   These separate title-pages read as follows :—

Vol. I.   Lyrics, Romances, / Men and Women. / By / Robert Browning. / London : / Chapman and Hall, 193, Piccadilly. / 1863.

Vol. II.   Tragedies and / Other Plays. / By Robert Browning. / London : / Chapman and Hall, 193, Piccadilly. / 1863.

Vol. III.   Paracelsus, / Christmas-Eve and Easter-Day, / Sordello. / By / Robert Browning. / London : / Chapman and Hall, 193, Piccadilly. / 1863.

Note : This edition was reprinted, from stereo plates, in 1865, the General title-pages reading "*Fourth Edition.*"

(3.)

[*Third Collected Edition :* 1868.]

The Poetical Works / of / Robert Browning, / M.A., / Honorary Fellow of Balliol College, Oxford. / Vol. i. / Pauline—Paracelsus—Strafford. / [Vol. ii, *etc, with contents*] London : / Smith, Elder, & Co., 15 Waterloo Place / 1868.

Collation :—Vol. i, pp. viii + 310.   Vol. iv, pp. iv + 310.

"   ii, "   iv + 287.   "   v, "   iv + 321.

"   iii, "   iv + 305.   "   vi, "   iv + 233.

Size post 8vo.   Issued in cloth boards, lettered in gold across the back.   Several times reprinted from stereo plates, no alterations being made in the text.

(4.)

[*Complete Edition :* 1888–1894.]

The Poetical Works / of / Robert Browning / Vol. i.
[Vol. ii, *etc, with contents*] / Pauline—Sordello / London /
Smith, Elder, & Co., 15 Waterloo Place / 1888.

Collation :—Vol.   i, pp.   x + 289.   Vol. ix, pp. vi + 313.

„	ii,	„	vi + 307.	„ x, „	vi + 279.
„	iii,	„	vi + 302.	., xi, „	vi + 343.
„	iv,	„	vi + 305.	„ xii, „	vi + 311.
„	v,	„	vi + 307.	„ xiii, „	vi + 357.
„	vi,	„	vii + 289.	„ xiv, „	vi + 279.
„	vii,	„	vi + 255.	„ xv, „	vi + 260.
„	viii,	„	viii + 253.	„ xvi, „	vi + 292.

Vol. xvii, pp. viii + 307

Issued in cloth boards, lettered in gilt across the back. Also two
hundred and fifty large (hand-made) Paper copies ; these were
issued in straw-coloured buckram boards, with white paper back-
label.

Illustrations.

Portrait of Robert Browning (1835) ....*Frontispiece* to Vol. iii.			
„ „ „ „ (1859)	„	„	vii.
Scudo of Innocent XII.............................	„	„	viii.
Portrait of Guido Franceschini	„	„	x.
„ „ Robert Browning (1882)	„	„	xvi.

** Vol. xvii, published in 1894, included an Appendix of *Biographical
and Historical Notes* by Dr. Berdoe.

PART VII.

SELECTIONS.

PART VII.

SELECTIONS.

[The two Tauchnitz volumes of 1872, and other exotic series of Selections, are not included in the following list, as they do not come within the scope of the present Bibliography.]

(1.)

Selections / from the / Poetical Works / of / Robert Browning. / London : / Chapman and Hall, / 193, Piccadilly. / 1863.

Collation :—Foolscap octavo, pp. xii + 411.
Issued in cloth boards, gilt lettered. The selections were made by John Forster. The volume is dedicated to Bryan Waller Procter (Barry Cornwall).

(2.)

Moxon's Miniature Poets. / A / Selection from / the Works / of / Robert Browning. / [*Publishers' Monogram*] / London : / Edward Moxon & Co., Dover Street. / 1865.

Collation :—Small square octavo, printed in half-sheets, pp. viii + 224. A portrait of Robert Browning, engraved by J. H. Baker after a photograph by W. Jeffery, forms the frontispiece.
Issued in cloth boards, gilt lettered, and covered with an ornamental design by John Leighton, F.S.A. This design is in gold upon the front, and 'blind' upon the back cover. The Dedication is to Alfred Tennyson. Also issued in Sixpenny Parts.

(3.)

Selections / from / The Poetical Works / of / Robert

Browning. / London : / Smith, Elder & Co., 15, Waterloo
Place. / 1872.

Collation :—Crown octavo, pp. xii + 348.
Issued in cloth boards, gilt lettered. Also dedicated to Alfred
Tennyson.
Reprinted frequently from stereotype plates.

(4.)

Selections from / The Poetical Works / of Robert Browning / Second Series / London / Smith, Elder, & Co., 15,
Waterloo Place / 1880.

Collation :—Crown octavo, pp. viii + 371.
Issued in cloth boards, gilt lettered.
In common with the First Series this volume has also freqently
been reprinted from stereotype plates.

New Edition.

In 1884 a new and cheaper edition of both Series of Selections was
published. These were exact reprints of the earlier volumes, but set
up in smaller type, thinly leaded.
The collation is :—
First Series :—Crown octavo, pp. xi + 288.
Second Series :—Crown octavo, pp. vi + 297.

(5.)

The Pied Piper of Hamelin / by / Robert Browning. /
Illustrated by Jane E. Cook, / author of " The Sculptor
Caught Napping," / King Alfred's Schools, Wantage, Berks./
Reproduced by the Autotype Company's Process of
Permanent Facsimile. / London : / This Illustrated Edition
of the " Pied Piper of Hamelin " is published with the /
kind permission of Mr. Robert Browning. / 1880.

Collation :—Oblong folio, pp. 12, *plus* 9 plates with page of
letterpress to each. The poem occupies pp. 8–12.
Issued in green cloth boards, gilt lettered.

(6.)

The Pied Piper / of Hamelin / by Robert Browning /
[*Publisher's monogram*] / London / Robt. Dunthorne / 1884.

Collation :—Small square octavo, pp. 16 [unpaged]. Printed, at
the Chiswick Press, in red and black.
Issued in mottled-grey paper wrapper, lettered upon the front.
The pamphlet was not placed upon sale. It was printed to
accompany Mr. Macbeth's etching, after a drawing by the late
G. J. Dinwell, illustrating Mr. Browning's poem, and was distributed only to subscribers for the special copies of the same.

There were also forty-one copies printed upon large paper. As
Mr. Edmund Gosse has pointed out in a letter to *The Athenæum*
of *December 12th*, 1896, p. 838, this separate issue of *The Pied
Piper of Hamelin* has the curious interest of being the only work
of Robert Browning produced upon large paper until the publication of the Collected Edition of 1888.

(7.)

Pomegranates / from an English Garden : / A Selection
from the Poems of / Robert Browning. / With Introduction
and Notes by John Monro Gibson. / " *Or from Browning
some ' Pomegranate,' which, if cut / deep down the middle, /
Shows a heart within, blood-tinctured, of a veined / humanity* " / *Lady Geraldine's Courtship.* / Phillips & Hunt, New
York. / 1885.

Collation :—Post octavo, pp. vi + 137.
Issued in white vellum boards, with coloured leather back-label.
The book was published in London by Messrs. J. W. Jarvis &

Son, then of King Willlam Street, Strand W.C.* It was set up by
Messrs. Henderson, Rait & Spalding, Marylebone Lane, London,
and the stereotype plates forwarded to America.

(8.)

The Pied Piper / of / Hamelin / by / Robert Browning / with
35 Illustrations / by / Kate Greenaway / Engraved and
printed in Colours by Edmund Evans / London / George
Routledge and Sons / Broadway, Ludgate Hill / Glasgow
and New York. [*No date, but published in the Autumn of*
1888.]

Collation :—Quarto, pp. 64.
Issued in Illustrated paper boards.

(9.)

A few Impressions / from / The Poems of Robert Browning. / By / Emily Atkinson. / London : Kegan Paul,
Trench, Trübner & Co., Ld. [*No date.*]

Collation :—Quarto, pp. 112, printed upon one side of the pages
    only.
Issued in illustrated paper boards, backed with canvas.

(10.)

PocketVolume / of / Selections / from / The Poetical Works /
of / Robert Browning / London / Smith, Elder, & Co., 15
Waterloo Place / 1890.

Collation :—32mo, pp. viii + 319.
Issued in marbled paper boards, backed with cloth, gilt lettered.

* Volumes of *Selections from Mr. Browning's Works*, as well as
volumes of *Biography* and *Criticism*, published originally in the United
States or elsewhere abroad, have been included in this Bibliography
only when they have been simultaneously issued in this country.

ADDENDUM.

HELEN'S TOWER. [See *ante*, pp. 51, and 156–157.]

This poem first appeared in the following pamphlet :—

Helen's Tower / Clandeboye. / [*Vignette of the Tower*] / Privately Printed.

The whole of the above title, including an ornamental double-ruled frame, is engraved upon steel.

Collation :—Quarto, pp. 10 ; consisting of Title-page, as above (with blank reverse) pp. 1-2 ; a leaf with " 11*th day of November MDCCCL. Thursday at 3 of ye clock did I Catherine Hamilton christen this Tower by ye name style and title of Helen's Tower*" upon its recto, reverse blank, pp. 3-4 ; and Text pp. 5-10. There are no head-lines, and there is no imprint.

Issued in stiff glazed paper covers, without letterpress. The colour of the wrappers varies in different copies of the book.

The above volume was issued in 1861, although Browning's *Sonnet* was written only in 1870. The latter, however, was not included in the copies originally distributed, but was added to those made up at a later date. Accordingly Browning's verses are frequently not to be found in such stray examples of the book as occasionally occur for sale.

To this interesting little quarto Tennyson also contributed a poem of twelve lines :—

" *Helen's Tower, here I stand,*
Dominant over sea and land," &c.

A

BIBLIOGRAPHY

OF THE

WRITINGS IN PROSE AND VERSE

OF

ROBERT BROWNING.

By

THOMAS J. WISE.

London :

PRINTED FOR SUBSCRIBERS ONLY.

1896.

Price Half a Crown.

RICHARD CLAY AND SONS, LIMITED, LONDON AND BUNGAY.

A

BIBLIOGRAPHY

OF THE

WRITINGS IN PROSE AND VERSE

OF

ROBERT BROWNING.

By

THOMAS J. WISE.

London:
PRINTED FOR SUBSCRIBERS ONLY.
1896.

Price Half a Crown.

RICHARD CLAY AND SONS, LIMITED, LONDON AND BUNGAY

A

BIBLIOGRAPHY

OF THE

WRITINGS IN PROSE AND VERSE

OF

ROBERT BROWNING.

By

THOMAS J. WISE.

London:

PRINTED FOR SUBSCRIBERS ONLY.

1896.

Price Half a Crown.

RICHARD CLAY AND SONS, LIMITED, LONDON AND BUNGAY.

A

BIBLIOGRAPHY

OF THE

WRITINGS IN PROSE AND VERSE

OF

ROBERT BROWNING.

By

THOMAS J. WISE.

London:

PRINTED FOR SUBSCRIBERS ONLY.

1897.

Price Half a Crown.

THE ASHLEY LIBRARY

PRIVATELY PRINTED 1897

RICHARD CLAY AND SONS, LIMITED, LONDON AND BUNGAY

A

BIBLIOGRAPHY

OF THE

WRITINGS IN PROSE AND VERSE

OF

ROBERT BROWNING.

By

THOMAS J. WISE.

London:

PRINTED FOR SUBSCRIBERS ONLY.

1897.

Price Half a Crown.

THE ASHLEY
LIBRARY

PRIVATELY
PRINTED
1897

RICHARD CLAY AND SONS, LIMITED, LONDON AND BUNGAY

A

BIBLIOGRAPHY

OF THE

WRITINGS IN PROSE AND VERSE

OF

ROBERT BROWNING.

By

THOMAS J. WISE.

London:

PRINTED FOR SUBSCRIBERS ONLY.

1897.

Price Half a Crown.

THE ASHLEY
LIBRARY

PRIVATELY
PRINTED
1897

RICHARD CLAY AND SONS, LIMITED, LONDON AND BUNGAY.

A

BIBLIOGRAPHY

OF THE

WRITINGS IN PROSE AND VERSE

OF

ROBERT BROWNING.

By

THOMAS J. WISE.

London:

PRINTED FOR SUBSCRIBERS ONLY.

1897.

Price Half a Crown.

RICHARD CLAY AND SONS, LIMITED, LONDON AND BUNGAY

A

BIBLIOGRAPHY

OF THE

WRITINGS IN PROSE AND VERSE

OF

ROBERT BROWNING.

By

THOMAS J. WISE.

London:

PRINTED FOR SUBSCRIBERS ONLY.

1897.

Price Half a Crown.

RICHARD CLAY AND SONS, LIMITED, LONDON AND BUNGAY